manticore
books with teeth

ERNST JÜNGER: A PORTRAIT

LENNART SVENSSON

BIC Classification:
BGL (Biography: Literary), BGH (Biograpy: Historical), DSK (Literary Studies)
978-0-9875598-7-6

M A N T I C O R E   B O O K S
WWW.MANTICOREBOOKS.NET

ERNST JÜNGER
A PORTRAIT

LENNART SVENSSON

TABLE OF CONTENTS

INTRODUCTION

FOR SOME YEARS I've been reading the works of the German author Ernst Jünger (1895-1998). I've mostly liked what I've read. More than that: his books seem to portray a world of its own, a world of ideals and meaning in contrast to the nihilism and materialism of our current age.

Jünger is said to be controversial. Maybe he is. I don't deny his more fiery aspects. And if some critics want to spend their time mulling over these aspects and warning about the fascist traits of Jünger's œuvre, well then, I can't stop them. I for one want to focus on the more subtle sides of his books, the essentialist and vitalist philosophy they are steeped in – the affirmative, life-celebrating aspects, those passages that tend to "see eternity in a grain of sand, and heaven in a wild flower". That was William Blake but Jünger has many similar lines in his work. You'll find them here and there in this book of mine.

This work is rather thorough. However, you could also call it an essay. As for biographies proper I'm well aware that we've had two Jünger biographies in German recently, Heimo Schwilk's *Ernst Jünger: Ein Jahrhundertleben* (2007) and Helmuth Kiesel's *Ernst Jünger: Die Biographie* (2007). I haven't read them. But I've read Schwilk's *Leben und Werk in Bildern und Texten* (1988) and some other works with

biographic material. Among those I'd like to mention Thomas Nevin's *Ernst Jünger and Germany: Into the Abyss, 1914-1945* (1997). Nevin has understood the gist of Jünger's work and has made some fine distinctions, however, I tire a bit of the finger of warning raised here and there. Nevin focuses on Jünger's life and works until 1945, and Elliot Neaman in his *A Dubious Past – Ernst Jünger and the Politics of Literature After Nazism* takes at look at the reception of Jünger's œuvre after 1945. Neaman also has a keen interest in Jünger the author and Jünger the man, giving us a lot of interesting details of his life. But the subtitle – "*a dubious past*" – annoys me. I don't find Jünger dubious at all. Now he wasn't a saint, but then who is.

It's a free world. You can if you will be wary of Jünger's controversial or subtler sides. But I for one won't go into "the Jünger debate". My aim in this study has been to look at what Jünger represents rather than at what he is, in this respect striving to highlight the fruitful aspects of his work, the neglected sides such as the esotericism and the idealism, the vitalism and the life-affirming traits. At the same time I don't deny that Jünger in the 20's was a radical nationalist dealing with fire; I have chapters covering that too. Wishing to write a book that's simple and hands-on, I sport "simple but not facile" as my ideal.

Maybe this is a fan-book of sorts. I like reading Jünger's books and this is my report. But I don't just give summaries; instead I delve into the works, reflecting on this and that and finding illuminating quotes along the way. And as for Jünger's life story I've collected facts from the above mentioned researchers and made it into a, hopefully, readable narrative. You could say: this is the Jünger biography I would have liked to read when I came into contact with his production in the 80's. And for the English reader who wants a concise, popular biography on this interesting author, well here it is. This is a Jünger book for the English speaking world, meant for the literature lover who doesn't read German (Schwilk's and Kiesel's biographies aren't, as far as I know, translated into English) and who doesn't for the umpteenth time want to hear that Jünger was a dangerous fascist,

only allowed to be read after some hallmark academic has touched him with his magic interpreting wand.

This book starts out with a thorough biography of Jünger's life (chapter 1). Then I look at the controversial sides of the man, such as his relation to Hitler and Nazism (chapter 2) and his role as an outsider, mentioning something on the reception of his works (chapter 4). After a look at his books on war (chapters 5-7) I treat central Jünger works such as *The Adventurous Heart, On the Marble Cliffs, Heliopolis* and *Eumeswil* (chapters 8-16). Chapter 17 is a summary of diverse, shorter Jünger works. Art and history are the subjects of chapter 18 and 19 respectively and the following compare Jünger with German and other authors (chapters 20-22).

In chapters 23-25 I look at Jünger's esoteric and religious creed. Then chapters 26-28 deal with science fiction. The book ends with chapters on humour and poetry and such.

Finally I'd like to point out: when in the following pages I say "the war diary" I refer to Jünger's Second World War diaries, in reality three separate volumes by the names of *Gärter und Strassen, Strahlungen* and *Jahre der Okkupation*, covering the years 1939-1948. And when I say "the late diary" I mean *Siebzig verweht*, Jünger's diary covering the years 1965-1996 (see the bibliography for details).

As for book titles I've used English titles when translations exist and have become household names, like *On the Marble Cliffs* and *The Adventurous Heart*.

When I refer to *Schwilk* I mean his 1988 pictorial biography and nothing else. Finally, the Jünger quotes in this book are translated from German by me throughout.

Härnösand, August 11th, 2014

LENNART SVENSSON

1. BIOGRAPHY

I begin this book with a biographical sketch of the life of Ernst Jünger. My sources have been his own diaries and the works of Schwilk, Paetel, Neaman, Nevin and Fabiansson(For bibliographical details on these, see the end of the book).

EARLY YEARS

Ernst Jünger was born on March 29th, 1895 in Heidelberg, Baden-Württemberg, Germany. For simplicity I shall call him "Jünger" throughout the book. He was the oldest of seven siblings of which one sister and two brothers reached adulthood. Jünger was closest to his brother Friedrich Georg, usually called Fritz (1989-1977). Fritz was a poet and an author who followed Jünger through the times, being an inspiration and an intellectual sparring-partner.

The father of this family was called Ernst Georg, earning his living as a chemist and a pharmacist. He can be described as a positive science disciple. The mother's name was Karolina, born Lampl. She was nicknamed Lily. Like most other wives of the bourgeoisie in those

days she was a housewife. She had French ancestry, visible among other things in her brown eyes, a trait inherited by Jünger.

Jünger was born as a citizen of the German Empire, a thriving nation newly united by Bismarck's wars against France, Austria and Denmark. In this German Kaiserreich there was some domestic strife (workers asserting their rights, and the Kulturkampf struggle between the state and the catholic church), but on the whole this epoch was harmonious and prosperous. Throughout Europe these were peaceful days. The only wars in sight were far off and easy to handle – in other words, colonial wars.

However, under the peaceful surface there were European conflicts brewing. For example France lamented the loss of the provinces Elsass and Lothringen to Germany after the 1870 war. Germany for its part tried to balance between France in the west and Russia in the east. The solution for Germany eventually became an alliance with Austro-Hungary, a great power in decline. In time Germany found itself in a long, drawn-out two-front war with Russia on the one side and France and England on the other, however this scenario was pure science fiction at the time of Jünger's birth. No one (except for the Polish banker Bloch, who in a famous pamphlet warned about an approaching great war) could surmise that Europe would be torn apart in a long war. If war would come everything would go swiftly and "be over by Christmas", the soldiers being "home before the leaves fall"; that was the common wisdom. War and belligerence was taken lightly, welfare and peaceful endeavours being at the centre of attention in 19th century Europe. It was la belle epoque with waxed moustaches, economic growth and technical progress such as it had been during the larger part of the century. The lesser crises and economical recesses were considered as anomalies in the greater picture of peace and prosperity.

As I said Jünger was born in Heidelberg, which is a mid-western German town. He grew up farther north, in Lower Saxony, in the towns of Hannover, Schwarzenberg and, from 1907, Rehburg. Living

in Rehburg he discovered two important things, the adventure novel and the world of insects. The latter he read about in the book *Der Käferfreund* (*The Beetle Friend*), beetles eventually becoming his main interest within the realm of entomology. He also came to collect butterflies, however, among other things beetles are more resistant against tear and wear when threaded on a needle and stored throughout the years. That was one reason why Jünger preferred these *coleoptera*, which is the Latin name for beetles.

Cultivating the entomological interest of Jünger was his scientific father, Ernst Georg. Except for the handbook he gave Jünger a butterfly-net, an ether bottle and other things you need for collecting and storing the insects. As for the adventure novels and other books that came in the way of young Jünger one could mention *A Thousand and One Nights*, Grimmelshausen's *The Adventurous Simplicissimus* (taking place in the Thirty Year's War), Cervantes *Don Quixote* and *Mein Braunes Buch* (*My Brown Book*) by Hermann Löns, a dyed-in-the-wool Saxon author. As a curiosity Löns fell in battle in 1914 as a nearly 50-year old volunteer, and sometime later in the war, in May 1917, Jünger himself led the company wherein Löns had served (4th Company, 73rd Regiment).

Other than that I haven't so much to say about the early years of Jünger. I choose not to deliberate on how he was "developed" into this and that by this and that circumstance, incident, milieu etc... I can't point out and say: this thing here affected him, this was a turning point, this was a defining moment. I leave that to the armchair psychologists. We are what we are; "wir können nicht anders sein" as Goethe said.

So I'll focus on some more or less interesting events in the rest of Jünger's pre-war life, without trying to analyze them overly much. For instance in 1910 he saw Halley's comet. "Maybe Wolfgang will see it again" the father said at the time, intimating the comet's 76-year cycle. But this youngest son was to be the first to die. Of his siblings only Jünger lived to Revoir Halley, as was the French title of Jünger's

17

Zwei Mal Halley (*Two Times Halley*) from 1986, a book deliberating on having seen the comet twice and how the world had changed in between. Among other things Jünger notes that Mark Twain also was lucky in this respect. Twain namely wrote in 1909 about how he had arrived with the comet and how he also expected to leave with it and actually Twain did just that, dying in April 1910. More on *Zwei Mal Halley* in chapter 17.

In 1911 Jünger and his brother Fritz joined Die Wandervögel, a German scout movement bent on hiking, camping and singing. Celebrating this life Jünger the same year wrote the poem *Unser Leben* (*Our Life*), the first text by Jünger to be published. It saw the light of day in *Hannoverland*, a Wandervögel magazine. More on this in Chapter 32.

In April, 1912, the Titanic went down, an event affecting Jünger according to Thomas Nevin. Jünger himself says, in his late diary, that this was a prophetic event for the age of scientific optimism, a similarly profound prognostic for the technical as the Dreyfus affair is said to have been for the political sphere. And of course the Titanic was a symbol of the illusionary in the ability of technology to bring happiness, a dissonant chord in the naive optimism for progress in those days. L'Affaire for its part can be seen as an omen of the role of anti-Semitism in the 20th century, how seemingly dormant attitudes become viral in politics. Nevin in this context also mentions Max Beckmann's painting of survivors of the Titanic, a modern *Medusa's Raft*, a striking image for the whole event. Not all the people of la belle epoque were self-contented optimists. (*Medusa's Raft* is a painting by Géricault, depicting a sea catastrophe of the early 19th century.)

In the fall of 1913 Jünger, getting fed up with his home and his school, left it all and fled to the south of France in order to join the French Foreign Legion. He was accepted, eventually reaching Algeria and the fortress Sidi-bel-Abbès. But life in the Legion was harsh and devoid of adventure and Jünger escaped, twice. And both of the times he was caught. Eventually he was freed thanks to the intermission of

his father. Ernst Georg wasn't actually mad at his son for this affair, maybe he was silently impressed, however Jünger now had to return to Germany and his schooling and everything else.

In 1936 Jünger wrote a doku-novel about this African adventure. More on this in chapter 9.

Jünger got his diploma for his higher school examination in 1914. Had nothing intervened he would have gone on to Leipzig University where he had registered. But now something did intervene, the Great War came, and this opened a new chapter in Jünger's life.

WORLD WAR ONE

At the very start of the war, on August 1st, 1914, Jünger volunteered for the German Imperial Army. He was placed in the 73rd Hannoveran Infantry Regiment: der Füsilier-Regiment "General-Feldmarshall Prinz Albrecht von Preussen". During the autumn Jünger got basic soldier's training in the bosom of the reserve battalion of the 73rd. At the end of December his unit was sent to the western front in Champagne. It was rather calm for the moment, not considering sniper bullets and randomly fired, single artillery shells, so calm or not you had to keep your head down.

The front lines were in deadlock here in northern France. The German general staff had, for the moment, resigned concerning the possibility of breaking through and bringing France to its knees. So this, then, was the Great War, the all-European conflict that some had foreseen. But no one could imagine this deadlock. However, it all had started and in some respects it could be said that Germany started it, even though the impression of a preventive war also can be at hand. Undoubtedly Germany was the dynamic centre of Europe at the time, in the same fashion as France had played that role a hundred years earlier. So Germany had declared war on Russia and France, these

two being allies, but even though the Germans were able to stem the Russian advance they couldn't break the backbone of the French. The mobilization and deployment of 200 German divisions had been in vain. Germany found itself in a two-front war with Russia and the Western powers, a nightmarish operational reality. As for the western front where Jünger had been transported there was a sort of mutual siege warfare with the armies of France, England and Germany shoe-horned into a fairly narrow combat zone, flanked by the Alps and the English Channel respectively. No one side could gain local superiority, lastingly break through the front-line and stage a decisive battle.

It was hard to get to grips with the enemy, hard to manoeuvre. And that could be explained by saying that in those days the defence, utilizing railroads to bring in reinforcements, was mechanized while the offense was not. For this they had to wait for the arrival of tanks in 1917. Until then it was the tedious story of fixed lines and trench warfare. It all sometimes erupted in material battles, Ger. Materialschlachten. This was for instance seen in 1916 when both sides on the western front tried to break the other by delivering massed artillery fire, at Somme and Verdun respectively.

As for the early days of 1915, when Jünger came to the front, they saw a deadlock after the mobile battles of 1914. It was the world of "All Quiet on the Western Front", of the everyday life of war in the trenches. As a private Jünger had to toil with digging and maintaining trenches and standing guard. A break in this routine came with the attack on the Lothringian village Les Eparges. Here Jünger was wounded for the first time, eventually being sent to Germany and Heidelberg to be cured. Meeting his father while on leave Jünger got the advice to volunteer for officer's school. It can be said that Jünger as a combat soldier had stood the test of stoic behaviour in the face of death. Furthermore he had his higher school education. So he applied for officer's school, got accepted and so received his theoretical and practical training in leading men in combat. In November 1915 he

formally became an officer, being promoted to first lieutenant.

In the year of 1916 both sides of the western front were planning large offensives. They both wanted to break the deadlock in the west with the means of Materialkrieg: saturating the enemy's positions with artillery shells, bombing them for days and then, hopefully, being able to break through with infantry and advance into the heartland of the enemy. That didn't happen but the battles as such are worth studying. The English for their part started their build-up to the Somme offensive in the autumn. In a fight planned to bind German reinforcements Jünger was wounded and sent to the rear. At the same time his platoon was obliterated in the battles at Guillemont. All this was part of the Somme-battle and these operations were truly fierce. The battles thus far were no picnic but now the war was on yet another level. It was symbolized in the arrival of steel helmets, which Jünger tells about in the chapter "Guillemont" in his war diary *In Stahlgewittern* (*Storm of Steel*). Arriving at the front at night and being guided by a certain aide, clad in steel helmet, for Jünger seem to signal the entry into a new world.

The first time Jünger was wounded was at Les Eparges, 1915. The second time was at Guillemont, 1916. Later that year, in November, he was wounded a third time, during a recon patrol in the St Pierre Vaast-forest. In December he received the decoration Iron Cross, first class. Concerning Somme it didn't, as intimated, result in a break-through; the Germans held their positions. However both sides suffered a large number of casualties this time of the war. At the same time the Germans launched their Verdun offensive, an operation on an even greater scale than Somme. But the deadlock remained, some people at this time even believing that the trenches and the locked front-lines would last forever.

COMPANY COMMANDER

In February, 1917, Jünger during four weeks underwent company commander training. Back in the combat zone he became the leader of an infantry company, a unit of about 200 men. He had six platoons to lead, they in turn with their officers and NCO's, and to assist him he had a staff, an aide-de-camp, a quartermaster and so forth. For the time being the situation was rather calm, the Germans being occupied with additionally fortifying the position they had held since the end of 1914, the Siegfried Line. The German general staff didn't plan any offensives in the west this year, instead being intent on knocking Russia out of the war.

When Jünger was off-duty he had his pastimes. For example he read the 16th century poem *Orlando Furioso* (*The Raging Roland*) by Ariosto, finding strength in its words about holding firm and to persevere. Other than that he hated the calm days. "When will this shitty war end?", he once wrote in his diary, in one of the many notebooks that later were elaborated and edited into *Storm of Steel*. This chance remark is not to be interpreted as an anti-war diatribe, but as a frustrated exclamation over the stalemate. Jünger was a sort of adventurer who enjoyed the din of battle. For the common reader it's hard to combine the words "first world war" with "adventure" but Jünger was no common soldier. He was a timeless mercenary type, a western samurai.

The rest of 1917 saw a lot of patrols and action. Jünger's prayers were answered. He also met his wounded brother on the battlefield of Langemarck in August. He had Fritz carried away to the battalion medical station, an episode that became a gripping poem by Fritz. In his 1934 collection *Dichte* he wrote:

Never will I forget, how you / found me in the cottage, / entering scouting, I hardly recognized you. / Like a gravedigger in the earthly realm you seemed, / covered by the earth, / up to the helmet

splashed with mud / from Flandrian meadows (...) / Silently, with tears we saluted / each other, the power / of this encounter gripping me / like a wonder in the land of Desolation...

According to Paetel Jünger treasured this poem more than the Pour le Mérite he received in 1918, underlining the difference between being honoured by a poet and being honoured by a king.

After yet another legendary patrol – "the hand-grenade battle at the St. Quentin channel", q.v. *Storm of Steel* – Jünger received an eminent German order: the Knight's Cross With Swords to the Royal House Order of Hohenzollern. This was in December of 1917. The following year for its part began placidly with Jünger and his company defending a certain part of the front. However, soon the preparations for Ludendorff's great March offensive began, the last German attempt to break the deadlock in the west. This could be launched since the Germans in 1917 actually had succeeded with the prime prerequisite to this, namely, knocking Russia out of the war. Now Jünger's company was withdrawn from the forward combat zone in order to practice the storming of trenches, the throwing of hand-grenades and how to bypass certain obstacles and push on into the second and third defence line.

Ludendorff's assault force of several army corps were amassed for the attack. And among them was Jünger's company. Here he suffered a severe setback: on the eve of the attack a grenade hit the waiting company and over half of the men were killed or wounded.

However, after some delays Jünger participated in the assault nonetheless. The artillery barrage preceding this March offensive lasted for several hours, truly a storm of steel. When advancing the first British defence line was easily broken through, the German infantry taking trench after trench. At the end of Day 1 Jünger's spearhead, having advanced some 200 meters ahead of the rest, could rest in the second British line of defence, having reached the enemy's artillery positions. That wasn't so bad for a day's work. And the attack

rolled on the next day. However, the British hadn't been completely routed and they could eventually launch a counter-attack with their reinforcements. Facing this attack the Germans lost it. Among other things Germany this time was under a naval blockade, impeding imports, and even soldiers at the front were half-starving. Having reached the rich stores of the enemy some troops just stopped to eat, it is said.

So Ludendorff's gamble failed. He had tried to reach Paris and for sure, it was close to succeeding for a while. But when faced with the fierce allied resistance the German retreat on the western front became a fact. However, it was an orderly retreat. There were still battles to be fought. Jünger for example fought at Copse 125, later on a famous narrative made public in book form. Then in the summer of 1918 Jünger was wounded in the lung at Cambrai. Recuperating in a hospital in Hannover he was reached by the news that the war had been lost.

The war was over. In November Germany agreed to a cease-fire, in essence a sort of capitulation. Jünger lamented it all even though he could seek some comfort in having received Pour le Mérite, the highest Prussian war decoration, shortly before the war ended. Moreover the war had seen him mature and evolve spiritually. During calmer times in the combat zone he read a lot, like Kubin's novel *Die andere Seite* (*The Other Side*) and entomological papers. Additionally there were names such as Gogol, Dostojevskij, Tolstoy and Wilde, and Sternes "Tristram Shandy", Rimbaud and Nietzsche. However as for Nietzsche, Jünger had already read him as a pupil at school (*The Birth of Tragedy* and *The Will to Power*). Finally he read during the war the epigrams of Schopenhauer, from then on a lifelong companion: the *Parerga und Paralipomena* of 1851.

More than educating himself this way the war had made Jünger more intuitive and less cerebral, less materialistic. He was led away from plain reason and orderliness into uncertainty and freedom, as intimated in this passage from *Der Kampf als inneres Erlebnis* (*The

Battle as an Inner Experience) with a reference at the end to the mythical Antaios:

> The son of an epoch thoroughly steeped in materialism I was drawn into this war – I, a cold, premature city-dweller whose brain was polished into a steel crystal through the contact with natural science and modern literature. The war changed me, it changed all of my generation I guess. My world view no longer holds that safety, and how would that be possible with the uncertainty that's been about for some years. From now on our actions have to be led by totally different forces, sombre and instinctive, however sensing that there is a profound reason to this realization. It could also be surmised that not everything that surrounds us are transparent and appropriate, instead being very mysterious, and this lesson would thus be the first step in a wholly new direction. Having again come into contact with the earth we must therefore, as that mythical giant, regain our whole force through this contact.

AFTER THE WAR

The war was lost. The German Empire had fallen as had the Russian and Austrian empires at the same time. New states appeared in Eastern Europe, democracy and independence being the new slogans. Germany was exhausted and starving but territorially it was still rather intact, not being partitioned as became the case after 1945. But it was weakened. The Versailles Treaty stated that Germany had to pay a substantial war indemnity and that her army had to be reduced in size. At the end of the war das Heer counted over one million men and now it was downsized to 100,000. Maybe this seemed feasible at the time but later on this became a lever for the Nazis in their rise to power. And in this agenda, the urge to increase the army in order to

balance the forces of the neighbouring Poles and French, the Nazi's had the support of the majority of Germans.

The war was over and Jünger was wounded in the lung. His regiment was dissolved but he remained in the army reserve. At first he went to his parents in Hannover, recuperating in the family home. During a leftist uprising he got visited in his home by members of the so called Spartakist movement, threatening to kill him. He was an officer and an enemy to the brave new worker's society in the offing. He was eventually given house arrest by the reds. Soon afterwards the Spartakist revolt was crushed, one of many such coups at the time, both left-wing and right-wing.

The Hannoverian Jünger home wasn't so merry, according to Jünger's "pseudo-memories" *Ännäherungen* (*Approaches*). The mother was paralyzed by the capitulation, seeing the past glories of Das Kaiserreich as in a haze. The father kept his stature but made himself no illusions about the future. Jünger for his part sometimes contemplated suicide and read about different drugs in his father study, eventually settling for opium drops against the pain in the lung. He knew about the risks of becoming an opium addict, using his will power in order not to fall into the trap. For example he had seen many drug addicts during the war, wounded veterans treated with prescription drugs having become slaves to the habit.

In 1919 Jünger was employed in the new, smaller army – der Reichswehr – as an active duty officer. He became platoon commander in the 16th Hannoveran Infantry Regiment. There were some things to do, such as launching patrols against smugglers in the British zone of occupation and looking for weapon caches, surplus weapons hidden by radical elements. There were still rumours about coups and they became serious in March, 1920, when a certain Kapp marched on Berlin in order to topple the republic. It all spread to Hannover where 2,000 people demonstrated in support of this nationalist. The city army garrison where among Jünger got the task to guard against any disturbances and uphold civil authority.

These days Jünger was living in an apartment at Hannover's Waterlooplatz, a city square commemorating the Hannoveran regiments participating on the winning side in the battle of Waterloo 1815. The square in question was lined by regimental buildings (Ger. Kaserne), forming one enormous parade ground. In 1920 Jünger was ordered to Berlin, eventually getting an apartment on Lützowstrasse facing the marketplace. Jünger's task was to participate in the writing of a new infantry handbook. From *Änneherungen*:

> The service was formally nice but you had to be alert. There were four of us working together: Hüttmann, Kienitz, Westernhagen and myself. That this post was blessed is proved by the fact the three others became generals, Kienitz even a commanding general. I saw him flashing by during the advance in France. The columns had to step aside, MP's on motorcycles leading the way for him with their air horns. In the defence of Berlin Westernhagen, trying to cross the Spree swimming, became the victim of Russian snipers.

As intimated Jünger was writing a field manual at this time and more of that was to come. Next he got the permission to edit his war memories during working hours, this in time developing into the famous *Storm of Steel*. Being published in 1920 in 2,000 copies on Jünger's own imprint Gibraltar it was soon followed by several editions on Mittler Verlag. Many copies were sold, however not in the realm of a milestone best-seller, not at once. "Slow but steady" seems to have been the motto for Jünger's literary career.

According to Heimo Schwilk Jünger these years socialized with expressionists such as Kurt Schwitters and members of Hannover's Klabund. Jünger himself wrote expressionist poetry of which one (1) example has survived. More on that in Chapter 32. As for reading Jünger these years delved into books by Baudelaire, Verlaine, Rimbaud and Huysmans. Above all Goethe became a main influence from now

on: this classical, Apollonian author with a keen eye for the world of plants and the discrete forces of nature, with his optimism and "everyday idealism", became a sort of guru. Jünger seldom mentions Goethe's name but the Weimar author's presence is immanent in much of Jünger's writings.

You could say: the lasting part of Jünger's outlook is more or less Goethean, best expressed in Jünger's elaborations on the Goethean line "im Innern ist's getan". For more on this, see chapter 14.

THE TWENTIES

Jünger later on didn't make much of his post war army years. It was bureaucratic work, devoid of creativity, with only the odd coup to crush. So in August, 1923, Jünger left the army and moved to Leipzig for higher studies. But it turned out that these academic years were as futile and uninspiring.

In Leipzig Jünger studied Zoology, Geology, Mineralogy, Biology and a discipline called Natural Philosophy under Hans Driesch, a biologist with a metaphysical slant. The vitalism he taught meant transcending matter and the empirical life-form in order to reach the invisible forces that essentially govern matter, living creatures and all. It was a Goethean school of thought, part of the idealistic trait that has survived in the German academy even into the post-1945 and post-1968 years. However, the mainstay of zoology that Jünger met at the university made him disappointed. It was too much fact and figures at the expense of forms and shapes; in short, too much quantity when quality should be the norm. It was too much of the instrumentalism and positivism that Jünger had from his father and too little of the contemplating, sublime form of observation, too little of the "sublime hunt" that Jünger was to embody as an entomologist. This according to Schwilk.

In Leipzig Jünger also studied philosophy under Felix Krüger. The lectures were also attended by a certain Hugo Fischer who would become a close friend, surfacing in disguise in Jünger books such as *Myrdun* and *The Adventurous Heart*. During his student days Jünger also served as a communications man for the national movement, being a member of Gerhard Rossbach's Freikorps.

As for Jünger's writing these years it took off after Mittler published *Storm of Steel* in 1922. Jünger exploited other aspects of his war years in the works *Copse 125, Feuer und Blut, Sturm* and *Der Kampf als inneres Erlebnis, 1922-1925*.

In 1923 Jünger met his first wife, Gretha von Jeinsen, descended from a Hannoveran family of officers and farmers. They married in August, 1925. The same year Jünger joined Stalhelm, the greatest German veteran society. He wrote for its weekly paper and also had *Feuer und Blut* published by them, this story of the epic first day of the 1918 March offensive.

Next year, 1926, saw some important events. In May Jünger's first son Ernst was born, nicknamed Ernstel (Little Ernst). Later in the same month Jünger just gave up on his zoology studies without graduating, from beginning to end an alien to the academic world as he said himself. He now became a full-time writer. The year 1926 could also have seen a meeting between Jünger and Adolf Hitler. Plans for a rendezvous in the Saxon town of Leisnig were made, but the Bavarian politician eventually had to send word that he couldn't come. Hitler was an avid admirer of *Storm of Steel* and he protected Jünger during the Nazi regime, like when Goebbels was bent on harassing Jünger. Hitler and Jünger never met in real life but in 1926 they at least switched books, *Mein Kampf* for *Feuer und Blut*.

In 1927 Jünger and his family moved to Berlin, settling in an apartment by the Warschauer Brücke. It was a worker's precinct but in his apartment Jünger had all the necessities for a writer, like jars with biological samples, his collection of *coleoptera*, well-filled bookcases and a long pipe with a porcelain head. This according to Ernst von Salomon in the book *Der Fragebogen* (1951).

THE NATIONALIST

The recently mentioned von Salomon was one of Jünger's many friends in the radical right movement at the time. The special kind of right-wing people that Jünger grouped with is called national revolutionaries (die Nationalrevolutionären). One subdivision of this group was militaristic, having been influenced by their war time experience. The other subdivision had combined nationalistic and leftist leanings, with a predilection for revolution and industrial mobilization. Soviet Russia was an ideal while the Western powers were seen as weak and decadent. These National Bolsheviks had a journal in *Der Widerstand*, edited by Ernst Niekisch. Jünger, from the beginning part of the militaristic wing, contributing to papers like *Die Standarte* and *Arminius*, from around 1927 began to approach Niekisch's National Bolshevism. Jünger was a radical these days, maybe with a negative approach: anti-Weimar, anti-Versailles and anti-bourgeois. However it is said that he never was an anti-Semite. In an article from 1929 he for example advocated that anti-Semitism wasn't a central topic for the national revolution.

Sketching a picture of German nationalism at the time it could be said that except for the national revolutionaries there were two other fractions. One was the traditional stock of conservatives, represented by Alfred Hugenberg's German National Party. The other fraction was the southern German, "völkisch" movement who adhered to racial theories and anti-Semitism. They were organized in the Nazi party, led by Adolf Hitler (Nationalsozialistische Deutsche Arbeiterpartei, NSDAP). There were differences between all these factions but they were at the same time united in their support for a German national renaissance, countering the stipulations of the Versailles Treaty and the dealings of the republican Weimar government. For the record Germany had some other notable political parties, like the Social Democrats, the Communists and the Catholic centre party (Deutsche Zentrumspartei).

Jünger wrote several articles in the years before 1933, numbering about 140. They criticized the Versailles Treaty and they criticized democracy in favour of a militaristic ordering of society. Nationalism and tradition were lauded in favour of materialism and cosmopolitanism.

According to Elliot Neaman, Jünger was influenced by Spanish and Italian fascism, gaining more inspiration from these stylish sources than from the more common, Bavarian ilk of Nazism. Jünger was something of an elitist who wrote advanced pieces, not a speaker who could reach the masses. At the same time the 20's Jünger shouldn't be white-washed into an outright anti-nazi, as some tend to do. Even as an old man Jünger admitted that the Nazis were right in advocating the abolishing of the Versailles Treaty, the treaty that forbade Germany to have an army able to defend the country.

In the Berlin of the 20's Jünger had a wide circle of friends and acquaintances. In politics he met people like Ernst Niekisch, Carl Schmitt, Friedrich Hielscher, Ernst von Salomon, Otto Strasser and Joseph Goebbels. On the artistic side he met people like Alfred Kubin, Ernst Toller, Arnolt Bronnen, Valeriu Marcu and Bertolt Brecht. It could be said that Brecht in no way was a close friend but the two of them undoubtedly met, they communicated, however cursorily. It all belongs to the picture of Jünger's Berlin days.

Jünger wrote some titanic monographs these years, like *Die totale Mobilmachung* (*Total Mobilization*, 1931) and *Der Arbeiter* (*The Worker*, 1932). At the same time he started to travel to southern destinations like Dalmatia, Italy, Spain and France. Books and pamphlets on these travels were *Dalmatinischer Aufenthalt* and *Balearische Gänge*. From the same era is the essay *Sizilischer Brief and den Mann im Mond* (*Sicilian Letter to the Man in the Moon*), being a manifesto for a unification of the scientific attitude with the mythical and artistic. You can see the moon both as a fairy-tale creature and as a celestial body open for our scientific endeavours. Jünger is not either-or, he's a man of double aspects.

Jünger's œuvre has a hard-to-define, grey area-tendency about it. Jünger's doings are an example of Wanderlust in diverse landscapes. And this is especially true when you consider that from this epoch, the 1920's-early 30's, we both have *Der Arbeiter* and the text on industrial mobilization as well as the travel stories and above all the classic *The Adventurous Heart* (*Das Abenteuerliche Herz*) of 1929. Here we find natural studies, childhood memories and short stories as well as some political statements and harsh words about this and that. This first version (another, thoroughly revised version came in 1938) is something of a cross-roads document, an anthology of the many moods of Jünger at this time.

THE THIRTIES

Jünger is said to have made a sort of re-orientation during these years, a kehre (turning) from nihilism and titanism in favour of a more affirmative, vitalist and spiritual world view. Jünger realized that not all in nature is work, as he had surmised in *Der Arbeiter*. The flight of a butterfly, a bird song, the wind in the willows – this is something that can't be objectively measured and made useful in energy and work. His brother Fritz more or less taught him this. At the same time Jünger turned down Nazi party approaches, like the offers of a Nazi mandate in der Reichstag in 1927 and again in 1933. In 1933 he also declined to be a member of Goebbels' newly formed Deutsche Akademie der Dichtung.

The Nazis were now in power. They wanted to abolish the Versailles Treaty, stop the dealings of the radical left and institute race laws. The state was to be reorganized on totalitarian grounds with Gleichshaltung and secret police. This secret police actually visited Jünger by this time, twice to be accurate. One time it was about his friendship with the anarchist Mühsam, the other it was about his

contacts with Ernst Niekisch, the national revolutionary, the police being out to find incriminating papers about this in Jünger's home.

These visits are said to have contributed in Jünger's moving from Berlin to Goslar in the Harz region, Lower Saxony (Niedersachsen) in 1933, the Berlin setting having become politically igneous. Jünger was right wing but he had friends like Niekisch who were strongly anti-Hitler, being persecuted for this.

In 1934 Jünger and Gretha had another son, Alexander. He eventually became a medical doctor, dying by his own hand in the 1990's.

The years 1936-39 the Jünger family spent in Überlingen by the Bodensee, Germany's greatest lake bordering on Switzerland and Austria. In time this 63 km long lake gave the impulse to the Great Marina which is the setting for the Jünger novel *On the Marble Cliffs*. In Überlingen the Jüngers lived in the so called Weinberghaus. The brother Fritz moved to the same city in 1937, remaining there to his death 40 years later.

In the thirties Jünger saw a growing reputation in France, *Storm of Steel* having been translated into French even in 1920, the book being followed by several others. During a Paris visit in 1937 Jünger met people like Joseph Breitenbach, Julien Green, Jean Schlumberger and Annette Kolb.

The year of 1939 arrived, a curious episode taking place this summer. Jünger was invited by Ribbentrop to the castle Fuschl in Salzburg where the foreign secretary offered him a job in the foreign service. However Jünger declined the offer. But you have to admit that he would have cut it as a diplomat, being educated and well groomed. In the spring of 1939 the Jüngers had moved once again, this time to Kirchhorst near Hannover, Lower Saxony. An old parsonage had been bought and here they stayed for the duration of the war.

In July Jünger finished his novel *Auf den Marmorklippen* (*On the Marble Cliffs*). In September the Second World War broke out. Jünger immediately got called up, editing the text of the novel while grouping

in der Westwalle on the Rhine. The book was published later that autumn. It sold well, becoming a sort of nom de clef among people resisting the Nazi regime. Goebbels had approved the publication and it remained in circulation, even though voices were raised for its withdrawal.

THE SECOND WORLD WAR

Jünger's Second World War began in his home in Kirchhorst, in the morning of August 26th, 1939. Lying and reading Herodotus, the historian of the Persian War, his maid came in bringing him his call up-order. Some days later he got the message that he had been promoted, from lieutenant to captain. The order was signed by the Army Commander von Brauchitsch personally, a nearly kingly gesture since in the old days these orders were signed by the kings themselves.

On August 30th Jünger reported for duty at Celle, the regiment's place of mobilization. He eventually became the commander of 2nd Company, 287th Infantry Regiment. You might wonder what this was like, as Jünger was, to serve in a German infantry company at the time. The following look at the anatomy of such a unit gives us the answer. Some crucial facts are from the site bayonet-strength. The German infantry company of 1939 had about 200 men, a common size since the days of the First World War. The 1939 company was led by a commander – the role of Jünger in his unit – with a command element of 10 men by his side. This HQ consisted of an aide to the commander, a command group leader, signallers and dispatch runners. There was no deputy commander (as in American infantry companies); if the commander fell then the leader of 1st Platoon was to take over the company.

The commander of such a foot marching company at this time either had a bike or a horse as his personal means of transportation. Jünger for one had a horse.

As for the supplies every company had its own field kitchen, a horse drawn stove called "Gulaschkanone" ("Gulasch" was a meat casserole common since the First World War and "Kanone" means "cannon"). A ration team of a cook plus two-three men cooked the food, mostly pea soup or lentil soup with the chance addition of meat, sausages and vegetables. In France there was often a good supply of food but not so in the East from 1941 and on. The supply vans also had stretcher bearers, ammunition carriers and teamsters, the material normally being transported on horse carriages. Sometimes a lorry was at the disposal. The supply unit consisted of 25 men and was led by a quarter master.

The company as rule had a machine gun squadron with two MG 34's. Then we had the mainstay of the company in the form of four platoons numbering about 40 each. The platoon as such was led by a First Lieutenant, sometimes by a well trusted Sergeant. The heavy equipment of the platoon (MG's, mortars) was transported on a horse carriage.

About this company you could say: apart from being equipped with machine guns and mortars and having the odd lorry and modern signals equipment, the appearance of it all was rather similar to the 1918 version of the same unit. The baggage train was towed by horses and the men of course had to march where ever the company was heading. The German infantry as a whole wasn't mechanized at this time. And Jünger himself as I said had a horse as transportation. The German war machine of 1939-41 won many victories and the personnel was well trained and motivated, but the look and feel of the line infantry was not always so high tech.

DER WESTWALL

In November 1939 Jünger and his company were deployed at der Westwall (erroneously named "the Siegfried line" by the allies) on the upper Rhine, facing the Maginot Line. It was close to the city of Greffern in the vicinity of Baden-Baden. The regiment was part of the 96th Division, 9th Army. In the subsequent attack on France 9th Army was in the reserve echelong, the spearhead being formed by such units as 4th and 12th Army.

As stated above Jünger left the army in 1923. In the mean time he had served in the army reserve, participating in manoeuvres and courses in order to brush up his officer's training and catching up with new weapons and routines. All the armies of World War Two had reserve officers like this serving in the line of fire. Jünger wasn't interested in an army career but serving as a reserve subaltern wasn't so bad either. Like it or not there is an air of adventure and expectation in the Jünger war diary of 1940 (later published as *Gärter und Strassen*), even though the events of Jünger's Second World War would be nothing like *Storm of Steel*.

The German attack in the west began in May, 1940. Spearheaded by tanks the German columns easily broke through a weak point in the allied line of defence and sped westward towards the English Channel. In this development Jünger's company mostly had to follow suit and gather up prisoners among the surrendering French. It wasn't a picnic, there were German casualties too, but not anywhere near as many as in the 1914 German attack on France.

Jünger for his part looked forward to some action. That much he intimates in his war diary. But he was mostly disappointed in this respect, quoting Herakleitos as a consolation: "we go down in the same river again and again, it is we and yet not we". The times change, you can't repeat what you've already done; the past is a thing of the past. Irrespective of an incident at der Westwall, where he had rescued

a wounded man in front of an MG-emplacement (see Chapter 7), Jünger wasn't directly in the line of fire in this war. Alright, he was there, he was a combat zone officer leading a company, but there weren't any substantial battles to be fought for him now as in the previous war.

Jünger aside the German onslaught was based on a clever plan, devised by Erich von Manstein. The idea was to 1) let the German panzers break the Anglo-French front-line in two, 2) push on to the sea and thereby 3) cutting off the British Expeditionary Force in Belgium. It was a concentrated deployment of armour, to be followed by a change of front and then an advance southwards towards the heartland of France. In this later stage Paris would be taken. This was a much better plan than the original World War Two plan for the French war, this being mostly a repetition of the 1914 so-called "Schlieffen Plan", with attacks on a broad front over Belgium which would have put the Germans exactly where the Allies wanted them.

Now we would see a massed, concentrated attack of armour like the world had never seen. At the spearhead, on a 100 km narrow front, were a substantial amount of panzer corps, units of one panzer and one panzer grenadier division each.

BREAKTHROUGH AT SEDAN

The German attack began on May 10th, 1940. And soon enough a breakthrough was effected along the river Meuse at the burgs of Sedan, Monthèrme and Dinant. A 50-70 km wide corridor of advancing armour ground down all resistance. And as planned the English were soon isolated in Belgium, cut off from contact with their French allies. The English army made a cunning retreat making it to the Channel, eventually being evacuated after having left all their heavy equipment behind. By this time the German panzers turned

south and kept the offensive going. The French resistance was weak and haphazard.

During all this Jünger went along with his foot marching company, taking care of capitulating French and handling refugees. His company was as mentioned part of the strategic reserve. In June Jünger got the Iron Cross, second class, for having saved the wounded soldier mentioned above. The operations rolled on with the challenges being mostly of the logistical kind (food, quarters). At the end of June France had surrendered and Germany had won a clear-cut victory, Jünger getting some home leave in the process. The rest of the year his company was stationed near the Teutoburger Wald in Germany. Then the company went on a mission as occupation troop in France.

In May 1941, Jünger's company was deployed at Vincennes outside Paris. Shortly afterwards Jünger was ordered to serve in the staff of the German army of occupation in France. His post was in the headquarters of the Military Governor in Paris, housed in diverse luxury hotels. At the same time Germany attacked Russia in Operation Barbarossa so Jünger could consider himself lucky: to roam the salons of Paris while the army was "eating mud" in Russia. In Jünger's defence it must be said that he never expected to spend the war in an army HQ. In his late diary [entry for May 20th, 1994] he writes about his visions at the time of partaking in hard-fought battles, like those in the First World War.

In the Paris staff Jünger among others got to know Hans Speidel, the model for der Chef in *Heliopolis*. Speidel among other things had Jünger work with plans for Operation Seelöwe, the invasion of England that never came to pass. Speidel also let him study the conflict between the Nazi party and the army of occupation in France. France was put under German military government but elements of the Nazi party wanted to share the influence. Early on, in May 1941, the SS-commander Himmler for example persuaded the then governor Otto von Stülpnagel in giving the SS a free reign in the country. Gestapo then on its own initiative could execute arrests,

searches and confiscations, not having to report to the nominal head, the military governor. This was the source of an ensuing power-struggle between army and party, and whatever Jünger learned in his study of the conflict we'll never know. These documents were burnt by him in the wake of the 20th July plot.

Stülpnagel's HQ was situated in Hotel Majestic on the Avenue Kléber, close to Bois de Boulogne. This Majestic isn't a hotel any more, it's a conference palace. For example the peace negotiations after the Vietnam War took place here. Jünger for his part had an office at the Majestic while living in the nearby Hotel Raphaël, on the top floor. Maybe this is mirrored in the attic dwelling of his alter ego, Lucius de Geer, in the royal palace of the novel *Heliopolis* (1949, see chapter 11). In that fictional palace a certain painter, Halder, is also living and he might have had his model in the painter and Jünger friend Claus Valentinier, who also lived in Paris at time.

During the French campaign Jünger wrote a diary. Soon after he edited it and published it as *Gärter und Strassen* (*Gardens and Roads*), the book being cleared by the Nazi censors. In the book Jünger mentions how he, celebrating his 45th birthday in the field, reads the 73rd psalm. And this was a snub against the regime; Goebbels is supposed to have stopped the publishing of the book when he checked on the *Bible* passage in question, an elegy over being followed by enemies.

Another thing in the book not liked by the regime was this comparison between Power and Spirit:

At certain crossroads of our youth it may happen that we are met by Bellona and Athena – the one promising to teach us how to deploy twenty regiments before a battle, the other promising to teach us the secret how to put together twenty words, forming a perfect sentence. And then maybe we choose the latter of these arts, which is rarer and not so easy to spot where it grows on the hillside. [Laon, June 12th, 1940]

39

This is a clear-cut demonstration of a *vita activa* versus a *vita contemplativa*, or as an example of "Ares versus the Muses". It could also make you think of the reflection of Dr. Johnson, the one of the young man put before the choice of following Charles XII or Socrates and thereby (says the Doctor) usually choosing the heroic way, choosing to follow the warrior to topple the Tsar rather than hearing a lecture in philosophy. But that's the young man's condition, to each his own – since Jünger wrote this when he was 45, at a mature age, and by then it seems right to sound wise and thoughtful. I mean, when he was young in 1914 he never doubted the wisdom of going to war. By then the old, wise man's recommendation of the glory of poetry in favour of killing would have been wasted on him.

THE EASTERN FRONT

The war was raging, Nazi Germany (so to speak) having re-started the First World War, Germany again being in a two-front war against Russia and the Western powers. Jünger for his part served in the Paris staff all of the war. And that was unusual for a German subaltern at the time. They could serve in staffs some of the time, but never all of the time. They had to serve in the combat zone also, in Russia or North Africa, but Jünger was protected by friends in high places. Proposals were made from party officials that Jünger should go out and smell some gun-smoke [q.v. the late diary, January 31st, 1983], but his superior, the military governor himself, General Karl-Heinrich von Stülpnagel, sternly refused and said that Jünger was needed at his post. That was a subterfuge in order to protect Jünger.

Karl-Heinrich von Stülpnagel, succeeding his cousin Otto at this post in 1942, had Jünger as a partner in conversations and deliberations, treating art and culture as well as more burning subjects such as the opposition against Hitler. Jünger wasn't a central figure

in this evolving conspiracy but he was there, he heard the rumours and he made an impression on his fellow Germans in this respect. In the fall of 1942 the general sent Jünger on a thinly veiled spy-trip to the southern part of the eastern front, with a view to sounding out the opinions among generals and regimental officers in preparing a coup against the dictator. Officially Jünger made his trip "in order to fill out some traits in the figure of the Worker", hinting at his 1932 monograph which was in part inspired by the industrialization and five-year plans of the Soviet Union.

Jünger got his orders, directing him to travel to Army Group A on the eastern front, the southernmost sector. The generals of the Army Group Centre for their part were already in on the conspiracy. The attack on Russia hadn't gone well. Having begun in June, 1941, the plan was to attack and conquer all of European Russia, i.e. Russia west of the Urals.

For this Operation Barbarossa Hitler mobilized well over 100 divisions, with one army group heading for Leningrad, the central army group heading for Moscow and the southern army group heading for Kiev, the capital of Ukraine. In December 1941, Kiev had been taken and Leningrad was under siege but the main onslaught had been stopped before the gates of Moscow. Now, in 1942, Hitler made a gamble in the south in order to stage a decisive battle and bring the Russians to their knees. It's true that the Germans got this Caucasian offensive (Fall Blau) rolling in the late summer, and that the Russians retreated, but in the cityscape of Stalingrad on the Volga it all got bogged down in small-unit warfare. The German 6th Army made a strenuous effort to take the city and this was underway when Jünger left Paris, on October 23rd, 1942. In his subsequently published war diary (*Strahlungen*, which roughly translates as beamings/shimmerings/emanations) this episode is called *Caucasian Notes*, forming a sort of dramatic denouement of the whole book, a heart of darkness if you will. For example, one time he notes: "They say that the Russians have broken through north of Stalingrad" [Vorosjilovsk,

November 24th, 1942] – and this is very efficient stylistically, just a matter of fact delivered *en passant*.

Jünger's Second World War diaries are replete with things like these, short notes with a deep under-text. Another memorable passage from this time is when he strolls along a muddy village street, entering a house and finding himself in a room where General von Kleist is standing leaning over the situation map. I would call this an unsought example of historical presence. More on this, on Jünger himself as a nexus for historical events, in chapter 19.

Jünger's father died on January 9th, 1943. With this Jünger aborted his Russian journey and returned to Germany. At the same time 6th Army had surrendered in Stalingrad, the intimated Russian breakthrough having been crowned with success. It was a turning point in the war. Irrespective of the Kursk offensive later in 1943, the Germans were now on the retreat in the east for the rest of the war.

PARIS

Jünger returned from the eastern front. As I mentioned his father had died. Jünger had a premonition of this a year before. It's all in the diary. By February 1943, Jünger was back in the Paris staff, staying there until the final German retreat in August, 1944. Among his daily tasks this time were censoring the letters of soldiers to their families, translations and signal intelligence.

This time also saw Jünger's Peace Pamphlet, an appeal of peace to the youth of the world. The text was published 1946 in Holland as *Der Friede* (*The Peace*). Before that it had an adventurous existence since preaching peace was illegal in the Nazi Reich, handwritten copies of the text circulating. Rommel himself considered it useful as an appeal to the public after a coup against Hitler. More on *The Peace* in Chapter 17.

As a captain of the army of occupation Jünger lived well. For example he had the permission to wear civilian clothes in his spare time and thus he socialized with authors and artists, some of which he had known before the war. Now he broadened his circle with the rich and well off, visiting dinners and social events. Among his friends were the director Sacha Guitry, the authors Marcel Johandeau, Jean Cocteau, Paul Léautaud, Banine and Céline, the book seller Paul Morand and the socialite Florence Jay Gould. It was a luxurious existence but Jünger didn't really have a ball. These were mentally trying times. The world seemed to come to an end to many by then, including Jünger.

Jünger wasn't involved in the 20th July plot but peripherally he knew about it. He didn't consider the murdering of tyrants to be useful, being an all too specific solution to the wider problem of the time, a problem called nihilism. He seemed to have meant that political changes were meaningless unless people's minds were radically changed at first. In his war diary we read: "Like suicides assassination attempts are mock solutions, transferring the problem to another however not better plane." [July 20th, 1944]

As I said: Jünger vaguely knew about the plans to kill Hitler. He never got to know about details but, Neaman hints referring to a certain Walter Bargatzsky, he remained a spiritual force of the conspiracy. This says it all and gives Jünger the credit he deserves. Other than that, with Neaman as the main source, this can be said about this historical complex – the plans to assassinate Hitler and seize power were discussed early in the war (or shall we say, mainly from 1942) by Speidel and von Stülpnagel in the salon of Hotel George V, another luxury dwelling of the Paris staff. Their talks were part of the army's coup plans; then there was a civilian conspiracy represented by count Schulenburg, now becoming the liaison between the George V circle and count Moltke's so called Kreisauer circle. A certain Hofacker was the liaison to the people around general Beck in Berlin and the Goerdeler group in Leipzig. In the Paris staff, according to

Neaman, apart from military and officials there were journalists and authors like Friedrich Sieburg, Clemens Podevils, Dolf Sternberger, Nicky von Grothe and Gerhard Nebel.

There was another military establishment in France along with the military governor: the field army staff under Rommel in La Roche-Guyon, this too being part of the conspiracy. Here they once expected a visit from Hitler, dealing with the allied invasion that had started on June 6th, 1944, but they didn't succeed in killing him then as planned. Thereby the focus was transferred to Beck and the Berlin circle. This eventually led to the failed Stauffenberg attempt in der Wolfsschanze, the East Prussian staff establishment, on July 20th, 1944. As is widely known, Captain Stauffenberg left a briefcase there with a time bomb next to Hitler. Then Stauffenberg exited the room and the building, seeing the explosion from the outside and making the conclusion that Hitler must have died in it. So he left for Berlin where eventually the conspiracy got well under way, the forces directed by the conspirators making arrests of SS people in both Berlin and Paris.

Stauffenberg's mistake was this: not waiting some minutes in der Wolfsschanze and actually get a confirmation of whether Hitler was dead or not. Stauffenberg only guessed that der Führer had died. However, he was still alive, only slightly injured. So when the news reached Berlin, when it was confirmed that Hitler was alive, it resulted in a counter-coup against the conspirators, having them rounded up and – like in Stauffenberg's case – immediately shot. Then there were mass arrests of incriminated officers and civilians, and the staff of the military governor in Paris was ransacked and closed.

As for Jünger he was off duty the fateful day (June 20th, 1944). He was beyond the reach of orders and staffs at the moment, thereby escaping immediate accusations of participation. A week later the allies broke out of the Normandy beachhead, the Germans being unable to check the massive onslaught of the American and British armoured divisions. The allies were closing in on Paris so the Germans packed their bags and left, the confusion of this hasty

retreat making it easier for Jünger to slip through the net of justice. Having arrived in Germany he was accused in a people's court but the case was dismissed. Jünger then got transferred to the army reserve and later he was discharged altogether. Then he served for a while in the Home Guard (Volkssturm).

General Stülpnagel, Jünger's Paris HQ superior, had been one of the conspiracy's leading men. He tried to commit suicide by shooting himself, only resulting in a wound that made him blind. He was then sentenced to death and hanged. Speidel for this part was imprisoned and tortured by the Gestapo. Later on he managed to escape.

As intimated Jünger was against the whole idea of assassinations. They only strengthened the tyranny. Maybe he, like the renowned army general von Brauchitsch, was of the opinion that "Hitler was Germany's destiny, and you can't escape your destiny". This at least we read in Bullock's Hitler biography.

1944-45

It was the year of 1944. Offensives from both the east and the west demonstrated that the days of the Third Reich was numbered. The bomber war intensified, nihilism ruled. The end was in sight but in the short run it all got worse. Earlier this year for example, Jünger's oldest son, Ernstel, had been arrested for having formed a resistance group against the Nazi regime. It was a demonstration of civil courage but at the same time dangerous; there were informers everywhere, a chance remark against Hitler came with severe penalties, and indeed Ernstel and a comrade were sentenced to jail.

Later on the punishment was transformed into combat duty but it was out of the ashes and into the fire, literally. Ernstel was weak from his prison days and didn't receive much soldier's training. He fell in battle as a panzer grenadier on the Italian front, November 1944.

Ironically it was on the marble cliffs of Carrara, Tuscany, in a marble quarry near Massa.

As intimated the allies had invaded France this year. They launched a seaborne assault on June 6th, 1944, eventually landing a substantial amount of army divisions, spearheaded by tanks and supported by a massive air force. The Germans could stem the advance for some time but at the end of July the front broke and France had to be abandoned. The allies took Paris on August 25th. Jünger for his part left the town in mid August. Eventually he settled in Kirchhorst, being an officer of der Volkssturm and doing his duty, however with a view to avoiding unnecessary bloodshed when the American tank spearheads arrived. And when they did arrive the road blocks were opened and the particular Volkssturm unit surrendered. Now Jünger, as can be seen in his 1940 diary, was a stern fighter bent on never surrendering, but this 1945 scene was a different story. In 1940 the stakes were somewhat equal, a professional army against another. Now, with ill-equipped civilian soldiers, it was probably the best thing to do to surrender as quick as possible. To hand over authority in this way also takes responsibility, it takes a man who knows what he wants, who knows what is useful and what is not.

Kirchhorst was occupied and so was the Jünger house, Americans settling in the yard forming – says Jünger in his diary – a veritable "Wallenstein's Camp", referring to a drama by Schiller about the Thirty Year's War. Jünger noted the soldiers' seeming lack of Prussian polish but overall the discipline was tight. When the soldiers had left he states in his diary that they were human. In this context it was better to have Americans on your doorstep than Russians and Mongols.

POST WAR YEARS

Nazi Germany was defeated and partitioned, occupied by the Western allies and the Soviet Union. The war was over and Nazism was called to account. For example, the person who wanted to clear himself of accusations of Nazi leanings could go to the authorities, answer a certain questionnaire and then receive a voucher saying you were idealistically cleared, "denazified" as the term was. These letters of indulgence were sorely needed for anyone in the grey area of Nazi accusations. You were either in or out, good or bad, condemned for ever or blessed as a new born man. In the literary realm this later developed into a whole genre, Ger. Rechtfertigunslitteratur, "justification literature". The typical example is Gottfried Benn, a poet who had openly supported the Nazi's in the 30's, who wrote *Doppelleben* (*Double Life*, 1945). This book, Neaman says, is one of the most hypocritical examples of this genre ever written. Jünger for his part never bothered himself with this, both refusing to undergo formal denazification and to creep to the cross with an apology like Benn's.

As I said Jünger had written a peace pamphlet, *The Peace*. In 1945 this work circulated in handwritten copies. According to Neaman the allied authorities were reached by a rumour saying that the content was liked by old Nazi's, thus igniting a press campaign against Jünger. It eventually resulted in a publication ban for him in the British zone where Hannover/Kirchhorst was situated. Its governor was Montgomery of Alamein by the way.

Before this *The Peace* was issued in 1946 by the Dutch publishing house Erasmus. Other books by Jünger surfacing by this time were *Atlantische Fahrt* (*Atlantic Journey*, 1947), published in England for German prisoners of war, and *Sprache und Körperbau* (*Language and Bodily Structure*), published in Switzerland. Then the publication ban became effective and Jünger didn't publish anything until 1949.

47

In 1948 Jünger moved to Ravensburg, Württemberg, situated in the French zone of occupation. Conditions were a bit more liberal here. Finally, in the next year, he published two milestone works: the war diary of 1939-45, *Strahlungen*, and the novel *Heliopolis*. They were greeted as major works even at the time of their issuance, partly because Jünger was one of the few German authors still living on German soil. Most others were in exile.

The Jüngers were now living in the landscape of Suabia (Ger. Schwaben), after Ravensburg only making the smaller transfer to Wilflingen by the Suabian alp foothills. Their home became the forester house of the von Stauffenberg family estate. Incidentally Jünger had depicted a Claus von Stauffenberg-type in the Sunmyra character of *On the Marble Cliffs*.

This forester house was a grand building, a palace in itself for a writer prince in the old sense and thus a sort of an anachronism. This was the era of Neue Sachligkeit and the threat of nuclear war, of kitchen sink realism and misery. But Jünger had never been in harmony with the Zeitgeist. Apart from that the Bundesland (state) of Baden-Württemberg where Jünger now lived was a classical conservative outpost, not very much affected by either Nazism or Neo-Nazism, Neaman says. In the same region for example, there lived friends of Jünger like Carl Schmitt and the first Bundespräsident of the German Federal Republic, Theodor Heuss. And in the central city of Stuttgart Ernst Klett came to reside, becoming Jünger's major publisher in the following years. The first Jünger issue on Klett was *The Glass Bees* (*Gläserne Bienen*, 1957). Previous Jünger issues of the 50's were *The Forest Passage* (*Der Waldgang*, 1951) and *Das Sanduhrbuch* (*A Book on Hour-Glasses*, 1954). Other Jünger events by this time was a trip to Sardinia and the reception of the Goslar literature prize. Goslar is a town in Lower Saxony.

By the 50's things had settled a bit: the German Federal Republic, the western part of Germany where Jünger lived, had risen from the ashes to become a modern, prosperous industrial nation. And Jünger

was accepted as a conservative writer, free from the mark of Cain. In a way he had come in from the cold. After all he had been a highly lauded figure in the Nazi state, his books being widely published in that era. As intimated Hitler held a sort of protective hand over Jünger the author. Almost every other author had either been in exile or hadn't published anything in those years. So for Jünger to make a transition into the anti-Nazi post-war years was a bit of an achievement.

Some details about Jünger's personal life and habits can come in handy here. For instance Jünger's entomological activities were fruitful. In Jünger's honour nine species of *coleoptera* were eventually named after him, like *Gackstroemia Juengeriana*. As for Jünger himself he owned a copy of the entomological encyclopaedia of Jan Swammerdam (1758) as well as a 30 volume catalogue on the beetles of the world. Plus, among other things, a 18th century edition of all the church fathers. Moreover Jünger collected famous last words. One of the tragicomic instances was this utterance of the American Civil War general John Sedgwick (1813-64), in the din of battle reportedly saying to his men: "Why are you dodging like this? They couldn't hit an elephant at this distance!" The next moment he fell off his horse, lethally struck by a bullet.

Now then, on with the story of Jünger's life. The rest of the 50's among other things saw a quick trip to the USA, in 1958. And in 1959 Jünger, along with Mircea Eliade, began issuing the magazine *Antaios*, dedicated to myth, religion and symbolism. It was named after an antique giant getting his power from the earth; when lifted up from it he became weak and could be defeated, as was exactly how Hercules conquered him. This Antaios became a new archetype for Jünger, in contrast to the Worker under whose spell he had been in the previous epoch. By then it was nihilism and technology, now it was Mother Nature and her wonders that led him on.

In the same year (1959) Jünger received das Bundesverdienstkreuz, an honorary order given by the western German state to artists, athletes, CEO's etc.

Apart from this worldly success Jünger was active in other worldly matters, having his surreal credibility already established by the book *Das abenteurerliche Herz*. Neaman gives us the merry picture of Jünger being invited by Salvador Dali in 1962 to contribute to a book, existing in one copy only, and with entries by Jean Cocteau, Jean Rostand, Bernard Buffet and others. Jünger's contribution was a passage out of *Fassungen*, calligraphy by himself on a sheepskin. The anthology was a mix of comedy, mysticism and surrealism and Jünger is said to have blended in well with this company.

In 1960 Jünger's wife Gretha died, known from the war diary as *Perpetua*. As intimated they had been married since 1925. Between the years 1960-65 Jünger's collected works in ten volumes were published. Having thus put his old work behind him, and having lots of energy for new endeavours, he started a new diary meant for publishing. This in time became the series *Siebzig verweht* (*Beyond Seventy*), ultimately running from 1965 to 1996, in other words from the year he turned 70 and on. Other 60's Jünger books worth mentioning are *Sgraffiti* (*Graffiti*), a book on this and that like *The Adventurous Heart*, *Sturm* (re-issue of a novel written in the twenties) and *Subtile Jagden* (*Subtle Hunts*), about his lifelong passion for insects and plants.

Later in the decade Jünger married the Germanic scholar Liselotte Lohrer, whom he knew from her work at Klett-Cotta where she had edited his works for many years. As a companion through thick and thin she is mentioned as *das Stierlein* (Little Calf) in the late diary. Among other things she accompanied Jünger on his travels. In these years he visited the Moroccan town of Agadir several times. It serves as the chief inspiration to the city of Eumeswil in the eponymous novel from 1977, this coastal town with its casbah, its river Sus and its marshes teeming with bird life.

LENNART SVENSSON

THE GOETHE PRIZE

Many writers have been recluses, enjoying the life of the eremite. Jünger more or less was forced into this lifestyle since in the 60's and 70's he was ignored by the intellectual elite, not being invited to symposiums and literary conventions. The years of the New Left with its partial admiration of Soviet Russia and/or Maoist China, its anti-militarism and nihilistic materialism were, on the surface, lean years for Jünger. But the back-catalogue of his books (like *Storm of Steel*) sold well and as a private citizen he could do what he pleased. And he wasn't totally bereft of invitations; in 1968 for example he visited Rome as a guest of honour at the German academy dwelling Villa Massimo.

He also published this and that. The year of 1978 saw a new collected works issue, this one in 18 volumes. And in 1977 he published the novel *Eumeswil*, a speculative novel summarizing his ideas on history, politics, myth, art and life. And in the years to come (i.e. in the 80's) he issued yet another novel, *Eine gefährliche Begegnung* (*A Dangerous Encounter*), a crime story taking place in 19th century Paris.

The leftist years had put Jünger in the shade. And still he was a controversial figure for the German mainstream. However, the 80's saw a renewed interest for Jünger in France. French intellectuals, weary of Freud and Marx, now began delving into the works of Heidegger, Nietzsche and Jünger. And as for Germany everything wasn't an intellectual desert, there were still conservative forces around, and in this respect the awarding of the 1982 Goethe Prize to Jünger was feasible.

In the same year Jünger was visited by Argentinian author Jorge Luis Borges. Borges had read *Storm of Steel* when young and was deeply affected by it. During this meeting they came to discuss the dystopia of Aldous Huxley and ant communities. Jünger considered these more complete than ours, the ants being happier than we are.

Borges for his part doubted it.

This survey has reached the 80's. The mid-to-late 80's in themselves were a prosperous, euphoric age with Reaganomics and market place hausse, but the early part of the decade saw a West-world in economic recession and with the imminent threat of a nuclear war in Europe. The word Euroshima summed it all up, embodying the fears of Germany becoming a theatre of nuclear war. In the midst of all this war fever some Nato-generals had had it, forming instead "Generals for Peace" and starting to propagate the issue of peace. They may have had a point in this, having been part of the nuclear war machine themselves. And in 1983 they sent a letter to Jünger, inviting him to join them in a peace rally against the placement of middle distance missiles in Germany. Jünger then answered (reprinted in the late diary) that he had stopped marching in demonstrations, nowadays rather siding with people than issues. Through texts like *Heliopolis* and *The Forest Passage* he had made a statement about defending life and fighting Leviathan and that should be enough, you might think.

Jünger was in the headlines now and then. In 1984 for example he participated in the French-German reconciliation ceremony at Verdun. The next year he was visited in Wilflingen by Francois Mitterand, the French President celebrating him on his 90th birthday. And in 1988 Jünger and German Bundeskanzler Helmuth Kohl visited Paris, celebrating the 40th anniversary of the French-German agreement of friendship.

In 1996 it is said that Jünger secretly converted to Catholicism. Then, lastly, he died, on February 17th, 1998, 102 years old. Present at the funeral were thousands of people and five generals of the Bundeswehr. This was not an ordinary author's funeral, not by any standards. Jünger was unique. "Germany's greatest author since Goethe" might be a fitting epitaph.

2. JÜNGER AND NAZISM

When dealing with Jünger a burning question might be his relations to Nazism. Everybody even vaguely acquainted with him seems to be interested in this.

A COMPARISON BETWEEN JÜNGER & HITLER

For starters, what unites Jünger with Adolf Hitler, the man who created and led the Nazi movement? What do they have in common? In the event I want to list the following points:

- Born about the same time (Jünger in 1895, Hitler in 1889).
- Positively shaped by the combat zone experience, the army becoming a spiritual home.
- German nationalists, in for the ideas of 1914 (country, loyalty, tradition) in conflict with the ideas of 1789 (freedom, equality, internationalism).

Then you have to look into the differences as well. They may both have been nationalists during the decisive years but Jünger, as intimated by Neaman, for example wasn't so influenced by the Northern heritage (with Wagner, *The Edda*) as Hitler was. Jünger of course never denied his German heritage, however, he found comparatively many of his influences in the south and in the common European heritage with a keen eye for things French. Following Neaman you get the picture of Jünger as an aristocrat, alien to the plebeian "have a beer and sing along" camaraderie of the early Nazi circles. Jünger himself later on saw Nazism as a product of the liberal democratic system, seeing Hitler as "the Napoleon of common suffrage". Had Germany been more aristocratic this would have been avoided, he seems to mean.

So Jünger didn't like democracy and common suffrage. The demagogy, the levelling and the standardization to him might have been too high prices to pay for "a government of the people, by the people, for the people". In early versions of *Das Wäldchen 125* Jünger wrote, "I hate democracy like the plague". He mellowed over the years, however it's equally true that he preferred the Wilhelmine Kaiserreich to everything that followed: the Weimar republic, Nazism and post-war Germany.

Now let's look at the Jewish question. My focus of attention is a certain article by Jünger in Schwarzschilds *Tagebuch*, September 1929. For example Goebbels lost his faith in Jünger after reading this, Nevin says. In the article Jünger criticised the fact that racism had become a central topic, ironically stating that a nationalist these days would seem to have to eat three Jews for breakfast, Jünger concluding: "To us anti-Semitism is no central topic." By that he meant "we national revolutionaries", the Prussian anarchists with a predilection for five year plans, militarism and nationalism.

Jünger was no anti-Semite. If anything he held the romantic view that the Jew should become more Jewish, abandoning his assimilation (q.v. an article in *Die Kommenden*, September 1930). By cultivating their uniqueness the Jews would become an anti-bourgeois, traditionalistic force he seems to have meant.

To the slightly snobbish Jünger, Nazism seemed to lack style. It was too Völkish, too much directed towards the lower classes and their tastes. Nazism to him lacked the spiritual, aesthetic and literary traits that inspired him. That's the impression I get from the studies by Nevin, Neaman and Jonasson.

In one respect Jünger's creed in the 20's was a bit facile. I think of his "Peter Pan nationalism", as a researcher quoted by Nevin calls it. The nationalist camp described by Jünger in those days tended to dream of eternal struggle, eternal war, eternal revolution, not spending much time about what would happen after the revolution. How to stop being a warrior and begin the peaceful struggle of building the land, this didn't bother them overly much.

Jünger in his polemical articles in those days envisioned a Bourgeois Man, a materialist devoid of faith and tradition, in the process becoming something of an Jungian Other, the archetypal enemy, against whom stands the Warrior who will fix it all to the best with his spirit of self-sacrifice and camaraderie, his sense of duty and discipline. The Warrior is an authentic man, restoring everything that has fallen with the advent of civilisation. Against this can be said: of course the warrior can be an inspiration in other struggles, as a paragon of self-sacrifice and courage. Here you can remember the pacifist who wanted to find the moral equivalent of war as an elevating and guiding force. But the Jünger of the 20's lacks a certain amount of distance. He reads too much into the role of the warrior, not realizing that it's just another colour on the palette along with the baker, the cook, the doctor, the priest and the teacher on so on.

Now war and the soldier's life are strong metaphors so Jünger can be forgiven for having fallen for their charms. You could only hope that a new generation of Jünger readers won't take his war books too literally (and even if they take them literally there won't be any wars to fight; I'm rather alone in this assessment, I know). You could use Bushido to raise yourself mentally but that's about it.

THE DREAMS

Hitler for his part remained a Jünger admirer until the end, *Storm of Steel* having made a lasting impression on him as a fellow war veteran. "Leave Jünger alone" is said to have been the standing Hitler order to Goebbels, in cases when the Reichsminister wanted to persecute Jünger for his atavism.

As for Jünger's relationship to Hitler on the personal level it was complex. As I said in chapter 1 they never met. It wasn't meant to be. But they met in the dream world. In Jünger's war diary it is related that Jünger had many dreams about Hitler. They are a field day for a dream analyst.

One of the chief dreams in this respect is referred to on October 26th, 1943 but never told in detail: a dream from 1938, experienced during a Jünger passage to the island of Rhodes. In this, Jünger tells us, Hitler is said to have met Jünger, pitting his strength against his and "offering him dominion over all earthly kingdoms" so to speak. Literally Jünger says that he "made a stance against Kniébolo and his minions in their centre of power." [October 26th, 1943] "Kniébolo" was Jünger's code name for Hitler.

On February 2nd, 1943, Jünger says that this dream became a guide for him in his daily life throughout the Nazi years. So this is a good setting of the scene, a mythopoetic way of looking at history in general and Jünger's relation to Hitler and Nazism in particular.

The rest of the Hitler dreams of the war diary are as follows. I leave them mostly without comment, it sometimes being best to let the words speak for themselves. In dream number one, Hitler only figures at the beginning, but I have to quote the whole passage, it being an organic, indivisible whole, a customary dream in three scenes:

> Lively night. First I met Kniébolo who seemed weak and melancholy, seeking contact. He gave me some beautifully gilded candy, telling me that they had presented him with large quantities

on his birthday. Then I saw an image of life like an obstacle course with labyrinths, reversed compartments and many obstacles which could only be passed in one direction; also gates leading out into the open. Then a new glow presented itself, in gold and blue. In a bowl I was shaking some crystals, the pebbles shining now in bright blue, now in pure gold, and during this act a faint rumbling sound rose from out of the vessel. [Kirchhorst, April 28th, 1939]

The next elaborate Hitler dream is one from Paris, April 16th, 1943:

During the morning hours a meaningful dream about Kniébolo, taking place in my father's house. He was expected there for reasons I've forgotten. Diverse preparations were made while I, in order to avoid meeting him, by habit went off into the more distant rooms. When I reappeared he had already left. I heard details about his visit, among other things and above all that my father had embraced him. Even when I woke up this struck me. In the circumstances this is the most important sign since the decisive meeting and confrontation, happening on the passage to Rhodes.

Then we have a last Hitler dream from Kirchhorst, March 20th, 1945. It's more clear-cut and preaching but with a fine detail, that of the insect collection:

This night another visit by Kniébolo, myself putting a room at his disposal for a conference with some Englishmen. The result was the proclamation of gas war. All things considered I realized that he would benefit from this, having reached such a degree of nihilism that put him outside of parties – to him every dead human being meant a gain, indifferent to which side he was on. I also thought: "Yes, and it's therefore you've had so many hostages shot and you will get a thousand times interest on this, at the expense of the innocent." And finally: "Now you've achieved what you wished

from the outset." All this in a mood of almost indifferent disgust since my roof was already shot through and I angered myself over the fact that it rained on my South American insects."

3. WITNESS

As we have seen Jünger was no Nazi, refusing to join the party, declining a Nazi mandate in der Reichstag and refusing to join Goebbel's sanitized Deutsche Akademie der Dichtung. It's true that Jünger remained a respected right-wing author during the Nazi years, but he slowly but surely drifted towards the resistance camp. As I've said he was no active conspirator in the 20th July coup but he was existentially against the regime. His sympathies lay with mankind, not with the torturers and the hangmen. Jünger witnessed the grim times he lived in. The following could be called reports from what Eliot dubbed "the dead land, the cactus land".

SYMBOLIC QUOTE

Jünger was a conservative in opposition to the Nazis, abhorring the barbarian traits of the regime. The following quote could symbolize it all, a sharp-edged image of the early days of the Hitler reign: "The

first execution under Kniébolo: the executioner, having taken off his jacket before the decapitation, reporting in his shirt sleeves, with the cylinder hat askew, the blood-dripping axe in his left hand and the right raised into "German salute": "The execution carried out." [Paris, March 20th, 1943]

THE BOMBER WAR

From 1943 on the allied bombings is something of a sub-theme of the diary, giving us a view of the bomber war over Germany from the perspective of the victims. This isn't about flying missions, encountering fighters and avoiding flak, no, it's about being on the receiving end of the aerial war. It's about literally feeling your house shake in its foundations and seeing phosphorus being poured out over the land you're living in:

> Tonight two parties of chess with Baumgart. Krause, having been in Hamburg both during and after the attacks, told about seeing twenty charred corpses lined up along a bridge railing, as on a grill. It was people being washed with phosphorus and with a view to throwing themselves into the water, having been burned to death before. Someone had also seen a woman, on each arm carrying a burned baby corpse. Krause (...) had been passing a house where the phosphorus poured in streams from the low roof, having heard screams but being unable to do anything. This reminds you of the scenes of Inferno or of a ghastly nightmare. [Paris, August 11th, 1943, after the Hamburg raid this year when 50,000 died]

Jünger's Kirchhorst house was in the countryside. So what he saw of the bomber war from there – and the diary is replete with it – isn't so horrifying in itself. Lots of planes in the sky: amazing but not bone-chillingly ghastly. More on this in Chapter 27. However, looking for

the infernal scenes of the Jünger diary I can give you these two:

(...) visit by a Lieutenant Sommer who has been in Hamburg. There, it was told, they had seen a group of children with grey hair, small old men, aged during a phosphorus night. [Paris, August 11th, 1943]

In the city yesterday I heard that the attack last night took many lives. Most were squeezed to death in the crowding in front of the doors to the aerial shelter bunkers. There are bunkers only accessible by steep stairs; some jump over the railing and down on those waiting in the stair, breaking the neck of those they land on. Harry once saw one of these entrances to Inferno; the groans and cries out of the dark mouth was heard far off into the night. [Kirchhorst, October 20th, 1944]

4. JÜNGER AS AN OUTSIDER

Ernst Jünger tends to generate totally diverse reactions: saint or sinner, fascist or hero of the resistance. Seeing it from an artistic point of view – and you can't ignore the artistic in the case of Jünger, since his life and his work blend into a single Gestalt – these differing reactions may in fact be the mark of mastership. For as Oscar Wilde said: "Diversity of opinion about a work of art shows that the work is new, complex, and vital" (from *The Picture of Dorian Gray*). In this chapter I will look into these issues – on what Jünger being a bad boy represents and how he's been received in diverse countries.

ON BEING CONTROVERSIAL

What exactly is "controversial"? I don't know. I only know that Jünger was and still is *umstritt*, to use a German term. Indeed, they fight (Ger. zu streiten) over (um) who he was, the critics of Germany, Sweden, France, England and the US and maybe even of Asia. From certain

voices we for instance hear that Jünger was lauded by the Nazis and therefore no one should read him. Against this others, from both the left and the right camp, says: it's no secret that Jünger's books were well received in the Third Reich but that doesn't disqualify him as a writer. His work is complex, not possible to reduce into a formula. Jünger isn't a saint or a sinner, he's "neither" as well as "both". That's what makes a writer great. See the Wilde quote above.

Of course Jünger is unusual. He did glorify war, he did talk about the need for spirituality in an age of materialism, he did stress the need for having contact with your ancestry as an individual and as a people. These tendencies are not in the mainstream of 20th century fiction.

There you have the outlines of this chapter. I won't go into a partisan debate over Jünger, like taking the conservative stance against radicals. If some intellectuals want to picture him as a monster I'm not overly concerned. I mean, If I wanted to I could counter the "Jünger-as-a-monster" argument by saying that the post war Jünger was a tranquil flower collector who only wanted peace and quiet, contented with blowing soap bubbles in his garden. You could whitewash him like that and quote from his work in this respect, even getting the soap bubbles into the picture...! But the Jünger œuvre in its totality says more than this, giving us more than pictures of the beauty of flowers and beetles. The post 1945 Jünger was still a kind of traditionally anchored nationalist. I'll show you some proofs of this, not with a view to making it into a political debate, just having the ambition to say that he was more than a respectable conservative contented with the quiet life.

I begin this chapter with a look at Jünger's German role during the 90's. There's a fairly political slant to this. Then, more or less leaving politics aside, I take a look at some critics in Sweden and the English speaking world who through the years have appreciated Jünger. These voices tend not to see Jünger as a controversial outsider – or do they? The Englishmen Stuart Hood and Bruce Chatwin surely liked some of Jünger's work but they were also puzzled by the man.

THE 1990'S: A NEW DAWN

As I showed in chapter 1 Jünger was mostly ignored by the German intellectuals during the 50's and well into the 80's. That is to say, he had his books published and they were widely read but he didn't count, he wasn't part of the current German discussion. Jünger was a man of the right and the Leitkultur of the times was leftist, not exactly pro-Soviet but not anti-Soviet either. Materialism, a denigration of tradition and a vague hope for "revolution", that was the post war intellectual atmosphere in Western Germany, the Bundesrepublik Deutschland where Jünger lived.

The left ruled, exerting a sort of hegemony. However in 1989 the movement suffered a setback with the dissolution of the Soviet Union, the worker's paradise on earth, an ideologically driven regime advocating anti-traditionalism, internationalism and pacifism (while at the same time warring and instigating insurrections all over the globe, including in the west). Soviet Russia crumbled and communism went broke and the forces of the right became resurgent throughout Europe, ushering in ideas of nation, faith and tradition. In Germany one of the spokesmen for this movement became the periodical *Junge Freiheit*, advocating conservative and traditionalist ideas. It was positioned in a formerly almost empty zone, the zone to the right of Germany's mainstream right-wing party, the Christian Democrats.

So where did Jünger fit into this? He had long since stopped taking part in the current debate by this time but it's clear that he liked *Junge Freiheit*. This paper still exists, by the way, as I write this in August, 2014. The title means "Young Freedom". After Jünger's death it was made public that Jünger had subscribed to the magazine. In *Junge Freiheit* 5/27/2011 a certain Thorsten Thaler wrote a piece called "Er hat Ihr Blatt sehr geschätzt" ("He liked your paper very much"). In it we read that Jünger always had the current copy of *Junge Freihet* with

him on his travels. He is said to have liked how *Junge Freihet* went against the Zeitgeist, occupying a grey area between the radical right and conservatism.

"So what?" you might say. *Junge Freiheit* is still blossoming, with many people reading it. But *Junge Freiheit* is a controversial subject in the still extant leftist Leitkultur of the west. And as for the subject of this book – Ernst Jünger – it should be noted that Jünger still held political views in the 90's. He wasn't totally apolitical, as he would sometimes seem.

BOTHO STRAUSS

In 1995 Jünger turned 100, being celebrated from many directions. Above all the Germans Heimo Schwilk and Günther Figal edited a Festschrift ("celebration publication") called *Magie der Heiterkeit: Ernst Jünger zum Hundertsten* (*The Magic of Mirth*). One of the entries was by German novelist Botho Strauss, previously known as a man of the left but by this time approaching the radical conservative camp. His piece was called "Refrain einer tieferen Erklärung" ("Refrain of a Deeper Declaration"). In it he praised Jünger as a literary pioneer, exploiting themes no one else in Germany wrote about. Like writing about the soldiery life (see chapters 5-7 in this book of mine), highlighting the warrior's way as a means to spiritual fulfilment.

Jünger seems to have affected Strauss in this way, sowing the seeds of western style Bushido in the quiet, neue Sachlichkeit-type of German author Strauss was (q.v. novels like *Mikado* and *Rumour*). It all began in 1993 when Strauss caused an uproar with his exclamation: "We have to restore Eros and the Soldier". This and other statements of his essay "Anschwellender Bockgesang" (like the criticism of materialism and nihilism of the current German society) wasn't well received by the establishment. Critique of the emptiness

of the consumer society may have been welcome, however not with these traditionalist leanings. Strauss became controversial...! Even in Sweden the waves were felt. And still in 2000 when his essay-cum-diary *Die Fehler des Kopisten* was issued in a Swedish version we learned from the media that Strauss was a dangerous man, best ignored.

Anyhow, I agree with Strauss. We have to restore Eros and the Soldier. And for this Jünger's books in question and Evola's *The Metaphysics of War* could be the orientation course, then moving on to Sven Hassel's books and top it off with Väinö Linna's *Unknown Soldier* (1954). War and love, Eros and the Soldier however have always been taboo: the soldier and the whore are eagerly sought after to do their required jobs but afterwards we despise them, because in their respective actions they expose the taboos of life and death. If we admitted this we would learn a lot about ourselves and our culture.

SWEDISH RECEPTION

I recently mentioned Sweden and now I'll examine the Jünger reception in this land. Then I'll finish this chapter considering some English views on Jünger.

As I promised in the introduction to this chapter I won't go into partisan debates on what Jünger is and is not. Briefly it can be mentioned that the Swedish radical left now and then occupies itself with Jünger bashing, this being one of their favourite sports. It's like a habit, a symbolic game. (For instance, in 2011 a major newspaper in a review of a new edition of *On the Marble Cliffs* in Swedish compared the protagonist of the novel with Norwegian terrorist Anders Breivik. That's the level of the Swedish Jünger debate, MSM style.) At the same time, as a Jünger fan you have to admit that Sweden is a good environment for Jünger publishing. The first translation to surface was

an edition of *On the Marble Cliffs* in 1950 and from then on we've had *Heliopolis, Eumeswil,* rich excerpts from the war diary, *Annäherungen* and about ten other books by Jünger converted into Swedish. The latest was *Storm of Steel* in 2008. And besides the customary bashing we've had responsible critics noting Jünger's fortes.

So then: you shouldn't complain, the Swedish reception of his works having been mostly positive. As for the critics with a keen eye for Jünger and his oeuvre you could mention Carl-Henning Wijkmark and Werner Aspenström. In Stig Jonasson's edited volume, the Swedish language selection from the Second World War diary (*Dagböcker från Frankrike och Tyskland under krig och ockupation,* 1975) we find, among other things, this quote from the Swedish critic Wijkmark, known to the English speaking world as the author of the Göring novel *The Hunters of Karinhall* (1972). It's true that Wijkmark didn't like the metaphysical traits of Jünger's writing but he also said this: "When Jünger is at his best – and he often is – his style forges impressions and reflections into a durable and shimmering alloy, a new and unique verbal metal."

This Wijkmark said in *Sydsvenska Dagbladet* 1958. Then we have, also from Jonasson's book, this note on Jünger quoted from the magazine *BLM* in 1950 by the poet and Academy member Werner Aspenström, noting the level of artistry in *On the Marble Cliffs*:

Both as a work of art and as a human document it can withstand a comparison to the best works of Kafka. Here we find the same mystical radiance – the shimmer of deathless art (...) – Orwell's famous allegory, *Nineteen Eighty-Four,* is in a totally different way straightforward and unambiguous but as a political satire making a more prosaic impression due to its relative lack of artistry.

STUART HOOD

Now as promised on to the English voices. Those I have chosen were on the whole positive to Jünger, not overly delving on the controversial side of the man and his work. Of course they mentioned Jünger's dark traits but they didn't for that matter leave him out in the cold. And yet they had problems understanding him, the elitist and metaphysical sides of his works alienating them. And these Jünger portraits have in some way established the Jünger role of outsider. I don't much resent it but as a Jünger reader you have to admit it.

Stuart Hood (1915-2011) was a Scottish novelist and a translator, his first work as interpreter being the English version of *Auf den Marmorklippen* as *On the Marble Cliffs* (1946). He did a fine job in finding old and colourful words for the imaginary, archaic world in question, like "quaich" for a type of small pot and "Chief Warden" for "Oberförster". It all started in 1945 when Hood was serving in Germany as part of the British occupation army, by chance getting his hands on a copy of *Auf den Marmorklippen*. Hood was a bit wary of the book since he knew Jünger as a right-winger, but this changed when he actually read it. I quote the following from Hood's "On Meeting and Translating Ernst Jünger", as seen on the site "Ernst Jünger in Cyberspace" from the subsection "Essays":

> It was with considerable curiosity and a certain distrust that I began to read *Auf den Marmorklippen*. My resistance was quickly overcome by a narrative which told the story of two brothers, two intellectuals – as might be Jünger and his poet brother Friedrich Georg – and how they coped with life under a primitive ruler, the Chief Warden, who was an incarnation of the Fascist ideas on blood and soil.

The book to Hood seemed to fill an empty space. This was the kind of resistance literature the allies had expected to surface after the fall of

Nazism. But no such literature came to light. And *On the Marble Cliffs* was issued already in 1939 under the auspices of the Nazi regime. This to Hood seemed "to be a literary act of considerable courage".

Having translated and published a chapter of the novel Hood then went on to translate the whole book. And in September the same year – 1945 – Hood went to Kirchhorst for a meeting with the author:

> In September I was taken to meet Jünger. The introduction was the work of a fellow-officer, a German refugee. Before the war he had had contacts with the circle round Stefan George, whose verses, pompously celebrating the idea of an elite brotherhood, he would chant in what, he assured me, was the authentic curiously nasal way. Jünger was at this time living at Kirchhorst near Hanover, having withdrawn there after his dismissal from the Wehrmacht in the days following the July Plot. I found a thin handsome man in his fifties, very correct and polite, ready to engage in a discussion of *Marmorklippen*, its meaning and the difficulties of translating it. Our conversation took place partly during a walk in the moor near his house, partly in his study which bore the mark of his fastidious and unusual mind. On the wall was the beautiful skeleton of a snake. Snakes, I knew from his writing, fascinated him by their beauty, renewed each year, as they cast their skins, and their deadly venomous power. There were small objects, stones, dried flowers, carefully chosen as if each one had a special significance. His language was precise, nuanced, cultivated.

Hood started to question Jünger about politics. Jünger said that in the 20's he had seen the Nazis as having "something to offer Germany but he had been mistaken". And, says Hood, "such political honesty was rare at the time; the usual assertion was 'Ich bin nie PG gewesen' (I was never a Party member)." Then they talked about German literature, Jünger having this to say about Thomas Mann:

He [Jünger] expressed his intense dislike of Thomas Mann and his style. (...) What Jünger could not stand in Mann, apart from his woolly politics, he explained, was his use of the German language. His own models, he declared, were French.

As for the translation of *On the Marble Cliffs* this was said when Hood met Jünger:

We talked about translation. I explained that in one passage I had used the Scots word 'quaich' meaning a bowl with two lugs because it seemed to me to convey the essentially archaic nature of the Chief Warden's court. The idea seemed to appeal to him.

Hood was puzzled by Jünger, being somewhat unable to figure him out. There was some distance felt. Well then, how should it be? Should authors as a rule be affable and jocular, and not talk in terse, nuanced and sometimes prophetic terms like Jünger? But Jünger was a kind of prophet, not being the other kind of heart-warming man. He was what he was. This could be an explanation to the alienation people are reported to have felt when meeting Jünger. Hood anyway sums up his essay in these words, frustrated at having met a human being and an artist with contradicting aspects to him:

I came away with a sense of having confronted an enigma. Here was a gifted writer who claimed to aim at the classical simplicity and clarity of the best of French writing and could yet produce passages steeped in cloudy romanticism; a man who had detailed expert scientific knowledge about insects, fish, snakes, flora, alongside a marked interest in the mystical. He found it significant, he said, that his elder son, killed in Italy, had fallen in fighting round the marble cliffs of Carrara. When I came to read his diaries of the war years dealing with the time he spent in Paris, in a city and culture he loved, I was struck once more by his fastidiousness, his constant

search for the strange, the rare, the exquisite – whether it was a print bought from a book stall by the Seine, a flower bought for a cultured Frenchwoman, an encounter among the intellectuals of Paris with fine minds and fine tastes and dubious politics. There is in his description of these times a kind of dandyism. He is in Baudelaire's sense of the word a flâneur who aestheticises horror whether they be the bombs falling on the outskirts of Paris or the description of the execution of a young German deserter. In such set pieces – the latter is an astonishing piece of writing – there is something fascinating and repulsive that can only be described as snake-like. Yet at the same time he was engaged on the dangerous business of collecting and storing in a safe place what he called (using Goya's word) caprichos: evidence of the horrors perpetrated by the Nazis. His was an anti-Nazism that sprang from aristocratic fastidiousness; which is in itself paradoxical for he is no aristocrat but the son of an apothecary with a shop in Hanover who embraced the codes of honour of a military caste while asserting that he was un homme de lettres.

As intimated Jünger wasn't easy to figure out, the man clearly having contradicting traits. But that's the privilege of an artist. "I contradict myself? Well then, I contradict myself!" as Walt Whitman said. Moreover Hood may have tried to depict Jünger as something of a poser and that's fair, Jünger indeed had something of the poser in him. To some extent Jünger the writer was a bit too stylistically conscious, being for instance obsessed with revisions and polishing his prose. However, unlike Hood I've never found Jünger repulsive.

BRUCE CHATWIN

Finally let's look at what Bruce Chatwin has to say, another Englishman somewhat puzzled by Ernst Jünger and yet putting the credit where the credit's due. Chatwin (1940-1989) was a prize-winning travel writer with works like *In Patagonia* (1977) and *The Songlines* (1987). The Chatwin text discussed, *An Aesthete of War*, was published in New York Review of Books on March 5th, 1981 [as found on the site "Texts by Bruce Chatwin".[1] Here Chatwin reviewed a French edition of the war diary as well as *Storm of Steel* and *On the Marble Cliffs*. And describing Jünger's style in the war diaries Chatwin has this, very much to the point:

> He writes a hard, lucid prose. Much of it leaves the reader with an impression of the author's imperturbable self-regard, of dandyism, of cold-bloodedness, and, finally, of banality. Yet the least promising passages will suddenly light up with flashes of aphoristic brilliance, and the most harrowing descriptions are alleviated by a yearning for human values in a dehumanised world. The diary is the perfect form for a man who combines such acute powers of observation with an anaesthetised sensibility.

Chatwin was a renowned world traveller with a keen eye for nature and things paradisical, and this is his take on Jünger the biology student:

> His pleasures in biology tended toward the Linnaean classification of species – aesthetic pleasures that offered him a glimpse of the Primordial Paradise as yet untainted by Man. Moreover, the insect world, where instincts govern behaviour as a key fits a lock, had an irresistible attraction to a man of his utopian vision.

---

[1] http://cecilecottenceau1.free.fr/chatwin%20website/texts.htm

To be honest Chatwin really appreciates the Jünger method. The review is about the war diaries (*Strahlungen*) and Chatwin does them justice. Here's another fine Chatwin characteristic of the mood of the war diary:

> The effectiveness of Jünger's technique intensifies as the war proceeds. The atmosphere in which he clothes the Military Command reminds one of a Racine tragedy, in which the central characters are either threatened or doomed, and ail numbed into elegant paralysis by the howling tyrant off-stage. Yet, though the clock ticks on toward catastrophe, they are still allowed to hope for the reprieve of a negotiated peace with the Allies.

And the technique that Jünger utilizes is of course that of noting details, depicting what you see, mimesis with a minimum of opinions and feelings, the feelings in question merged into the images.

In the 70's Chatwin once visited Jünger, he goes on to say:

> My own visit to Jünger five years ago was an odd experience. At eighty, he had snow-white hair but the bounce of a very active schoolboy. He had a light cackling laugh and tended to drift off if he was not the centre of attention. He had recently published a book describing his experiments with drugs, from his first sniff of ether to lysergic acid, and was about to publish an enormous novel called Eumeswil. The ground floor of the house was furnished in the Biederrneier style, with net curtains and white faïence stoves, and was inhabited by his second wife, a professional archivist and textual critic of Goethe. Jünger's own quarters upstairs had the leathery look of a soldier's bunker, with cabinets for beetles on the landing and a sea of memorabilia – fossils, shells, helmets from both wars, skeletons of animals, and a collection of sand-glasses. (In 1954 he wrote *A Treatise on the Sand-glass* – a philosophical meditation on the passage of time. If I had hoped for more

memories of Paris under the Occupation, I was disappointed. In answer to questions, he simply recited an excerpt from the diary, though occasionally he would rush to the filing cabinet and come back with some pièce justificative.

It's the same old story: the fan who wants to meet *The Man Himself* and goes away disappointed. Oscar Wilde again springs to mind here: "To want to meet an author because you like his books is as ridiculous as wanting to meet the goose because you like paté de foie gras." By this I mean: Jünger's private persona may have been that of an officer or a school master, strict and correct and not especially warm and cordial. But that's not the whole issue here. There's always a gap between the public and the private persona. Having read an amazing, funny and enchanting book you can't always expect the author in question to be just that: amazing, funny and enchanting. It's the same with actors. Who doesn't, for instance, like Christopher Guest as Nigel Tufnel in the comedy "This Is Spinal Tap", which is spot on in parodying a heavy metal musician; however in private Guest is reported as not being especially funny and outgoing. And of course he has the right to be whatever he feels like off stage. You can't punish a man for being funny on stage and lacking that self-same quality off stage.

Returning to the subject of this book I'd say: it's futile to discuss Jünger's persona per se, to minutely detect how he was in that or the other respect. As I stated in the introduction it's more interesting to look at what he represents.

5. STORM OF STEEL

Storm of Steel was Jünger's first book, his debut as an author. It was originally issued in 1920 and it's still valid as a combat zone narrative. Some even say that' it's a deathless classic, something like the *Iliad*. Hector is as heroic as the First World War Jünger. Well, why not...? To me Jünger's book is one of the best war books ever, up there with the Finnish Väinö Linna's *Unknown Soldier* (1954) and the Danish Sven Hassel's *Wheels of Terror* (1958). You have to agree with André Gide when he said that *Storm of Steel* is "genuinely credible, real, honest".

When here looking at *Storm of Steel* I will focus on the elements of leadership, of leading men into battle. And I will begin in 1916.

STEEL HELMET

Gone are pantaloon rouge, gone are dragoons and lancers, and gone is the hope of imminent victory. No one says "home before the leaves fall" any more.

It's a new order in the combat zone. It's a world of tactical air forces, hour-long barrages and constant patrol duty. And it's good-bye to der Pickelhaube and time for the steel helmet. In other words, it's the autumn of 1916 when Jünger's company arrives at Guillemont on the western front near Somme. Marching through the night through a desolate landscape, far away lit by impacting artillery shells, they're met by a guide in a steel helmet, the first soldier thus geared that Jünger sees. Compared to the ornate Biedermeier style of the Pickelhaube we here have a symbol of a totally different world. The soldier in question seems to Jünger to be "the inhabitant of a new, tougher world".

Not that the war thus far has been a picnic. Having volunteered for combat duty in 1914 Jünger has been wounded and seen some of the war himself. However, he likes what he sees; the style of *Storm of Steel* is hands-on and matter-of-fact, without any of the rhetorical chauvinism of the time, but in no way is this a cold and indifferent story. Between the lines you can feel that Jünger is in his element, not exactly being the war-lover but not far from it. He's a western front samurai, a model soldier evolving into a leader and an officer. And what the book says about leadership is one of its prime qualities. It's not a formal lecture on the subject, it's a collection of unsought examples. And that's what makes it so efficient. "I learned more from your book than during two years at the Military Academy", a reader once told Jünger, quoted in the diary *Gärter und Strassen* from 1942.

Many books have been written on how it is to be a private, to be a lost particle in the confusion of battle. See for example Remarque's *All Quiet on the Eastern Front*. *Storm of Steel,* on the other hand, tells us what it means to be a front-line officer, having to take responsibility and make decisions, often tough ones. See for instance the chapter "Retreat from Somme" with Jünger's platoon defending a forward position saturated with enemy shells and about to be overrun by the British. At one point some soldiers return from a certain depression saying "we can't take it anymore, let us be relieved..." Jünger however

must order them to return, having no reinforcements and no choice. He's virtually sending them off to die but what should he do? The company commander in turn would have flayed him alive had Jünger allowed the men to evacuate the position in question. The whole of the battalion's position depended on this.

COMBAT PATROL

An exemplary chapter illuminating combat leadership and tactics is the chapter "Régnierville". At the end of 1917 Jünger's company is given the mission of launching a combat patrol, sallying forth into the French lines in order to catch a prisoner. No one thinks that the patrol will change much in the strategic situation, nevertheless patrols like these were needed to keep the personnel in shape morally. The preparations were thorough, going on for about a week in advance. And during the event itself as many shells were fired as in an 1870 Franco-Prussian war battle, Jünger comments. That says something of der Materialkrieg.

After some scouting plans are drawn up. The 40 men chosen for the assault have been given special training, mainly in throwing hand-grenades, an efficient weapon in trench warfare. Except for hand-grenades Jünger equips himself with two pistols and a knife. We might call this infantry unit a symbol of the rebirth of an old arm: the grenadiers, the heavy infantry. They flowered in the 18th century, being attached to every battalion of line infantry. Now, in 1916, all the infantry had to be heavily equipped: steel helmet, loads of hand-grenades and the rifle mainly carried slung across back. That was the style of the German infantry shock troops at this time.

After some preparation fire over the enemy lines to keep the enemy down the patrol eventually got going. A breakthrough is effected, the unit pours through at a point in the defences, and then it's more or

less a case of "let action determine the matter". Luckily the standard of the soldiers was high, they knew how to fight without due orders for everything. That was the ideal of Einzelkämpfer, of every private soldier being his own leader, that Germany's army lauded. Jünger for his part didn't give much orders during the patrol, feeling a bit lost in the haze of trenches. In advance he had seen a survey of the land, he had a map, but in action he somehow lost orientation.

As for the mission itself some casualties were inflicted on the enemy. But the patrol failed with its stated mission: to catch a prisoner. Jünger & co eventually made their way out of the maze, having lost about half of the 40 men in dead, wounded or captured. Having returned Jünger was questioned at the battalion HQ. A staff officer reviewed the movements, asking Jünger why he at a certain T-crossing turned right and not left. Now this may be a fair thing to ask by a staff officer, a man with a bird's view of things. However for the man in the field it isn't so easy, not having the same possibilities of overview. He has to make decisions based on insufficient data. "Don't just stand there, do something" as Colin Powell said, that's how an infantry leader should act. It's sometimes better to act wrongly and then correct the decision later, rather than to stand hesitant. Vitesse, vitesse, de l'activité as Napoleon said. That's how it's done, that's the style of the man in the field. Then the staff officer can be wise after the event as much as he pleases.

Jünger was even sent to the division headquarters to explain himself. The operation wasn't outright a failure but it was questionable. But in the end no reprimands were issued, instead medals were awarded and leaves were granted for the surviving. It was just another combat patrol on the western front, a mostly self-serving operation. As such it might even had been to Jünger's liking, even though he mentions things like "horrifying" and "like a labyrinth in a dream" when remembering it.

A decisive moment in the life of Jünger the leader comes in 1918. When waiting for the attack in an impact crater his company is

struck by a random grenade, knocking out 60 of the 150 men. Seeing this cauldron of sooty, bloody, screaming men he rushes up and away, trying to get away from it all. Then suddenly he remembers being an officer, having responsibility; he's the company commander an inner voice tells him. So he returns to the crater, starting to lead the rescue work.

This little escape of Jünger's is the only time when he looses it, his only behavioural lapse in *Storm of Steels* 300 pages. Even the fighting machine Jünger is human. Another human moment is when he sees his brother Fritz lying wounded in a bunker during the battle of Langemarck. Jünger details four men to carry Fritz to the rear. And this is the humanely right thing to do but tactically these four men could have been needed at the front. But of course Jünger had to do what he did. Sometimes you just have to. An officer who never lets his human side shine through is some kind of a monster, a robot.

IMAGES

Storm of Steel takes place in a somewhat monotonous flat country, latticed with trenches. This is the archetypal western front trench world, so to speak. Now sometimes there is mentioned wooden grounds and villages, but any such items seem to get levelled by the artillery in due time. It's a desolate world but Jünger's descriptions aren't moody and sombre, on the contrary he can find details that enlivens the reader. Like this image of some tank wrecks:

> Some had humorous, threatening or lucky names, and symbols and war paint, neither leaving out the four-leaf clover, the happy piglet or the white skull. (...) Dwelling in the interior, cramped and damaged by grenades, with its haze of ducts, shafts and steel wiring, must have been trying even outside of battle, during which these juggernauts in order to avoid hits crawl over the fields of death in circuitous patterns, looking like giant beetles.

Another observation are the planes he spots during the March offensive, 1918. The style of this passage isn't overly original but the unmistakeable feeling is always there. Here you have to remember Matthew Arnold's definition of good style: "having something to say". And this is what Jünger has to say about the aircraft in question:

> Over the cloudless sky a squadron flew, equipped with signal flags in black, white and red. The last rays of the sun painted it delicately pink, like a flock of flamingoes.

That's the forte of this book: images. There aren't so many reflections, Jünger's prose being efficient and fruitful when describing nature, action and concrete facts. As a reader you're awarded with ever new vistas and visions, not having to hear that this and that experience is tedious or enlivening or whatever. *Storm of Steel* is a classic because of its tight style and tight narrative, however, without it ever being strict or sterile. "It is simply right" as someone said of the Icelandic sagas.

LEADERSHIP

Leadership was said to be the theme of this chapter, how to lead men in combat. And except for what I've already said *Storm of Steel* has some more lessons on the subject.

Jünger came to the western front early in 1915, serving as a private. Then in February he was sent to a preparatory course in military matters. Exactly what he learned there he doesn't say. Then he had his baptism of fire at Les Eparges in April when he got wounded, and being a convalescent he got the advice from his father to volunteer for non commissioned officer's (NCO) training. Jünger followed the advice even though the ambition to become a leader wasn't his principal ambition at the time:

I fulfilled his [the father's] wish even though, to me, at the beginning of the war it seemed more tempting to partake as a private soldier, only being responsible to yourself.

You could say: Jünger was still a bit naive, still being the romantic adventurer. I admit that by this time he was free from his initial, pre-war naiveté, the vision of a war filled with "manly deeds, a joyous fire-fight on blossoming, blood-soaked meadows" as he says in the beginning of the book. In the trenches there was only routine and toil, this he discovered quickly. It was the stalemate after the mobile 1914 battles. But to be free from these routine tasks you have to become a leader and this may have been the stimulant in volunteering for NCO school.

Jünger went to such a school, spending the summer being trained "in the different techniques applied for leading small units in the terrain" as Jünger says. What more did he learn? He doesn't say but I guess they had to learn about the weapons and organization of the enemy, and receiving practical weapons training (machine gun, hand-grenades) as well as knowledge about mines, tactical trench digging and supplies. Back in the combat zone as a sergeant Jünger soon got to apply his leadership qualities. One day, leading his section to the regimental quarters at Douchy during a French offensive, suddenly...

(...) the black cascade of a grenade erupted before us, the projectile hitting the entrance to the small village cemetery next to the road. This was the first time that I had to make a decision as a reaction to unexpected events. "Spread out to the left – move it, move it!" The column dispersed, advancing by rushes over the fields; I gathered the men to the left and led them in a circuitous path into the village.

Jünger guesses that they had been spotted from an observation balloon, a stationary balloon with an observer who by wire gives

the artillery the coordinates to fire the shell in question. Thus he led his troop out of a threatening catastrophe, mostly by intuition but intuition needs a theoretical ground to be able to blossom.

Later on Jünger took some more courses and became an officer, always endowed with the same talent to lead. The best example of his leadership quality in my eyes is in the chapter "Langemarck". Jünger and his platoon is isolated in no man's land, the enemy pressure is felt but some friendly forces are nearby. The shelling is so severe that it doesn't matter if they retreat or advance – so Jünger makes the decision to advance. After a while he gets a substantial following, they close with the enemy and then have to fall back again. After a council of war the decision is again made to advance. Afterwards they get the confirmation of their bravery in a French report saying that the Germans stood their ground at a certain river. This was an official confirmation that the contribution of the individual matters. The decision by Jünger to stand fast, plus the impulse to advance since retreat would be as dangerous – that in my opinion is the epitome of fighting spirit and leadership.

6. FIRST WORLD WAR BOOKS

Jünger wrote many books dealing with the First World War as he knew it. First we had *Storm of Steel* (1920), treated in the previous chapter, his elaborated diary of his four years in the combat zone. Then he wrote two books embellishing some elements of *Storm of Steel*: *Das Wäldchen 125* and *Feuer und Blut*. They emerged in the mid 20's as did a short novel taking place in the trenches, *Sturm*. I will look at all of them in this chapter. But first some reflections on the possibly best war book Jünger wrote, the fiery philosophy of *Der Kampf als inneres Erlebnis*.

DER KAMPF ALS INNERES ERLEBNIS

Der Kampf als inneres Erlebnis surfaced in 1922, the first book Jünger wrote after his debut. The title means *Battle as an Inner Experience*. In mapping what goes on in a man's psyche while in the combat zone Jünger ventured into dangerous lands. To fight in a war means to kill and to kill is a taboo. Remember the fifth commandment. In war we

retreat to basic instincts, directed by the reptilian brain. So then, how can battle be spiritually elevating, as Jünger maintains?

In his slightly pedantic way Jünger tries to analyze what makes the battle experience so special. Had he been an academic it could have been unreadable, like Kant analyzing what it is in humour that makes it funny (q.v. *The Critique of Aesthetic Judgement*, 1790). But Jünger was no academic. He had been in the combat zone and he had the vivid language to convey what happened there.

For the elite soldier combat becomes a spiritual act, something of a super meditation. You live on the edge, in the process raising yourself mentally. Other authors who have treated the role of the warrior philosophically are Julius Evola (q.v. Chapter 21) and the shamans Taisha Abelar and Carlos Castaneda. The last two equalled the venturing into the lands of magic with going into war. Only the mindset of a warrior could prepare you for the challenges of a sorcerer. That gives you a clue of what it's all about.

So what is the mindset of a soldier? It's having the willpower to endure. It's about looking inside, searching inside yourself for those inner reserves that make you go on even if you're hungry, tired and scared. Fighting horror means coping with the reality of death. That's what every soldier has to learn or else he won't last long in the combat zone.

It's about getting used to the idea of dying, knowing you're in the Valley of the Shadow of Death. Then what, what about the intimated raising of the spirit, this spiritual experience per se when you fight? Jünger compares it to intoxication and ecstasy, like the ones experienced by poets and saints and even loving couples. Here we have a definite taboo: as in the love act, mighty spiritual forces are released in battle and you have to exercise some willpower in order not to have the two blend, the love drive and the death drive. This is bordering on insanity. Modern psychology knows this. That said, battle could then be seen as the ultimate love act? Jünger intimates as much:

It's an ecstasy beyond all ecstasies, a liberation breaking all bonds. It's a rage without consideration and limits, comparable only to the violent forces of nature. Here man is like the raging storm, the roaring ocean and the booming thunder. Then he blends with the All, rushing towards the dark gates of death like a projectile to its target. And with the purple waves breaking over her he is long since unconscious of the translocation. It's like a wave sliding back into the heaving ocean.

This is rather bold and to the point. Evola's take on the subject in *Metaphysics of War* was more academic, true as such, but not anywhere near this literary experiment of Jünger's. Jünger probably hadn't read any of the classic texts on war – like *Bhagavad-Gîtâ* or *Hagakure* – but he could be said to know them anyhow, intuitively. And he boldly went where no man had gone before in intimating the connection between war and love. Okay, Freudian psychology knows this too but they can't express it on the stylistic level that Jünger can.

CAPTURING THE SPIRIT OF WAR

Jünger tries to capture the essence of war. The First World War gives him the paraphernalia but the conclusions are more or less eternally valid. You have to be a writer of no mean skill in order to say it the way Jünger says it. So you could say he was a natural since this was only his second book. Jünger had yet to become a novelist but these lines from *Der Kampf als inneres Erlebnis* are a clear-cut example of a novelist to be:

The steely characters roaming the skies with eagle eyes peering through rotating propellers, characters crammed into tanks daring a hellride over the roar of the crater fields, characters in encircled

strong-points surrounded by heaps of corpses crouching behind glowing machine guns and facing a certain death: they are the best of the modern battlefield, suffused with a reckless fighting spirit, of a strong will who discharges itself in a hard, concentrated, well-aimed thrust.

The passage goes on to depict the infantry, the shock troopers who Jünger himself led in combat. In lyrical yet sober wordings this is Jünger's picture of the elite soldiers of the world war:

Observing them silently cutting their way through the barbed wire, digging storm steps, comparing their luminescent watches and orienting themselves towards north by the stars, I realize: this is the new man. The storm-trooper, the elite of Central Europe. A whole new race, cunning, strong and filled with will. What reveals itself here as a vision will tomorrow be the axis around which life revolves still faster and faster. This war (...) is the forge in which the world will be hammered into new borders and new communities.

In the same vein with have this, a hymn to the everlasting glory of the infantry:

It was a completely new race, embodied energy loaded with the utmost power. Limber, slim, sinewy bodies, sharp faces, energetic eyes under the helmet. They were over-comers, steely natures set for battle of the most gruesome kind. Their advance over the fractal landscape meant an ultimate triumph of fanatic horror. When these daring troops broke into demolished positions where pale figures were staring madly at them, unknown energies were released.

BALANCING ON THE EDGE

Writing about the urge to kill is, as intimated, a risky business. Along with breaking the taboo of killing there's a fine line to tread between the sublime and the ridiculous. And Jünger might cross it sometimes. Judge for yourselves: "(...) the allure of bloodshed, hanging over war like a red sail over a black galley, in its impossible voyage only comparable to eros". These grounds can be dangerous to tread for a nihilist, fearful of the forces dwelling inside him beneath his well-ordered humanism. But the aristocrat of the soul, the differentiated man with will-power over his impulses, can benefit from having Jünger as a guide on this journey under blood-red skies.

Jünger salutes war, paying homage to it like a religious act. Battle is character-building, lifting you up spiritually, making you come into contact with the essence of reality. Jünger acknowledges the elements of battle going beyond battle, the elements of life, vitality, prâna and life force:

> The will to life floats by here, the will to battle and to power, even at the expense of life itself. Compared to this nocturnal and never ending attraction to battle all values becomes naught, all concepts empty. You notice the expression of something elementary, enormous, something ever-present and eternal, even when men and war for long have ceased to exist.

COPSE 125

The next Jünger book on war was *Das Wäldchen 125*, surfacing in 1925 and translated into English in 1930 as *Copse 125*. It's about the week-long battles in the western front terrain mentioned in the title. The gist of it all is in the chapter "English Advances" in *Storm of Steel*.

Other than the action itself Jünger muses on warlike subjects, talking about the spirit and the discipline needed to create an army, about the will to win, and how technological know-how and cooperation with machines is a centrepiece of modern war. How man and machine is one single phenomenon is stated thus:

> The mechanization of war doesn't only mean increased power, it also makes the highest demands on the men fighting it. The best men will have the best machines and the best machines will have the best men; the two are inseparable.

The same year as *Das Wäldchen 125* Jünger issued *Feuer und Blut*. The narrative itself was now down to about 24 hours, depicting the D-day of the spring offensive in 1918, in itself the subject of the memorable chapter "The Great Battle" in *Storm of Steel*. To make it into a book Jünger filled the pages with reflections on this and that, like the beauty of the machine:

> The machine is beautiful. And it has to be beautiful for the lover of life in all its fullness and violence. (...) Haven't we noticed that when seeing a bullet train flashing through the landscape, race drivers heading for the straight after the banked curve; when metal birds have circled over our cities and when in large glass-covered halls we've been standing between crank shafts and shining flywheels, with the mercury pillars of the manometers rising and falling and the red pointers of the instruments on the wall trembling – haven't we noticed that in all these actions there must be an abundance of life, of luxury, of a will of totally transforming life into power.

LENNART SVENSSON

STURM

Sturm was written in 1923 as a serial for a daily paper, not being published in book form until the 60's. That's odd since this a pearl of a novel, maybe one of Jünger's best, its only fault being that it's a bit too short. A novel has to have a certain amount of pages to reach that elusive epic quality and *Sturm* only has 80 pages or so. Now of course there's a form called short novel or novella, once common in continental Europe, and *Sturm* can be said to fit into that category.

Sturm has everything that Jüngers First World War books has and then some. Above all there's an element of tragedy here. We don't see that in his more programmatical war books. *Sturm* has a certain level of complexity, with a combat soldier and his every day life at the centre of attention and then, along with this, scenes from a book he's writing. And he writes about a writer lauding war and heroism, but at the same time the life of the writer is hailed as a life worth to live. The joys of peaceful society, like standing in a book-shop and discussing authors and editions with a cunning assistant, is nicely depicted. I know of no other war book that so has conveyed the charms of peace without making it with resentment and angst. Jünger in *Sturm* moves from peace to war like scenes in a dream, seamless.

Sturm shows us the strength of the novel as an art form. Jünger often wrote diaries and factual prose, in the process making himself into a sort of Gestalt or immaculate hero that hides the quality of the work itself. Jünger the Monument stands before us in *Storm of Steel* and all the other war books as well as in the war diary and the late diary. But *Sturm*, being a novel, is more easily accessible since you don't have to relate to the narrator, identical to Jünger the Great. In writing fiction he is beautifully reduced to the Narrator, thus allowing you, as a reader, to encounter the scenes and the people more directly. "The novelist is a liar telling the truth" is a proverb that springs into mind here.

I could quote this and that from this novel. Jünger's prose is often very quotable. But I'll content myself with one of the more fiery passages since this chapter was about war books. The main character on a city leave has a sort of battle hangover, longing back to the combat zone: "He was thinking about nocturnal patrols after short, brutal bursts of fire, violent assaults, steel helmets, hand-grenades." Voilà in nuce the soldierly lifestyle, to raise yourself spiritually by living on the edge. To me this is the essence of Jünger's First World War books.

7. MILITARIA

I n almost all of Jünger's books we can find things military, be they attitudes, terminology or concrete memories of his life in the combat zone. His 1915-1918 trench life served him as a constant inspiration, the Prussian army having been like a second home and battle itself like a second birth to him. And I find nothing shocking in this. Death and destruction aside no one has ever taken damage by doing military service. Jünger is a fine example of the military as a lifestyle. This might sound controversial, I know. But this isn't about rigorism, about forcing your existence into a rigid form; it's about seeing life through a systematic but passionate temperament, a sort of western Bushido.

LANGEMARCK

Approaching 100 Jünger was a bit surprised at still being alive. Reaching old age was never an ambition for him, having instead wanted to die in combat like the volunteers at Langemarck in 1914, the student recruits who went singing to their deaths. Thus you can interpret this entry in the late diary:

The one hundred years approaching. Plautus: "Whom the gods love die young" – that is, at Langemarck. [Wilflingen, January 14th, 1995]

However, he wasn't allowed to die in the battles of 1914-18. The battles raged on and he participated in many of them. After he war he was an active officer for a while, and when starting his civilian career he kept a connection to the military by remaining in the Army Reserve, as was common for many veterans. Participating in diverse manoeuvres and courses during the inter war years he could join the forces in 1939 as a captain. Having eventually served in the west almost the whole of that war he was discharged in 1944.

He never served again but he kept the military as an ideal. He benefited spiritually from his years in uniform. His second baptism of fire at Guillemont, when the war became even more intense, is said to have made him immune to catching fire even though later times were highly igneous also: the contemporary situation was conflagrant but he, Jünger, was immune to it [Wilflingen, August 12th, 1988]. But he didn't go unscathed through the war. He had some shrapnel embedded inside his body, reportedly enough to make airport metal detectors react.

Jünger was in the infantry, not the cavalry, but the infantry officer's training at the time included riding, infantry officers traditionally going by horseback to the battlefield. Still in 1940 Jünger made his entry into France as a company commander this way, the rest of the company marching by foot. He knew riding and once wrote a pamphlet on the subject, a hands-on instruction in how to ride. In the novel *Heliopolis* riding becomes a symbol for the cavalier army lifestyle, like the scene with the captain de Geer riding up on the Pagos hill and visiting the war academy. Riding in the morning breeze with the gulf beneath him and fragrant aromas in the air he is reminded of his youthful days, feeling free and fluent.

Then we have a person in the novel *Eine gefährliche Begegnung*, riding in a park in 19th century Paris. Jünger talks about "this entry

into the centaurian element" and that's an original metaphor. Even more steeped in the cavalry lifestyle is the captain Richard of *The Glass Bees*. In the pre war years he serves in a Prussian cavalry regiment, calling East Prussia "a land made for riders", the glory of being a cavalry officer being well captured. Then the Great War comes and the horse soldiers literally have to dismount, instead becoming motorized infantry. This circumstance was hard to many historic cavalry men, like George S. Patton shedding a tear when the American cavalry was disbanded in the 30's making way for mechanization. Then he became as passionate about tanks but that's another story.

Manuel Venator in *Eumeswil* is also a kind of warrior. Notwithstanding that he's an academic he knows how to act when the alarm is sounded and a certain post has to be manned, should there be an uprising in the city and the casbah where he serves has to be defended. Moreover Venator in the novel speaks about equipping a retreat in the woods, situated in a deserted bunker. He would need weapons, like a rifle for hunting but also for shooting intruders:

> At night time I would change the sniper sight for a flashlight and illuminate the intruder. The shot would follow immediately after the light beam.

This is a quote from a novel, however, you could say that the 80 year old author had his soldiery spirit intact.

THE METAPHYSICS OF WAR

Jünger in his diary often muses about the nature of war, with or without the aide of his experience as a combat veteran. An entry with a metaphysical slant is for instance the following from his Russian outing. It's about the invisible, intangible side of war, how invisible

powers partake and why we must restrain ourselves in applying force. We know these issues from international law but the Jünger take on it is original. War doesn't simply consist of what we see, there's a discreet background to it all:

> It's the divine part that's separate from the battle, keeping the struggle away from bestiality and demonic violence. Even Homer knew it and respected it. The really strong, the one predisposed to rule, is characterized by appearing not altogether as an enemy, as a person filled with hate; he also has responsibility for the adversary. Having more power than the others is demonstrated on a higher level than where the violence exists, which only convinces subaltern natures. [Beloretsenskaja, December 11th, 1942]

Another abstract war observation is this one on fire and movement, the basic elements of battle. During the western offensive in 1940 he notices the quickness of the progress, old stumbling blocks like Verdun being bypassed in no time:

> Once again fire seems to have got behindhand in the eternal race between fire and movement, the rapid units often having operated well ahead of the infantry. Thus the major once installed himself in a castle, about two day's marches ahead of his infantry; the lady of the manor who didn't quite know the German uniforms said that the rooms were in order, but they were for an English HQ who had announced their arrival the same day. This reminds you of the Seven Year's War. [Landifay, May 31th, 1940]

This could be compared to the entry for July 10th, 1943, still on the theme of fire and movement:

> For a few days a great battle has been raging in the centre of the eastern front. It seems to offer a whole new vision with a concentration unusual for this theatre, the forces having

outbalanced each other, lessening the movement while increasing the fire.

It was about Operation Zitadelle, the panzer battle at Kursk. Here you could add that fire is more important than the movement; the movement is there to enable firing at the enemy. To simply move doesn't lead anywhere.

As final words on the subject of war in general here's a Jünger quote in the late diary, with the author remembering what his father said after the First World War:

Now we won't see war for another 100 years. [Wilflingen, January 17th, 1991]

The old man of course was wrong in this. "Versailles is nothing but a 20 year truce" as a French politician said at the time. The First and the Second World War belong together forming a continuous historical unit, like all the Coalition Wars of 1790-1815, or the Thirty Years War. Jünger seems to have seen it thus since sometime after 1945 he fittingly said that we now are living after Actium, evoking the image of the end of the Roman civil war in the first century A.D., another almost 30 year long war. After Actium it was time to close Ara Pacis and sing nunc est bibendum.

Thus it was: the time after 1945 was mainly peaceful, the "cold war" being mostly a phoney war as I see it, a futile attempt to draw us down into hell once again. The wars in the post 1945 period were mostly cabinet wars, small wars in a time when peace dominated, as between 1815 and 1914.

NO CAREER OFFICER

Jünger was no career officer. As soon as the battles ended in 1918 he lost interest in the officer's life. He stayed on in the army because of the steady income in an unsecure time. But he was more of an adventurer than a common army soldier.

The French President Mitterand once told him:

> Under Napoleon you could have been a marshal. [late diary, 3/23/1993]

That somehow rings true: in a less formalistic army he could have made it to the top. Here we must remember that all the others who got Pour le Mérite during the First World War, and still served in the Second World War, became generals: Schörner, Rommel and others. So had Jünger wanted it he could have become a general, serving through the years and meeting the demands in question, but he didn't.

Jünger was satisfied in being a captain in the Second World War. Career-wise he was in the doldrums, ending the war in the same rank. But I guess he didn't see it as a stalemate; he could easily have volunteered for combat duty on the eastern front and thus being given the opportunity to rise through the ranks (becoming battalion commander, serving in a divisional HQ, attending General Staff courses etc.). Jünger now played the role of an outsider in the combat zone, like when he visited the eastern front in 1942. He once visits a battalion HQ and this is like a vision of what could have been: Jünger could have been this major leading his men in a trying battle. I mean, you could speculate, couldn't you? Anyhow it's a vivid picture of the everyday war on the eastern front, of an abrasive, grinding battle in a combat zone otherwise known for its rapid movements:

> Visiting the battalion commander, Captain Sperling, in his shelter of oak logs. The roof was supported by hefty pillars. Two makeshift

beds, on the walls shelves with conserves, mess tins, rifles, blankets and binoculars. The captain was tired and unshaven, like one having been up not only this night, having run from tree to tree in the dark, humid forest, waiting for an attack with shells from the Stalin Organs gushing up earth and tearing down treetops. One dead, one wounded. And the same night after night. [Navaginskij, December 21th, 1942]

Jünger didn't have to serve like this on the eastern front. But he made himself no illusions in that respect. The call could come at any moment, knowing that the general (Stülpnagel) could become a Pontius Pilate being forced to hand him over:

But in that case there would be a washing of hands with a little perfume: "My dear J, your talent needs a wider field than I can offer, so therefore I've put you on the transfer list." When celebrated you have to put on a brave face. How to raise your glass to say farewell: such gestures are well caught by Shakespeare, putting all academic historians to shame. [Paris, October 6th, 1943]

Even in post war years and to the end Jünger retained his soldiery persona. For instance the burial in 1998 was visited by five generals. And the last entry of the last volume – volume V – of the late diary intimates the role of the soldier:

The day begins with signatures, with Liselotte sorting out the relevant from the mail. (...) The handwriting is still presentable – "an old warrior doesn't have a trembling hand". [Wilflingen, December 15th, 1995]

THE CAMPAIGN OF 1940

Jünger wrote and published several diaries about the Second World War, the first being *Gärter und Strassen*, covering the years 1939-1940. To be exact it starts in April 1939 and ends in July 1940. The war itself began on September 3rd, 1939. As I said in chapter 1, Jünger got called up in August. By November he was the commander of 2nd Company, 287th regiment, eventually deploying on die Westwall, the German defensive line along the country's western border. So then, what noteworthy things does he relate during the waiting game ("The Phoney War") and the offensive into France? What entries are of interest given the fact that Jünger was an active officer serving in the field? What telling details of the military kind are there to quote and relate? As for the seemingly uneventful run-up to the Blitzkrieg of May 1940, the aptly named Sitzkrieg, Jünger partook in one incident rendering him the Iron Cross. It wasn't comparable to his exploits in the First World War, that's at least his own verdict on this affair, but as a fact he had been exposed to enemy fire this March 29th and that was the criteria for getting the medal. To be decorated with the Iron Cross exposure to hostile fire was a prerequisite.

The company by then was deploying on the eastern banks of the Rhine west of Baden-Baden. On the western banks were the French. The day in question was Jünger's 45th birthday and he had celebrated it in the conditions allowed in the field. Since they quartered in solid fortifications and no major operations was at hand it was a rather nice birthday given the situation, Jünger treating his fellow officers with brandy, cigars and candy and receiving gifts. In the afternoon however there came a call from the line soliciting stretcher bearers, so Jünger went over to Point 47 to have a look.

This strong-point had a bunker in the form of a gun emplacement, visited by the time by an artillery sergeant and a corporal from the nearby fire control post. The sergeant wanted to take a photo of the

emplacement from the front, catching some bullet marks in the gun's protective shield. Followed by the corporal (who had his doubts about this affair) the sergeant had ventured out past an earthen wall and down the Rhine slope. At this exact time a French machine gun from a fortification on the other side of the Rhine had opened fire, forcing the two artillery men to duck and thus isolating them in a kind of No Man's Land.

Jünger took a look at the grounds and then decided on a rescue mission, and for this taking a different path than the two artillery men had taken. Cutting through a barbed wire obstacle and followed by his ADC Spinelli Jünger crept over the ground, protected from view by vertically hanging camouflage covers made of bamboo matting. From the point where these covers ended there was about fifteen steps to the casualties lying on the ground.

Having ventured out in the danger zone Jünger and Spinelli soon reach the corporal, still alive. The sergeant is dead and the two rescuers plus the corporal carry him away:

> Having proceeded thus for a couple of steps we were caught in the fire from the French emplacement, the bullets flying around us, piercing the thick poplars, being crushed against the bunker, sweeping zinging through the barbed wire and ploughing furrows in the ground. We hit the dirt...

During the continued firing the dead serves as a kind of protective shield for Jünger, the corpse's arm for example being hit. Jünger also notes cascades of earth and a smell of red-hot metal. Finally they get cover from a friendly gun, suppressing the French MG. And so the adventure was over, the three of them plus the corpse soon reaching safety. A later conduction found that the sergeant had died from a bullet hitting him in the back of the head.

So what's the point of this story? The point is that the 1940 Jünger hadn't lost his nerve, hadn't lost his taste for martial action. As

intimated his Second World War wouldn't become the fierce battle field of his prophetic visions, instead being rather uneventful. But at the same time there were a lot of things to do and see, even if the challenges weren't mortal in nature all the time.

ADVANCING INTO FRANCE

On May 10th Jünger's company receives the order "all leaves are cancelled", signalling that action is imminent. And soon they get to advance westward into France, mopping up behind the tank spearheads. But "mopping up" in this context doesn't mean combat operations, it's about taking care of capitulating French soldiers, ranging streams of refugees and the like. As for the battles Jünger sees traces of them near Martelange, a Belgian town bordering on Luxemburg, on May 25th:

> On this road there's evidence of clashes between recce patrols, very surveyable, as if arranged on a tactical exercise. There were small piles of empty cartridges by the roadside, next to them soldier's graves, then traces of tanks having crossed the fields whereof one had remained on the field of honour, and finally a road block and even here graves with Belgian helmets on them.

Then it's on to "the dead land, the cactus land", urban variety: the French towns and villages deserted by their inhabitants. Jünger notes the change in mood even among the officers, the presence of the dead land affecting them too. Everyone agrees that there has to be a firm grip on discipline or else anarchy will ensue. No pillaging, pay for everything you can, and only if you miss something out of your field equipment – like a spoon – you may take one. This may sound fastidious but you have to draw the line somewhere.

There's some magnificent desolation in the landscape Jünger describes in the entry of May 27th:

> Marching off at eight. Everywhere the same deadly silence I noticed even in Belgium. The landscape is deserted, you only see soldiers marching along the roads with their horses and carriages. It was still morning when we entered Sedan. The city for the most part lay in ruins, big houses having been levelled by hits, others having been bereaved of their fronts revealing like in architectural cross-sections whole room interiors and resplendent halls as well as spiral staircases hanging in the air.

THE DEAD LAND

The images are abounding in this empty, deserted space left behind by the armoured spearheads: no smoke from the chimneys, no people about, and looking through windows Jünger could often see whole made tables but no dinner guests. In one word: the dead land.

There are also mysterious and mythic traits to this land. Sending forth his quartermaster to reconnoitre leisurely, only to report remarkable images, the man in question ventures ahead on his bicycle and returns with reports: for instance he had seen that music instruments were among the things first destroyed, which Jünger interprets as "Ares' enmity towards the Muses", this mythical phenomenon for example being depicted by Rubens. Mirrors on the other hand were left unscathed, the quartermaster seeing this from a practical perspective: they are needed at shaving. But Jünger guesses that this too has deeper meanings, unclear what.

This is from the entry of May 27th (place: Boulzicourt) and added is this more light hearted aspect:

Along with the demonology is the fact that in spite of the rapidity of the advance there's always people taking their time to put up absurd objects in the windows of the deserted houses: stuffed birds, opera hats, busts of Napoleon III, manikins and the like.

By the end of May they advance in the vicinity of Reims, a region where Jünger was stationed in the First World War in 1915. Then he was engaged in lethal battles, now he doesn't see any dead bodies except for those of animals: carcasses of horses, dogs and cats are disturbing elements in the picture. Of course it's still no picnic, death is out and about and the cannons roar, but it's safe to say that this campaign was watered with wine, brandy, Cointreau and every other fluid and beverage the Germans could find in the well equipped cellars. And in reasonable amounts Jünger himself consumed one or another bottle.

RUSSIA

The French campaign lingers on throughout June. Then France capitulates and Jünger and his company concentrates on fulfilling routine duties. And as I said in chapter 1 he was eventually transferred to the HQ of the German occupation army in Paris, in the summer of 1941 as it was. I have nothing to say about this in itself interesting post, being kind of bereft of telling details. Instead I will move on to Jünger's spy trip to the eastern front in 1942. I have already given the background in chapter 1 so here I can focus on interesting details.

Going east Jünger doesn't have to "eat dirt" at the front, he's only there to observe and visit HQ's and the like. But the Russian front is also a dead land:

Technical objects are in pristine condition – railroads, cars, aeroplanes, loudspeakers and of course everything belonging to

LENNART SVENSSON

the world of weapons. In contrast there's a shortage of everything organic: food, clothing, warmth, light. In an even higher degree this is true about the spiritual essentials: joy, happiness, good spirits and the generous, benevolent, musical disposition. And this on one of the most fertile lands in the world.

As for the meaning of "musical" in this respect, see notes on *The Music* in Chapter 25. This entry from Rostov November 23rd, 1942, continues to relate the misery of the eastern combat zone behind the front, with suffering civilians in tattered clothes, apathy, toil and no end in sight, and added is a chance remark of historical significance:

In the crowd many uniforms, even Hungarian and Romanian, and sometimes completely unknown like Ukrainian volunteers or people from the local security service. After dark you hear shots from the abandoned factory precinct near the railroad station. This afternoon soldiers on leave waiting for their trains were interrupted and hastily sent to the front in quickly assembled units. They say that the Russians have broken through north of Stalingrad.

And they had, creating the encirclement of the 6th army leading to the major German defeat there in January 1943. More on this in chapter 1.

Jünger's eastern front séjour – the section is part of the book *Strahlungen* and is called "Kaukasischer Aufzeichnungen" (Caucasian Notes) – gives us the Jünger war in nuce: cruelties, cultural notes (like meeting a young Russian woman who likes the author Friedrich Schiller) and even entomological outings, such as finding "a Diaperis boleti with red legs" in the valley of Psjisjs on December 25th. And on top of this is the Russian operation Uranus threatening to cut off Jünger and the 17th army on the Kuban steppe. And like that army he had a narrow escape: when receiving the note that his father was deadly ill he got the permission to return to Germany, his father

however having died before he got home. Jünger's farewell to the eastern front could be symbolised by this entry from Kiev, January 9th, 1943:

> At six o'clock take-off with an aeroplane painted green and bearing the name "Globetrotter", piloted by a prince of Coburg-Gotha. Two hours later we flew over Don lying there green and frozen, with a streak of white ice-floes. On the roads long retreating columns were seen. When landing in Rostov for a short interlude the air base was full of bombers being loaded with enormous bombs.

THE END OF THE WAR

Back in Paris the year 1943 passes by without any noteworthy military entries, at least not quotable in the context of this chapter: in the form of telling details. So I move on to 1944 where we have one passage that they point at when showing what a mindless, no, cruel aesthete he was, enjoying his wine while bombers filled the sky. Judge for yourself what kind of man wrote this:

> Alarm, overflights. From the roof of Raphaël at two times I saw giant bomb clouds rising from the region of Saint-Germain while the squadrons flew away on high altitudes, their targets the bridges over the river. The way these strikes are executed, against the supply lines, reveal a sharp mind. At the second time, by sunset, I held in my hand a glass of bourgogne with strawberries in it, the city with its red towers and cupolas radiating an intense beauty, like a flower being overflown before a deadly fertilization. [Paris, May 27th, 1944]

Operationally these bombings were part of the allied preparation for D-Day, destroying – as Jünger noted – bridges, and this to impede the Germans from reinforcing whatever bridgehead the allied chose to land on. With the landings afoot and the Germans trying (in vain) to eradicate the bridgehead Jünger sees reinforcements on a Paris street, a good quote revealing how Jünger's officer persona is still intact:

> On Boulevard de l'Amiral-Bruix heavy tanks were pausing on their way to the front. The young soldiers sat upon the steel behemoths, expectant and in a state of apprehension mixed with melancholy I remember so well. From them I sensed a tense emanation of the proximity of death, of the glory from hearts ready to die in the flames. [Paris, June 7th, 1944]

Jünger then retreats with the rest of the German army from France. And eventually he is discharged from the army, being transferred to the Home Guard. As an officer you have responsibility, and as the commander of an ill-equipped unit of local civilians in arms Jünger in Kirchhorst, April 1945, only has one order when the American tank spearheads arrive: open the tank obstacles when the first enemy vehicles are in sight. That was his last order and the American entry then rolled on without resistance, Jünger himself seamlessly retreating into the civilian life, symbolized by the handing over of his target shooting pistol to an American tank company commander, "a chivalric man" [April 13th, 1945]. Jünger has his other weapons dug down in a far-off potato field.

The district is occupied by Americans. There were some incidents, like Jünger having a pistol pointed at him by a soldier wondering what he did in his barn, the gun muzzle touching his chest. This is the moment of truth, Jünger however keeping his cool:

> I put away the hay fork I was holding. Everything became still, almost solemn. [April 12th]

When asked what he is doing there Jünger states that he is the owner of the house. Then the pistol is lowered. Jünger says:

> That was the second time in my life that I had felt a gun muzzle for such a reason, the first time being when visited similarly by some Spartakists searching our house in 1918. Both times this touch marked the translocation to a new zone. Again I felt this enormously tense atmosphere, this listening into the silence.

It was in other words a close encounter with death. And that's what it is to be an army officer: to be acquainted with death in one respect or another.

The Jünger house yard these days come to look like a riff-raff military camp, "like something out of Wallensteins camp", referring to a Schiller play about the Thirty Year's War. The discipline and spirit of the American army differs from that of the German, however the discipline is there:

> Watching the soldier guarding the house I see him sitting leisurely in a wicker chair. Nevertheless, he holds his rifle like a hunter on the beat. His commander passes by unceremoniously expect from being addressed with a "Sir" with noticeable respect.

Then we have this passage that may close these notes on the military side of Jünger's Second World War. It's about having been occupied by Americans, a slim chance considering the repute of the eastern allies at the time:

> Early this morning the Americans marched off. (...) So what shall you say about everything you've seen and heard during these days? Human beings have passed by here. And thereby everything is said. [Kirchhorst, April 14th, 1945]

8. THE ADVENTUROUS HEART

Many Jünger books defy description, living as they do in a borderline between genres and forms, consisting of reflections, anecdotes, visions and stories presented in a more or less systematic form. *The Adventurous Heart* (*Das abenteuerliche Herz*) was the first Jünger book of this kind consisting of short pieces of prose, ranging from observations of everyday life and fiction to musings and philosophical reflections, everything in a precise and pedantic prose, however not pedantic as in boring but pedantic as in enchanting, if that's possible. And it is, in Jünger's hands.

THE MASTER KEY

The first version of *The Adventurous Heart* was published in 1929. In 1938 a second version was issued, having had 220 of the 263 pages of the original revised or changed altogether. This was probably a ruse to evade the eagle eye of the Nazi censorship. So definition-wise this was hardly a revision; the 1938 version is virtually a new book.

Be that as it may. The 1938 version is now a classic in itself, being

for example the one translated into English by Telos Press in 2012. And in this chapter I too focus on the 1938 version. The translations into English presented here, however, are mine throughout.

One of the many intriguing pieces of this volume is "Der Hauptschlüssel" ("The Master Key"), about the art of entering into the essence of things. This is one of many clues to Jünger's idealistic philosophy, of his partly obscure way of looking at things:

> Every meaningful event looks like a circle whose periphery can be wholly measured by daylight. During the night however the periphery disappears to be supplanted by the shimmer of the phosphoric centre, like the petals of the Lunaria that Wierus tells about in his book *De Praestigiis Daemonum*. In the light the shape, in the twilight the creative powers appear.

More on the metaphysics of *The Adventurous Heart* in Chapter 24.

IN THE DISTRICT OF THE BLIND

A nice short story in *The Adventurous Heart* is "Im Blindenviertel" ("In the District of the Blind"). Strolling in a city the narrator soon finds out that he's in the district of the blind. One clue is a dance parlour where the mats have certain inlays of cork for the dancers to feel their way with. There's also a bar where a blind man is kept by the proprietor as a curiosity, as a conversation partner for people to ridicule, giving him a theme to elaborate on which due to his blindness tends to end up in the wrong. The guests, the seeing, then get an easy sense of superiority.

The narrator however wants something else. And here the humanism of Jünger is shown in an unsought way. Inviting the blind man to sit down he thinks about a subject in which none of them has any advantage over the other. Finally he has to – "and so we had a wonderful conversation during our breakfast about the unforeseen."

NIGROMONTANUS

The Adventurous Heart hasn't aged at all, giving us the whole spectrum of the Jünger world-view in pieces rich in reflections, scenes and symbols. I'll give you two more quotes, the first one centering on the fictional teacher *Nigromontanus* who has some similarities with Hugo Fischer (se Chapter 20). However it could be said that the name *Nigromontanus* is borrowed from a short story by Goethe. And in some way this *Nigromontanus* is a kind of Jüngerian self portrait. In "Die Vexierbilder" ("Enigmatic Images") we hear about Nigromontanus' fascination with materials that change, like iridizing glass and some precious stones. But the images in question mean more than that:

> He [Nigromontanus] had a collection of masked pictures, emanating like magic out of monochrome mosaics. They were made of pebbles which during bright days couldn't be distinguished from others, however during twilight they lit up like phosphorus. In his house he had ovens on which, when heated, proverbs in red appeared, and in his garden terraces on which a burst of rain elicited black symbols. You could also be enjoyed by the ornaments in his room and on his tools, like the meander in which alternately the bright or the dark rock arose, or vortexes drawn on the surface now showing the observer its front and now its backside. He had transparencies on which everyday motives turned into cruelties, or where the horrifying turned into the beautiful by the rays of the light. He also liked the kaleidoscope of which he had samples built, in which cut precious stones easily formed into roses and stars, a struggle between freedom and symmetry.

THE COLOUR BLUE

That's how it is with *The Adventurous Heart*: finely wrought gems of prose that you feel like quoting, not having much to add. So I'll finish this chapter with yet another quote from the book in question, letting the lines speak for themselves. They are about the colour blue and all its marine manifestations:

> The deep sea embodies this colour and reflects it variously, from matt cobalt to bright azure. There are seascapes of a sombre silkish hue or sapphiric lustre, then again surfaces of hyaline lustre over a bright bottom and by the cliffs vortexes, with the stream spreading out wondrously and flashing of colours from bouquets and starfish. Any lover of the sea can recall moments of perplexity and then bright, spiritual joy before such dramas. It isn't the water or the infinity of the water creating this joy but its divine, neptunian power living in every wave.

9. AFRICAN DIVERSIONS

A remarkable episode in Jünger's life was when he joined the French Foreign Legion in 1913. Some years later, in 1936, he wrote a novel about it. It's a documentary novel of sorts, Jünger in the process having made the hero into a 16 year old. In reality Jünger was 18 at the time. An English translation of the book was published in 1954 as *African Diversions*. The German original title was *Afrikanische Spiele*.

LA LÉGION

The telegram said: "The French government has released you. Go and have your photo taken."

The practically minded father did indeed have a keen eye for the photogenic, the iconographic, the symbolic if you will. A photo to remember this incident could be a fine object on the mantelpiece. So Jünger obeyed and went to the photographer, letting himself be portrayed in the uniform of the Legion with képi on his head and the sabre hung over a chair in the background. What catches you in this picture is the look in Jünger's eyes, seemingly gazing into

impossible lands. It's an adventurer and a dreamer we see, and even if this particular adventure had failed nothing of it is seen in the young man's demeanour in the photo.

So he had been in the French Foreign Legion. With some distance, both temporally and ideally, he made it into a documentary novel in 1936 entitled *Afrikanische Spiele* meaning "African Games", a play on words on the current Olympic Games in Berlin that year (in German it's called Olympische Spiele). Novel or not it could be used to reconstruct this episode in Jünger's life, bearing in mind that he in reality was 18 and not 16 as the book's hero. I know it's a bit risky to say that, based on a novel, this was Jünger's 1913 African adventure, but I take that risk. How did the pre-war Jünger youngster feel and act? This might be the answer.

It was the fall term of 1913. Just at the beginning of it Jünger fled from his upper secondary school, leaving his home and all in order to seek the big adventure, being fed up with books and rules and safety. He went to France and succeeded in being enlisted in the Foreign Legion, an army unit for overseas stationing.

The enrolment itself took place in Verdun, a city in northern France. Then Jünger was transported south with Marseilles as a way station. In this Mediterranean port he has an encounter with a medic trying to talk him out of it all, saying that life in the Legion is nothing but hardships and monotony. The colonial cities are nothing but copies of Europe, there's no adventure there; you'd better return to your studies...! Ignoring this advice Jünger moves on to Northern Africa, to Oran in Algeria. Seeing it for himself he eventually finds the Legion life boring. This is nothing like the adventure novels about daring explorers venturing into the heart of the continent, returning with riches in gold and slaves. It's drill and weapons duty in the company of raw brutes; not all legionnaires are scum but the environment as such isn't the right one for a dreaming young adult.

For the record it can be said that the Legion in those days wasn't so careful with whom they recruited, being a substantial force that

needed to fill the ranks. Nowadays the Legion is an elite force where criminals and such are refused out of hand. Then again, in all of its history the Legion has been a fighting force, not just some riff raff. You can't have criminals and expect them to withstand the horrors of war, you have to have a fair soldier material to work with. For as Sven Hassel said: at the first sound of gunfire the criminal runs away while the soldierly type bites the bullet and overcomes.

Jünger however realised that he had to get away from this dead-end. And this he did, escaping with a companion. They soon got caught. Some lesson on the hardships of life: you can't always quit when you feel like it. However, help seems to be at hand: the medic in Marseilles in the meantime has notified the foreign ministry in Berlin, they in turn informing Jünger's parents of the situation. Grasping the nettle the father made these suggestions to his son:

- Learn French
- Learn drill and to shoot
- Register for the corporal's course

This made some sense but Jünger rejected it all. Joining corporal's school is another dead end, a career for Dummköpfe as he sees it. Moreover, to eventually go to NCO school would be a too distant goal and as for officer's schools the Legion had none, its officers coming from the regular army.

ESCAPE

Jünger then escapes another time. But parallel to this his father has succeeded in having him released from the Legion altogether. See the telegram I quoted in the beginning. The father is as ever cool about it, forgiving his son this folie de jeunesse. There's no punishment

awaiting the returning Jünger, instead he is promised a trip to Kilimanjaro when he has graduated from upper secondary school. And back in Marseilles Jünger gets a message from the good army doctor, saying: "You experience everything and its counterpart." That's a fine proverb summing this adventure up. Romantic dreams and harsh reality go hand in hand, sometimes intensively so as in Jünger's outing to the Legion.

Sometimes your dreams are crushed but you have to dream nonetheless. "We're not defeated because of our dreams but because we haven't dreamed intensely enough", Jünger said years later in the novel *Eumeswil*. So the lesson is: dream on. And if you go out into the world seeking adventure, see to it that you have your picture taken...! The picture of Jünger as a legionnaire is one fine symbol of the author, a bit posing but only a bit. Today they say, "picture or it didn't happen", and this we also know from history, like how the Wright brothers' flight came to be established as the first motorized flight even though there were others who were at it in those days. The photo of the first leap, the first controlled motorized flight at Kitty Hawk on December 17th, 1903 has become a symbol of man's endeavours, the picture elevating it from the historical to the timeless realm.

10. ON THE MARBLE CLIFFS

On the Marble Cliffs is a complex work, existing on many levels. To be precise I don't hold it above the rest of Jünger's books but of course it's among the top five, if I should express it like that. First of all the title is very apt, combining as it does beauty with danger. Jünger himself had that ambition with the title and I must say he succeeded. As for novel titles in general *On the Marble Cliffs* is especially rich in connotations, the marble part symbolizing tradition and beauty, the cliff part symbolizing danger and then some. This book was published in English in 1947. The German original is from 1939.

WHY DID THEY WITHHOLD THIS BOOK?

I'd like to start this chapter on a personal note. I'm a Swede, born in 1965. I had a mostly okay schooling in the bosom of the leftist liberal Swedish system of those times. Moreover I read the papers, I searched around for gurus and leaders, for spiritual fathers showing you the way. As for books and authors nothing really turned me on. Of course you had some English and American science fiction to lighten you

up, there was a modicum of meaning and inspiration in the fantasy, crime and thriller books of the day, but the officially approved writers and novels all seemed to be of the doom and gloom kind.

In school and in mainstream media they told us to read Kafka, Orwell, Harry Martinson and Karin Boye. This and their contemporary epigons was considered serious, edifying fiction in those days, a monstrous monoculture of scepticism, materialism and – to add insult to injury – a spate of irony to top it off. Now then, to put it short: what a relief it was to eventually find the books of Ernst Jünger in all this waste land of nihilism and angst. My teachers and the media had kept silent about him but I found out about him nonetheless. He was after all published in Sweden in those days, in the 70's by a certain Cavefors' förlag. So the Swedish versions of *Eumeswil* and *On the Marble Cliffs* became a watering place for me, magically conjuring up totally different lands compared to the standard fare of fiction, intimated above. Not that *On the Marble Cliffs* for its part was a simple idyll; instead it was danger and beauty combined, it was melancholy over the corruption of a virgin land, and a fatalistic struggle ending in retreat and exile. But the overall mood of it all, the atmosphere and tenor of the book was totally different from anything I hitherto had encountered, excepting maybe Tolkien.

And of course I don't despise Kafka and the rest. It's just that they're missing out on so much of reality. The kitchen sink authors lauded by the teachers of my generation were unable to even write words like "beauty", "meaning", "essence", "value", "wonder" and "abundance". But Jünger had them in his vocabulary. To read them in his prose was like a revelation. That's what makes Jünger into such a unique and unparalleled voice of our times.

WHAT IT MEANS TO LIVE

The narrator and his brother are standing on the Marble Cliffs looking out over the Great Marina, a lake lined with small burgs, farmland and vineyards. To see this is what it means to live, he says:

> In the early morning the fullness of the sounds penetrated up here, delicate and pregnant like things seen in a reversed binocular. We heard the bells in the cities and the guns saluting the wreathed ships sailing into the harbours, as we did the song from the pious companies going on pilgrimage to the saint statues and the flute music from a wedding procession. We heard the jackdaws croaking around the weathercocks, the crow of the rooster and the call of the cuckoo, the sound of the horns blown by the squires when the hunting pack went through the gate of the castle. How wonderful it all sounded hearing it all the way up here, how roguish, as if the world was sewn like a many-coloured fool's cap – but also inebriating like wine in the morning.

Jünger sometimes has a tendency of making his heroes into Heroes with capital a H, characters a bit too perfect, a fault that Robert Heinlein also has been accused of (in for example *Stranger in a Strange Land*; otherwise see my comparison between Jünger and Heinlein in Chapter 26). It often becomes a bit too monumental, too rigid. However, in *On the Marble Cliffs* Jünger made room for the common man or woman to play along in the drama, she could also have her say, like the maid Lampusa who laughs at the plant collecting of the brothers, and at their putting up little porcelain signs in the garden for every flower. She herself sows haphazardly and gets a triple harvest compared to what her tenants get, the narrator and his brother. The story gains a lot by letting the hero in this fashion seem a bit too punctilious, giving him human proportions in the process.

ERNST JÜNGER – A PORTRAIT

This book has it all: there's a balance between milieu descriptions and reflections, between background and action, between nature and people. For instance all the minor characters feel alive, from Father Lampros and the nihilist Braquemart to Count Sunmyra and the mercenary Biedenhorn. *On the Marble Cliffs* as a novel may have led a somewhat obscure existence from its inception but there's a renewed interest for it these days, as in all of Jünger's œuvre. There's something timeless in its message of learning to see a wonder in every flower and the optimal in every fellow human being, as brother Otho puts it.

Jünger is different. There are other ways of ending a story than having the protagonist changed into a cockroach – than having a damaged spaceship steer out into nothingness – than having him say that he loves Big Brother. Instead you can give it all the human touch. At least you can try. "Il faut essayer de vivre" as Paul Valéry said: try to live, at least try...! Voilà a fine ideal – and this without at the same time having it sounding like a Sunday school lesson, without avoiding the difficulties. With this in mind you still have to give the reader some hope.

Okay, some plots may demand that all goes astray, and of course you shouldn't bowdlerize classics like *1984* and having them end happily. That's not my point. But I'm fascinated by *On the Marble Cliffs* for having such a structure that allows for anything to happen, for a piece of hope in all the darkness. That's its forte, for instance visible in the end game with the backwoods people gaining ground as forerunners of the Forester General's advance, the narrator's siding with the mercenaries seeming to be a losing proposition – and the battle seeming to be lost with the Marble Cliff habitat abandoned, but not until the child has had it's say, the young Erio with his ladle hitting the kettle and calling the snakes to battle against the invading lemurs.

This is some mythical tour de force, unique in 20th century literature. It is, to quote Jünger from another context, an image of the kind that you otherwise only see in your dreams. And with the additional support of Shakespeare I'd say that *On the Marble*

Cliffs is "the stuff that dreams are made of", both happy dreams and nightmares. Therefore you can't praise this novel enough.

ORIGINS

Back in the day when Jünger was asked about the meaning of *On the Marble Cliffs*, if it for example was about Nazism, he abjectly refused all such interpretations. The novel was a timeless comment on Power versus Spirit, on the struggle between clarity and culture versus occultism and raw brute force. That was Jünger's constant position when asked about the underlying pattern of his novel. However, at the same time he admitted that the character Prince Sunmyra anticipated Count Stauffenberg. Sunmyra in the novel becomes the victim of the Forest Ranger and his shadowy forces but the narrator in the end treasures Sunmyra's severed head, keeps it stored in a certain pot with preserving herbs and finally lays it as a cornerstone under a new-built church.

Sunmyra isn't literally Stauffenberg. But the character invites to such an interpretation and Jünger himself did it, as in the war diary entry of May 1, 1945. In a wider sense he was on the track of something with having Sunmyra in the novel: an old aristocrat taking up arms against tyranny. That's what Stauffenberg represented and Jünger knew that something like that was about – not that he knew Stauffenberg, but he did in fact meet with another dissident aristocrat before the war, a certain Adam von Trott zu Solz. In an appendix to a modern edition of *Auf den Marmorklippen* (the appendix is dated December 10th, 1972, the Ullstein edition in question is from 2006) Jünger tells us a bit vaguely about this, not naming either names, places or dates, but it seems to have been in Goslar sometime before the Second World War. Visiting his brother Fritz who lived in the same town by the Bodensee Jünger had already gone to bed when

some late visitors arrived so he stayed between the sheets, letting Fritz entertain the visitors.

So Jünger himself didn't participate in this fateful meeting but he remembered the name Adam von Trott zu Solz (he doesn't expressly mention him in this note but says "the one who later got executed", the aristocrat in question meeting this fate in 1944) and he remembered the atmosphere that somehow could be sensed even by the half asleep author: an atmosphere of wordless consensus as he says in the appendix. And he had seen the car of the visitors approach up the wine hill, the headlights dimmed. And these dimmed vehicle lights and then some we get in the book version of the meeting, the novelized transformation of it all into "the visit by Sunmyra".

And some days later in Goslar, after a drinking bout with some other notables, Jünger dreamt of a string of lakeside cities on fire, the flames mirrored in the water, and this spurred the whole vision and mood of the novel eventually written in 1939: *On the Marble Cliffs*.

So without reducing the novel into a "roman à clef" there was some or other things, in dreams and IRL, that spilled over into the finished product. It wasn't about Nazism but the Nazi and contemporary connections can't be ignored. You could say: the novel is about tyranny as a phenomenon, including but not exclusively about Nazism.

CHARACTERS

On the Marble Cliffs displays a rich collection of characters. We have the above mentioned prince Sunmyra, pale and frail yet strong and belligerent, a romantic dreamer aroused from his sleep and ready to act against darkness, mirroring in a way the statue of the Bamberg Horseman (der Bamberger Reiter) in Bamberg cathedral: a heroic medieval knight, seemingly distraught but essentially a true rock of

LENNART SVENSSON

resistance. Mythologically he is in my book juxtaposed by the knight depicted by Dürer in his 16th century engraving "The Knight, Death and the Devil", a no-nonsense fighter with a literal devil-may-care attitude, a man of a hard mindset and yet no mere barbarian. And this character could be said to be represented by another *Marble Cliff* figure: Biedenhorn, the commander of the mercenaries. The brothers at the centre of action get some help from him at the end, and before that he is lovingly depicted as the timeless solider, without higher ideals but reliable when it comes to battle and a jovial friend to his brothers in arms.

Then we have Braquemart, the nihilist and technical expert, a man without illusions but neither is he altogether a mindless barbarian. His likes were out and about in Nazi times, and they haven't disappeared only because the Reich went down; on the contrary, the world of today seems to be governed by Braquemarts, forming the middle management and apparatchik roles in the nihilist Empire having the west-world in its clutches. By my description Braquemart may seem like a boring acquaintance but what makes you endure the company of Braquemart and his brothers could be their sense of education and culture, their traits of ease and style. That's what makes this man memorable, as a symbol for the mauretainan life form, this use of "mauretanian" being a genuinely Jüngerian invention and recurring in other works such as *Heliopolis*, the war diary and *Eumeswil*. Mauretanians are a grey area people of educated nihilists and cunning operators, not expressly cruel but they can be that too, not altogether despicable but in all a breed of somewhat petrified souls, unable to inspire mirth, joy and happiness.

On the Marble Cliffs has more characters than that: the Forest Ranger, whom we never meet face to face but is said to be an archaic fellow, like an old Home Guard colonel arousing ridicule among the younger officers because of his old fashioned attire when he once a year attends the autumnal manoeuvres. But who gets the last laugh in this respect, regarding the Realpolitik side of things? The Forest

121

Ranger more or less triumphs at the end, conquering the Great Marina. Then we have the more positive characters like father Lampros, a priest who has a small but significant role in all this, and then other supporting characters I've already mentioned like Erio and Lampusa. Everyone, high and low, are brought along to enact the human drama that is *On the Marble Cliffs*.

11. HELIOPOLIS

Heliopolis (1949) is a sweeping novel in the grand tradition, feeling a bit constructed but nonetheless enchanting in many of its parts. If you're looking for a traditional novel with a plethora of characters and interiors, with catching landscapes and interesting discussions on traditional subjects, this is the novel for you. But beware, it's not a common best-seller, not easily read, even in comparison to other German authors. Herman Hesse and Thomas Mann are more accessible in this respect. So if you want to read a novel in German (*Heliopolis* hasn't been translated into English) *Heliopolis* isn't a beginner's first choice. Then again, it's a classic and impossible to bypass when talking about Jünger.

BETWEEN THE PALACE & THE CENTRAL DEPARTMENT

The city of Heliopolis has its name for a reason, steeped in sunlight where it lies at the bay, vaguely reminiscent of the Italian city of Naples. This City of the Sun however is an original creation of Jünger's,

a timeless town where the sun shines in every chapter. And rightfully so. It's a novel with the sunny lifestyle as a background, balanced with intrigues and power struggles and the plans and aspirations of its main character, Lucius de Geer.

Heliopolis takes place in the future, after some undisclosed catastrophe. There's a talk of mythical "fires", the city has been partly damaged, but not much of it is actually seen when the plot is unravelled. The city has ridden out the storm, now resting comfortably by the sea like a jewel. And here we have the captain de Geer serving in the Palace of the Proconsul, taking part in the struggle against the Central Department. The Proconsul rules the city on behalf of the Prince, an absent but still existing royalty symbolizing legitimate power. So the novel is about old power versus new, legitimacy versus demagoguery, light versus dark. Here you could add that the de Geer faction of course isn't made up of angels, they're men like their counterparts.

The dark forces are active but the main impression of Heliopolis is that of an idyll with parks, well kept villas and palaces except for the blocks with tenement houses and offices. As intimated de Geer takes part in the intrigues, fighting for tradition and stability against the machinations of the modern powers embodied in the Central Department and its ruler, der Landvogt (the Land Marshall or Bailiff). Finally de Geer comes into conflict with his peers due to a disciplinary matter so he has to resign. What then shall his next move be? He rides off to the Pagos mountain, asking his old guru Pater Foelix what to do.

The Pater is a bee-keeper. As a digression, pointing to his beehives, he says: the bees don't actually work, they gather nectar because of a discreet joy, a silent celebration of life. This is elaborated into a meditation over human endeavours and human economy, the Pater saying:

> We could learn from the bees what work is. No enterprise can bear fruit if there isn't a sparkle of love in it. The joy of life keeps it

all together, much stronger than the economy or the brute force. It's like a farmer ploughing in the morning sun or a blacksmith standing at his anvil or the fisher lowering his nets: in all of them we can surmise a sense of satisfaction that is unmeasurable. You can notice it even in the marketplace and the hubbub of the city. In this sense of satisfaction lies the true treasure of the world, the solid gold, the harvests and the profits being merely the yield. This is also true for the industry – no economy can blossom if it isn't founded on love. Benevolence has a golden hand.

Emerson springs into mind here: "Nothing great was ever achieved without enthusiasm." Jünger paints a picture of the joy that makes the world go round, a hymn to the discreet forces of life, going from part to whole, from the drop of nectar collected by the bee to entire harvests.

THE BEEHIVE AS A SYMBOL

Talking about bees there are a lot of them in the Jünger fiction: here in *Heliopolis*, and in *The Glass Bees* where the artificial bees tended to kill the flowers they had sucked, and in *On the Marble Cliffs* where a certain Father Lampros also was a bee-keeper. The bees in the Jünger fiction become a symbol for life, stronger than the titanism of the Worker Jünger had previously hailed.

Returning to Heliopolis, what did Pater Foelix advise de Geer? What should the captain do with his life when he had to resign his commission? The Pater led de Geer to the realm of the Blue Pilot, the commander of one of the spaceships mankind has sent out by this time. To move out in a greater space, to roam the spatial vistas to de Geer seems like a feasible way out. With his woman he becomes a space cadet and leaves the city with the next ride.

Like *On the Marble Cliffs* this book still has something to say to us. As intimated it teaches us what makes the world go round: Eros

and esoterica, not mass media and materialism. There's a tangibly positive message in this book, shining like the sun of the title itself. And this is seldom noticed by the Jünger scholars, stuck as they are in the sterile landscapes of *Storm of Steel*, *Der Arbeiter* and *Die Totale Mobilmachung*. Why is it so hard to appreciate Jünger's esoteric and metaphysical side, exposed since *The Adventurous Heart* in 1929? As I said in the introduction I want to lift the mysterious, spiritual side of Jünger in this book. And an English translation of *Heliopolis* could do its part in giving the English speaking world a view of this side of Jünger.

A WEALTH OF PASSAGES

Heliopolis has a wealth of fine tableaus, passages depicting life in all its beauty and splendour and with a tinge of melancholy. As in this scene where Jünger tells us about the island Vinho del Mar just off the Heliopolis coast, an island mostly deserted but still reminiscent of its glory days:

> In better times rich Heliopolitans had built a series of Roman country houses by the southern beach of the island, meant for quiet days and celebrations of the wine-harvest. (...) Since the establishment of the Land Marshall on the neighbouring island the joy had abated, emptying the villas and seeing the walls and arbours decaying, the statues in the gardens being covered by ivy. In the mid-day heat the snakes sunbathed on the colourful mosaics, and by midnight the owl soared soundlessly out of the round ox-eye window into the park.

THE MOMENT OF HAPPINESS

Heliopolis is a treasure house of wisdom and enchanting scenes. When you've grown accustomed to the somewhat cumbersome, 19th century-ish style then you're hooked. The narrator takes his time, he goes slowly but surely along in trying to capture the essence of Heliopolis, lecturing on everything under the sun and symbolising it with a wide array of images and pictures.

There's wisdom, there's lecturing. Some passages are like miniature essays. Like in the chapter called "The Symposium" with Lucius having gathered his friends, the painter Halder and the author Ortner, for an academic get-together, just like the one Plato described in his eponymous work. They are there to drink wine and talk about certain subjects in an ordered but free structure. Halder for one talks about the peculiarities of painting and Ortner about his art, on writing in general and novel writing in particular. Then they touch on philosophical subjects, such as the ethics of suicide. Then, seemingly unsought, they discuss "the moment of happiness" and whatever that means to each one of them. Lucius for his part illustrates his view of it with a story from his days as a secret agent. A certain day in a harbour "beyond the Hesperides" he was to meet up with a certain contact, the rendezvous being in the evening so he could spend the day as he chose:

> Until then the day is mine in a new and unfamiliar way. The fine threads with which habit and duty binds us are cut off and thereby freedom fills me as in a dream. I'm going to spend a day outside the law, as if I owned the ring who makes you invisible. I now understand the secret joy of the dwarf in the fairy tale: no one knows my name. The incognito of the prince is here mixed with that of the criminal, equally absorbed in his plans. Temptation has got me in its grasp.

This is a congenial description of being "the accidental tourist", like William Hurt in that eponymous 1988 movie: as a traveling businessman he often found himself in exciting world cities with time to kill, not having planned to go there as a tourist. So he was free to do a bit of casual sightseeing, maybe experiencing happiness in the process. As for the fairy tale dwarf it's the Grimm story of a dwarf who would win a bet if the other one didn't figure out his name. However the other one did find out the name, spying on the dwarf in his secret lair where the gnome triumphantly sat singing: "No one knows my name!" But in the song he did say it – Rumpelstiltskin – and thereby the bet eventually was lost. As for "the incognito of the prince" the kings of old sometimes used to travel in their realms anonymously in order to step out of the ruler persona for a while.

So Lucius was sitting at the symposium talking about his take on the moment of happiness. Visiting a southern town, having to kill time, he approaches a happy state bordering on magic. He says:

What magical power such moments reveal for us. As if I had been drinking strong wine or enjoyed Indian drugs the world is changed. In the same measure as I abstain from desiring, from acting, the dominating influence grows stronger. Sitting by the breakfast table a dark servant pours my coffee. In seeing the smile, the glint in his eyes, I realize that I am the unknown guest which he serves every morning. (...) I could now break the spell in giving him gifts, in pulling him down on his knees and revealing to him dreams and wishes unknown to him. Instead I increase my power by remaining silent and abstaining from it all. That's the overture, followed by walks by the harbour, through the bazaars and the conglomeration of quarters. Seeing the eddying crowd increases my joyous mood. The less I know their names, their occupation, their language, the clearer the secret meaning emerge. They're illuminated from within. You realize that the life of men is based on a myth as simple as hieroglyphics. We approach happiness when we enter that myth.

What makes this passage original is the mere mention of "happiness", of taking it seriously. Every other writer of today seems to deny that any such thing as happiness exists, bent as they are on promoting nihilism, sarcasm, atheism and defeatism. The only other modern writer I've seen talking about happiness is Lars Gustafsson (q.v. Chapter 22).

Lucius continues his train of thought:

> Fleetingly fast the sun rises to zenith and then goes down towards the sea, time flying by in a wondrous, painless course. The lively pictures fall into me, catching fire in me. The people live inside of me: I can feel their thoughts, actions, sufferings when I see them. They stream into me like veins conjoining in my interior.

Jünger/Lucius then continues to catch the mood of happiness in fitting metaphors. It's "the eye as a sun", "the spirit as conductor of the life melody" and so on. And the conclusion seems to be that happiness lives within us. The passions are said to gather their nourishment from the spirit world, and by the time "we touch the treasure the desire consummating us dies out". Thus it's better to remain at the threshold of the dream, at the borderland of imagination, the feeling being at its strongest there.

This Jünger essay on happiness is like an exposition of désinvolture, which I talked about in Chapter 25: to partake in life but not being engaged, with a Zen Buddhist calm seeing life passing by. A subtle form of active-passive meditation, in the middle of the hubbub. With a pious sentiment neither attaching yourself to luck or bad fortune, success or failure, almost like a stoic apatia taking you to the realm beyond good and bad.

GUNNERY SERGEANT SIEVERS

In his Heliopolis dealings Lucius comes across a fascinating character, Gunnery Sergeant Sievers. At the end of the book Lucius is going to launch a semi-private commando raid, and as a captain in the proconsular army he has the means to acquire the materiel needed. Visiting the arsenal of the castle and meeting its manager, the NCO in question, we get to see a symbolic representation of the artillery man, the fire-worker or fire-maker, a technically skilled labourer of death. Sievers is a moderately passionate figure, calm but loaded, always prepared:

> He was a short man, almost brownie-like, certainly having to stretch under the measuring-rod in order to get accepted into the ranks. But he had found his place in life, indicated by three rows of decorations on the left side of his chest. Those who knew how to decode this to soldiers so dear hieroglyphics understood that it mostly concerned actions like stormings and close-quarter fights. Then there were decorations for having lead operational demolitions. The princely order of the silver eagle for its part was a sign of long and faithful service. The little man was straight-backed, moving about with a resilient agility. There was both joviality and a rock-hard willpower in his character. Due to an old wound he dragged his foot a little. The blue eyes were open and firm and a fiery red beard with white traces edged his face.

Lucius for his part is a contemplating gentleman officer drawn to cultural doings, while Sievers is a stiffened professional bent on continuing the struggle at all costs. Both are opposed to the oppressive regime of the Land Marshal but Siever's recipe is more hands-on: bomb the Central Works, even if it means civilian casualties. Siever's creed is summed up like this, in his own words:

Where you plane the shavings fly, as they say. And when cutting hay flowers and bird's nests aren't spared. The world is governed by order and orders has to be obeyed. When the Proconsul have weighed for and against people like me don't bother their heads. That's how it's done and everything else is insubordination. As a fire-maker I'm responsible for the ignition. And that won't misfire as long as old Sievers is still in business.

Lucius then privately reflects on the type Sievers represents:

His pedigree was martial: the old quartermasters and bombardiers had been thinking like him. In the service of kings they had made their way into castles, then crushing cities and fortresses and sinking ships at long distances.

When technology had turned the wars into battles between machines these old fire-workers had come along, somewhat reluctantly, but having assessed the situation they kept on doing their duty. They had to, otherwise they would have been out of work. The endpoint of this development was Hiroshima, a city by the sea obliterated by technicians, by the modern heirs to the fire-workers and with some help from airmen.

So was Sievers and his kind responsible for it all? "The bill didn't add up" Jünger admits. However, the fire-worker in question isn't an evil man. Primarily responsible are the politicians, pursuing politics as a game.

THE MINING SECRETARY

The arsenal where Sievers dwells is in the interior of Pagos, the hill west of the city on which the Prince has his hothouse and on which the war academy also is situated. And on the same hillside, within

subterranean localities, lives a certain Mining Secretary. The title is hard to translate: in German it's Bergrat, an official in charge of mines etc., and moreover an honorary title for some government officials (that's at least how it is in Finland: "Bergsråd"). The name "Bergrat" [to be divided as "Berg" (mountain); "Rat" (councillor)] to me seems to convey the concept of a mining official and then some, like a latter day mountain king with his own modern grotto, exactly like the one we see in *Heliopolis* – a connoisseur of minerals and precious stones, the steward of the city's gold reserve. The Mining Secretary is a shady figure, a troglodyte ("caveman") in a literal however not figurative sense, the latter role being reserved for the Land Marshal and his torture expert Messer Grande.

The Mining Secretary thus becomes a remarkable grey area figure in the mosaic of Heliopolis. He lives in a fully equipped modern habitat in the Pagos mountain. With Lucius having come inside it is depicted like this:

> [After a hallway Lucius entered] the main hall, already embedded into the rock. It was cold in spite of a fire in the hearth. (...) [A door was opened] up on the emporium in the high hall with the old man stepping forth. (...) Lucius went up the spiral staircase, half embedded into the rock and half projecting into the hall as a free spiral. The Mining Secretary wore his grey suit and on his head the kind of little green hood the stonecutters wear during work.

The reason for Lucius' visit is to take a look at the man's collection of precious stones. A petrified sea anemone appears like this:

> Resting on a basis of oak the piece of anemone was exquisite. Even though its mirror was completely free from dust the Mining Secretary carefully wiped it with a piece of cloth. It must have been cut out of a fathom-wide block that had been cloven. The surface was slightly curved and its violet tinge was so deep that

it bordered on black. A velvet brown edge enclosed the dark core. The zoophytes, embedded in shining white, crystallized marble, looked like ice flowers, the grinding having hit them lengthwise and making them look like thin magnolia buds or, in cross-section, developing their radiating pattern. In between the tentacles twisted, here and there broken in their joints and looking like strewn out coins.

What does this mean then? It's a fossil making you reflect on creation itself, on the dawn of time when the shapes where stamped out according to their ideal forms:

Lucius looked at this petrification with the wonder that always gripped him before such early creations: the hieroglyphics of the first documents. There was also fear in this wonder. In the mathematical, radiating shape of the construction lay something inexorable, the reflection from the highest workshops, the sublime loneliness of the shiftings and reflections of the first day of creation, even before Leviathan was invented. Here the same character ruled as in the old scriptures without vowels and periods, here you found the gleaming skeleton of the life plan, its law inscribed in crystal. Before such treasures man's eye fell through a slit into the forecourt of an architect lit all too brightly. All the sciences led towards this perspective.

THE MOON CRATER

Lucius looked at this anemone in the abode of the Mining Secretary, the same figure appearing in the novel's chapter 1 – "The Return From the Hesperides" – with him and Lucius aboard a ship heading for Heliopolis. After their conversation the Secretary dictates to his aide by cell phone – his "phonophor" – a mysterious text about a

geological expedition, performed by a certain Fortunio. That it takes place on the moon isn't mentioned but the dropping of such names as Mare Serenitatis and Caucasus, a plain and a mountain range (Caucasus Mons) on the moon, firmly establishes the scene. So what did Fortunio see there? Jünger imagines this geological formation at the bottom of a crater, a giant emerald with a wealth of other treasures embedded:

> The crater was formed like a green chalice with foam glistening at the edge and with spiral bands leading down to the bottom, spectrally shimmering out of the depth, leading me [Fortunio] to dare the descent by these bands into the green shaft. Soon enmeshed in the interior of the crystal, now translucent in the strong light coming through it, I noticed that its mass wasn't entirely made of emeralds but contained other minerals as well, many-coloured veils diminishing its lucidity. Bands of opal dust, looking like the rain of sparkles from magnificent smithies, shot through it. There were inset nuclei in all forms, shapes and colours that we see in field and meadow among seeds and fruits, these resplendent stones now lying spread out over the surface like jewels in a king's crown or inlays in a reliquary, now shining matt out of the depth of the foundation.

Jünger seems to say: the world is enchanted. And you don't even have to go to the moon to experience it; as we saw Fortunio did liken the lunar beauty in question to earthly forms and environments. And his coda to it all, the dominating feeling visiting him after this lunar outing, is this:

> Happiness took a hold on me as it takes hold of the suitor entering the chamber of his beloved, being filled with calm when knowing what I had found.

Heliopolis is filled with gripping passages. You just can't quote them all. But if I may present just one more it'll be this one, from the sea journey opening the book, with this unsought vision of the town finally lying before the travellers, giving us the novel's and thus Jünger's creed in nuce:

Heliopolis, the legendary city with its palaces and villas, its squares and swarming quarters, appeared mightily in the sunshine – like a grand metropolis, attracting the ship like a magnet. You could already hear its hubbub as if from a bright mussel in which the foam of the sea has united itself with precious soils. All since heroic times men had been living by the bay, the golf being ploughed by the primeval keels. Up on Pagos the caves revealed images of early hunts and out of the ground idols could be unearthed. Dynasties of gods and kings had come and gone and the fundamentals of the city rested on the humic layers of bygone cultures, the great fires leaving rusty red traces in between. Innumerable were the ones who had lived, loved and thrived here, all gone now, all harvested by death. Seeing it thus the city became slightly unreal, reminding you of the blossoming of an old tree, soon to be blown away by the wind. The first dwellers drew their furrows around it. Since then it had never ceased to grow even though it had seen its fateful days too, being touched by the red sickle. Still its ground seemed like an arable land constantly producing new harvests in invisible barns.

12. THREE TREATISES

As a societal thinker Jünger has a lot to say, unifying social commentary with ethics, the situation of society with that of the individual, in texts like *The Forest Passage* (1951, English translation 2013) and *Über die Linie* (1950). And in *Der Arbeiter* (1932) he caught the gist of modernization, the force transforming idyllic villages and farmlands into monotonous industrial areas of malls, apartment blocks and highways.

THE FOREST PASSAGE

A walk in the woods to the post war Jünger became a symbol, the walker in the woods embodying a rebellious ideal in a time adoring progress and materialism. In the woods you found the silent answer to everything, resisting the temptations of modern civilization and becoming truly free. It didn't even have to be a real forest; the wood in this respect was as intimated a symbol for freedom.

But of course Jünger tended to go out there, for real, in a real forest, having done that since childhood, from his early outings in the Hannoveran moor to the late walks in the Wilflingen forests. However,

in *The Forest Passage* (Der Waldgang, from Wald/wood, Gang/walk) he tried to take it all to a more theoretical level. If I have to be critical the book is lacking in some respects, Jünger being a bit hard-headed and non-spiritual. Just walking in the woods, what's the existential use in that if you don't' have a fully spiritual outlook...? Jünger for instance criticizes the act of forming yoga schools. This you shouldn't do he says, this is harmful and introverted. This contradicts what he says in *Eumeswil*, where he states that if you have ten anarchs living in a city this improves the climate, making it easier to breathe. An invisible change is effectuated even though nothing concrete is made. And I would say that the presence of a yoga school or something similar improves the climate, be it in a city, be it in the world as a whole. If more people meditated and focused on divine and eternal values, then we would have less crime and violence.

The anarch in *Eumeswil* of 1977 is like a heir to the forest walker of *The Forest Passage* of 1951. Jünger is the self-same anarch, Jünger is the self-same forest walker, and in each book he gives the one or the other formalization of his current outlook. Now then, the forest walker indeed has some good points. He is a man of resistance, resisting the demands of society, even the demand of voting in general elections. He reminds you that even the (when writing the book) current Stalinist Russia has elections. But in the kind of elections where you can only vote Yes or No, writing Y och N, der Waldgänger simply writes W. That's W for Waldgang. That's a strong symbol and a defining moment of the book, reminiscent of similar moments in Ayn Rand's *We the Living* (1936) and Robert Silverberg's *A Time of Changes* (1971). It's like the TV series *The Prisoner*: I am not a number, I am a free man…!

You have to break free from every oppression, be it Stalinist or currently Western. Having spiritually left the Titanic that is our consumer and control societies the anarch lives here and now on his virtual island. The media and politics of today rules with fear. It's a regime of terror. They frighten us with phoney wars, invented flues

and the possibility of an asteroid colliding. All this you have to shut out, going out into the Forest and be free. Now this is easier than ever today when mainstream media loses ground and people can choose new channels of information, devoid of the constant fear-mongering of the state controlled ones.

Ezra Pound once said that he who doesn't have order within himself can't create order around him, and that rhymes with what Jünger says in *The Forest Passage*.

ÜBER DIE LINIE

In Jünger's production *The Forest Passage* was preceded by *Über die Linie* (1950), a similar clarion call for the conscious individual to realize his might against the Powers that Be. Live here and now, conquer fear and so on. Other than that *Über die Linie* (a title hard to translate but meaning something like "About/Across/Over the Line") dealt with nihilism, a wide concept that Jünger wasn't totally negative to. But then he meant nihilism as a personal, ontological phase to go through.

Nihilism in this vein could have a cleansing effect on the mind. However, institutional nihilism such as the one we see in today's society, where nothing exists but eating, sleeping and fornicating, where economic growth is the ultimate goal, this nihilism is dangerous. It's life threatening and sterile, a titanic form of existence.

To focus on the subject of personal nihilism it can be said that this nihilism isn't totally sterile. It's better than defeatism which to Jünger is the worst attitude possible, a negative approach leading to premature death. Nihilism on the other hand is a living and vibrant stance of the mind that has lost its childhood faith, experiencing how everything seems to be meaningless. The old gods are dead so where to find new ones? Nihilism comes in handy here as a temporal

solution, making you believe in Nothingness (since nihil in Latin means just that, nothing). This however is not a goal, it's a way station. You zero position the system. But then you have to move on. If not, you start to worship death and decay.

Exactly how to move on from Nothing to Something is hard to say. But you can begin with this, Jünger says: to conquer the fear of death. And having done that you're indestructible, impossible to defeat. "People who don't fear death are infinitely superior to even the greatest earthly power", Jünger says in *Über die Linie*, evoking the image of Leviathan as a symbol for the Powers that Be. Free from the fear of death, having realized your memento mori, you can steer free from both personal and societal nihilism, a man impossible to be affected by the terrors and demands of society, a society whose media outlets are only out to scare you, its technological systems trying to obliterate all joy and love.

Frightened people are easy to govern. But people who have left fear behind them form a subtle resistance movement, people resistant to the ravages of titanism. Tying the bonds of love and friendship we can cultivate gardens, "oases in the desert around which Leviathan moves in anger."

How we as individuals reach this loving mental state, that's up to ourselves. Free will has to reign – our own free will, yours and mine:

> Your own chest: this is the centre of the desert and the ruin world. Here is the cavern where the demons gather. Here every man dwells, independent of class and position, in direct and gallant struggle, and with his victory the world is changed. If he's the stronger Nothingness retires. The treasures, having been covered, are left at the beach. They will outweigh the sacrifices.

DER ARBEITER

Der Arbeiter (*The Worker*) from 1932 could be seen as a portrait of societal nihilism in action. Here we don't have to dwell on the fact that Jünger himself was a kind of nihilist when he wrote it. The book is complex and has something to say to us even today. Here I will analyze the book from a societal point of view (in Chapter 28 I will look at its dramatic qualities).

The age of technology, of industrialization, of total, material mobilization: that's the world of the Worker, a modern homo faber commanding nature's forces and having the whole world march in a machine rhythm. The woods and the seas are devastated, everything has a prize but no value, culture is defined in terms of consumption, old city centres are raised to the ground to give room for structures of concrete and glass. We now see the reverse side of such a development, critics of this kind of civilization are out and about and have been for a while, but the age of the Worker isn't over yet. Outside our cities the landscapes of malls, offices and highways stretch for miles, in the West as well as in the East. Material expansion is in most people's mind. Our politicians talk about economic growth as the only standard of progress.

The Worker still rules the world, with industrial methods spreading to all areas: health care, the military, the school. A doctor shouldn't be curing individuals, no, he is to cure the X number of patients in order to be worth his money. A solider isn't supposed to be valiant, he shall only fulfil a prescribed number of tours, in some cases reducing battle to a mere body count. And the teacher shouldn't convey wisdom; to stick to the teaching plan is the only goal.

Now then, the cure to all this. We saw it in subsequent Jünger books, like the ones I talked about earlier in this chapter. Other books in the same vein, how to regain sense and proportion, friendship and quality of life in this age, were *Heliopolis, Eumeswil, Besuch auf*

Godenholm and *The Glass Bees*. I cover them all in this book, *The Glass Bees* being up in the next chapter. – The main cure against titanism and nihilism, Jünger intimated, was to get to grips with the desert inside, our internal, mental desert lands. If we don't like the sterility of the Worker's world we have to look at ourselves, looking inside, to get the answer. Are we Workers ourselves or are we sentient beings with a spiritual dimension?

It's not enough to say, "re-establish the eternal values by giving resources to the church, the school, the authors, the artists". We have to live the change, be the change. It's all in the mind. The suitable Jünger recipe is in the words "im Innern ist's getan" ("it's decided within"), like Goethe said. This became a glorified a sub-theme of everything Jünger wrote in the post war years.

13. THE GLASS BEES

The *Glass Bees* has an odd structure for a novel, the events taking place during one day and at the same time being almost totally devoid of concrete action. Maybe the book can be seen as a "throw away", the closest Jünger ever got to writing something like that. Artistically it's kind of embryonic but it still has some value. It also has the distinction of being translated into English, published by the American company Noonday Press in 1960.

> We can't break out of our bonds, not out of our inner essence. And we can't change much either. We may change, true, but it's done within the bonds, within the limitations.

This the narrator of the Jünger novel *The Glass Bees* of 1957 tells us. Maybe this wisdom is applicable on Jünger himself: once an officer, always an officer; once a pedant, always a pedant; once an esotericist, always an esotericist. As for the military background the narrator of this novel, Captain Richard, has been in the cavalry. He lovingly looks back at an archetypal belle epoque, the pre-war world where a cavalryman was the thing to be. Then they rode out into the Great War, having to dismount before the obstacles of barbed wire and

massed artillery fire. In time they became armoured troops. The drama of the two world wars is telescoped into one. As intimated this is about an archetypal development; it's not specifically about "1914", "France", "Germany" and so on, but it isn't totally other-worldly either. Certain city and district names anchors the plot in Europe but the overall effect is what you may call familiar-unfamiliar, a true tour de force for a novel of speculative fiction, of slipstream or whatever. It's neither an ordinary novel or a generic SF novel, that's what I'm trying to say. It's a novel of ideas.

In the olden days there were horses and cavalry, the solider's life was easy, then the Great War changed all that. Jünger catches this emotion rather well albeit in a stiff, first person narrative. Then it's on to technical developments, the old world of horsepower giving place to a world of machines. And central among the machines in this novel are robots of diverse kinds, both for entertainment and useful things as well as for war and power. The inventor of them is one Zapparoni, a technical wizard and media mogul in one, a mix between Nikola Tesla and Walt Disney if you will. And Captain Richard is about to apply for a job in Zapparoni's company. That's the whole plot. He gets the job. The book was supposed to have a sequel but it never materialized, thus giving the story a kind of truncated ending.

Whatever Zapparoni would have done with his robots we never get to know. Conquer the world, like some Jules Verne anti-hero...? But the novel is nonetheless fully readable, giving the reader proverbs such as these:

- Where hate is sown the harvest can be nothing but weeds.
- He who looks too closely into the kitchen looses his appetite.
- Help can reach you from unexpected quarters, above all from the weak ones.
- To decide the age of a person is unimportant; spirit has no age.

Having landed his job at Zapparoni's, Richard goes home to his wife. Happy ending...? On this it's said in the book: there are no more happy endings, happiness just isn't abounding in these times. But there's moments of happiness and there's the freedom of the moment.

This is a fine proverb, however a bit too pessimistic for my taste. But as I said, there's wisdom in this novel. It's all over the place. One quote in particular could highlight this. For the following, imagine the vaults where certain speculators are said to hide away their art master-works, vaults with a grave-like atmosphere. Jünger:

> A work of art dies and withers away in a room where it only has a prize and no value. It has to be surrounded by love in order to shine. It has to fail in a world where the rich doesn't have time and the educated no money.

14. JAHRE DER OKKUPATION

F irst it was called *Die Hütte im Weinberg* (*The Hut on the Wine Hill*). Jünger mentions this shed in the entry of May 13th, 1945, a Biblical symbol for his condition as a conquered German in a land of ruins: "Only Sion remains like a hut in the vineyard, a sentry's shed in the pumpkin field." That was from Isaiah 1:8, a fine metaphor however a bit vague for the common reader. For later editions an editor suggested the name *Jahre der Okkupation* (*Years of Occupation*), a title more in sync with the neue sachligkeit of the post war German Federal Republic.

FLOWERS BLOSSOMING

Jahre der Okkupation is the last volume of the oft mentioned war diary. The first book in the series was *Gärter und Strassen*, covering the years 1939-41, the second was *Strahlungen*, going from 1941 to 1945. In the book at hand we get Jüngers journal for the years 1945-1948. And as such it's about everything under the sun and then some. The best Jünger books used to be of this kind, without structure, just

giving you short texts on whatever he felt like talking about. And especially the diary gives you this kind of freedom as a writer.

In spite of the grim times there's thriving in this book. The flowers are blossoming and that gladdens Jünger. "Whereof is the consolation you get from watching flowers?", he asks in the entry for April 14th, 1945, answering:

> It's undoubtedly tellurian-erotic since the flowers are the love organs of Mother Earth, her love drive. The festival of flowers is solemn since even the splendour of animals can't equal it.

And once again the consolation: "When the world seems shaken in its foundations the look at a flower can restore the order." [October 15th, 1945]

The same date Jünger goes on to say that the plant is a lens for the invisible, for Goethe's Urpflanze, i.e. "the original Plant", the Platonic idea of the plant, the Tree of Life if you will. And on April 14th, 1945, the flower becomes a symbol for paradise, for cosmic presence here and now. Oh these flowers, so silent but yet so telling; in every garden, in every ditch...

> (...) mosaics and ribbons of hieroglyphs shines at us. Where is the possibility, the existence of higher worlds more visible than here? It's divine nectar, the wine of eternal youth expressed in these cups.

This is central to Jünger's creed: the eternal is mirrored in the temporal here and now, the ability to see the invisible with the help of the symbol. It's the metaphysics of everyday: a hint of eternity mediated by a chance observation, far from the dry idealism of the academy.

EVERYTHING IS DECIDED WITHIN

A centrepiece of the whole Jünger oeuvre are the last lines of *Jahre der Okkupation*. He begins the passage in question by quoting Goethe, without giving the source: "Doch im Innern ist's getan" ("everything is decided within"). As I've said elsewhere in this study these lines stem from Goethe's *Wilhelm Tischbeins Idyllen*. Jünger was thinking about this when on December 2nd, 1948, he writes about having posted a letter. Now, he says, when doing this we always wonder if the letter will reach its destination – but that's a bit beside the point since having thought about the receiver (when writing the letter etc...) the letter so to speak is already there. The letter has already had an effect, like an arrow completing its course in the invisible, in the transcendental realm, the supernatural beyond the Beyond. "There is always a second addressee to our words, deeds and thoughts".

Regardless if the letter reaches its destination it feels good having posted it. The sheer mental process of writing the letter gives you comfort, gives you inner cleansing. Something in the world has been changed by the writing: "It is a sacrifice fulfilled, even if no one reads it."

The same could be said about the worries and concerns for your dear ones who are lost, imprisoned or dead; this was written by Jünger right after the Second World War but it's generally applicable. Maybe we'll never know what happened to them, maybe one day you'll get to know that the one you worried about is long dead, and then you've worried in vain:

> We've been thinking about him as if he lived. And yet there is something wonderful in this "as if". We should be thinking about every dead as if he lived, and about every living as if he were dead. Thus we're aiming our wishes higher, towards the eternal person. And stretching the bow enough we will experience the wonderful moment when the answer is there. Because everything is decided within.

HOW AND IF TO EDIT

The lines I just quoted to me are another fine example of the metaphysics of everyday. It's also a fine example of the worth of a stylistic diary, a consciously edited diary. Jünger made it no secret that he rewrote passages before having them published in book form. An unwritten rule says that a diary should be more or less in the raw; beyond corrections etc. you shouldn't improve lines and wordings. But if the result is like the piece just quoted then I stand for this kind of edited diary.

The finely edited, stylistically refined journal is an established form. André Gide also published his "Journals" this way they say, seeking the exquisite wording for the final form, never bothering that it becomes less authentic that way. Now of course there's a charm to the more rawly printed journal too, like the one of Witthold Gombrowiz (1904-1969). But Jünger's journals are classics and – I figure – those who complain about falsification because he reworded this or that years after the event before publishing it – they are in the wrong. Polish or no polish, the Jünger diaries are sincere.

15. ANNÄHERUNGEN

Approaches: Drugs and Ecstasy might be a suitable English title for *Annäherungen: Drogen und Rausch* (1970). An excerpt has been published in English in Myths and Symbols – *Studies in Honour of Mircea Eliade* by Chicago University Press in 1969. The title then was just *Drugs and Ecstasy*. But the theme of the book is how you can approach the essence of reality by different means, not just by drugs. Being close to Reality is to be in der Nähe of it. When you're approaching something, then an Annäherung is made.

THE DRUG AS A METAPHYSICAL VESSEL

To reach beyond everyday reality you may need drugs, some people say. Some religions have a tradition of drug use, like Indian Shivaism and the shamanism of Mexican Indians. Then of course these religions also say that the Beyond can be reached by other means such as intuition, meditation and power of will. And in order to cut to the chase, what did Jünger himself say on the subject? He did use a lot of drugs over the years, not exactly in great quantities but he verily tried this and that. And did the drugs work for him? I'd say

he made some interesting discoveries but in all, to me, this book – *Annäherungen* – is not so clear-cut on the subject, not so positive. Jünger seems a bit disappointed after all his experiments with heavy drugs, having learned that there is no easy way to the Essence of Reality. Approaching the divine by means of exotic drugs is not so easy. Drugs and their mysteries are a reality but bourgeois, common drugs like wine is as efficient as opium, he intimates.

How then about the subject of "taking drugs to become a better writer"? Forget it is the message of *Annäherungen*. Personally I don't want to sound like a prissy but you can lead a full life without any drugs at all. Even Baudelaire himself warned against drugs in the relevant study *The Artificial Paradises* (1860). Jünger says about this work that Baudelaire here delivers,

> (...) the main objection posed against the drug: that it is a false path to trust pharmacists and magicians when you want to reach heaven. As genuine and honest ways he [Baudelaire] mentions fasting, prayer and work but also "noble dances".

Of course, Baudelaire also did say: "we have to inebriate ourselves", in *Pétits poèmes en prose* (1869). There the idea is that we can use cultural means as well as drugs. Reading and writing, listening to music, creating images: this is also an approach.

DIVINE REFLECTIONS

Jünger's *Annäherungen* is about drugs, casting a wide net to capture the essence of the subject. Cocaine, opium, chloroform, LSD and everything else is covered, both through Jünger's own experiences and by means of cultural history. Then the book has musings about more or less unrelated things, side-tracks well worth following for the avid Jünger student, illuminating his overall creed.

Let's begin with some divine reflections.

Jünger often occupied himself with gods, ancient and heathen pantheons, his late diary being full of references to Titans and Olympians gods. That's fair, but why didn't he also delve into the Christian universe of angels? They are, in my book, a sort of gods or demi-gods too. In Christian terms it's always said: don't worship archangels! I agree to that. But discussing the roles and doings of the Biblical angels could give an esotericist as much as studying the Greek and Norse gods. The Christian angel pantheon for one has an interesting juxtaposition in angels of the light versus angels of the dark, devas versus asuras in esoteric terms. That pattern is also discernible in the Greek system with Titans versus Olympian gods: rough and tough creatures versus more shining ones. Jünger often talked about the Titans having no festivities, all work and no play being their creed, and that strikes me as a defining character of asuras too.

As for the Norse gods Jünger makes an interesting note in *Annäherungen*, about how Wagner failed in the Asa gods. The divine characters in *The Ring of the Nibelungs* were noteworthy creations, Wagner conjuring them out from the shadows of history – this was a bold enterprise Jünger says, mentioning how Nietzsche for his part was ecstatic about Wagner having the goddess Erda in a central role, the earth mother rising out of the ground – only to just leave her in the next moment. Jünger is as disappointed as Nietzsche and goes on to say that these gods didn't quite make it as convincing supernatural creatures, they remained independent and hemmed in by the word. But what could we have expected...? A mystery play for Asa believers...? I guess Wagner did everything he could as a human and an artist in order to make the gods come alive in this theatrical vision. The Wagnerian gods are a bit too human and realistic, like Wotan mulling over problems and quarrelling with Fricka. More restraint could have been exercised, thus making the divine more credible. But in all the Wagner *Ring* was a fine effort in creating a modern yet traditional Northern gudasaga, a tale of the gods.

151

Jünger's interest in polytheism seems to have been awakened by his brother Fritz via *Griechische Mythen* from 1943. Ernst Jünger often discussed gods, Titans and divine matters in the late diary. And in *Eumeswil*, his final message in the subject of gods and all, seemed to be: the gods will return. The 20th century was titanic but the 21st will be divine, we will go from atheist nihilism to a deeper esotericism and spirituality. I guess he is right in that respect. Conversely the gods won't go away only due to some liberal nincompoops stating that the *Edda*, the Greek myths and the Christian legends are fairy tales.

SIDETRACKS

Now for some more sidetracks from *Annäherungen*. Jünger for example mentions that Baudelaire was a night person, therefore being attracted to Poe like a brother in spirit. Then we had the light person Goethe – who in his turn was fascinated by the night person Byron as a "complementary colour", which was interesting. It's like they say about marriages; on the one hand we have the like will to like, on the other there's the phenomenon of man and wife being completely different, complementing each other (the one logical the other intuitive, one energetic the other phlegmatic etc.). Jünger moreover, says about Byron that to him creating came too easy which is very clarifying; we are thus given a clue to such elements as I woke up and found myself famous and the ease with which he wrote his versified causeries. No pain, no gain.

Hereby a song of praise of the ordinary, the banal, given in the form of an anecdote out of *Annäherungen*. During the inter-war years Jünger once heard of someone aspiring to be a new Napoleon, for the enterprise reading the same books as the famed Corsican (mathematics and tactics) and planning to become an artillery officer, this rendering him sarcastic comments from people. However the

problem, Jünger said, was only a lack of imagination, the young man in question could be talented anyhow. And besides, imagination isn't everything:

> If imagination took control the world would soon look like a jungle or a lunatic asylum. The world however is less dependent on the great ones than on the simple people and their sober frame of mind. In this respect it's like a household where it's more important that the mail man or the chimney sweep comes than Fredrick the Great or Napoleon.

Annäherungen is filled with pearls of wisdom. Here are some, without comment:

- "Future" is a term favoured by thinkers unable to live in the present. This Jünger says concerning the Nietzsche who (in *Der Fall Wagner*) proclaimed that "The Germans themselves have no future."

- This, Jünger says, is "the first time in historical time that we're entering an astrological sign not representing an animal", i.e. Aquarius. The meaning of it Jünger doesn't elaborate on and that's fine, being an example of his prophetical style.

- "Universities have always been a safe haven for barbarianism, camouflaged as academic liberty". Jünger here has the drinking habits of student fraternities in mind, a phenomenon known throughout the western world in one form or another. Toasting and ceremonies can be another aspect of these academic social traditions, but academic drinking habits are for the most part nothing but alcoholism with a student-like flavour.

- Occult: according to Jünger Dostoevsky's *Svirdrigalov* says that ghosts only show themselves to sick persons, and that for a reason: in sickness (and in inebriation) you reach altered psychic states, moments of non ordinary reality to speak with Castaneda. And if these visions make you wiser they are more than mere hallucinations, then they are – you could say – hallucinations, illuminating experiences.

THE WORLD OF DRUGS

I just mentioned hallucinations and visions and this brings me back to the drugs, the true subject of *Annäherungen*. Jünger there for example quotes "the addict's lament": "Once I lived like gods"... Even to a teetotaller like me the meaning of this lament is gripping: to have lived in the artificial paradises and urging to go back but having a hard time doing so since the dosage has to be bigger every time, such as for example heroin addicts have confessed (q.v. the song "Mr. Brownstone" of Guns n' Roses: "I used to do a little but the little wouldn't do, so the little got more and more"...).

Then again, the will-driven esotericist makes do with the mere idea, "to live like a god", and uses it to raise himself to the divine realms. This is the basis of true satori, enlightenment, peace and quiet: you can reach it with will force (and patience). It's simple but the simple is difficult, as Clausewitz said. True salvation is reached by realizing: there is only here and now. Living with this Leitmotif is to live like a god. And this without taking any substantial drug.

Common sense and drug taking, do they belong together? Yes they can co-exist, like for instance what the character Guido says to Jünger in this book: you don't need to regularly indulge in drugs, you can avoid the weekly drinking bouts, however if you want to experience these orgies then it's enough to do so three times in your life: when

coming of age, before the wedding and on your deathbed. That's a fine symbol of the ceremonial, of the rite of passage-role of drugs.

Well then, how about drugs and creativity? I touched on the subject above. Here it's also true that common drugs can unlock blockages – in vino veritas – but the routine drug taking should be avoided Jünger seems to say. In the drug itself there's only emptiness. The risks of regular drugging are that "the turnover grows at the expense of capital, emptying the basic reserves". [*Jahre der Okkupation*, September 19th, 1945]

Why then even take drugs? This is why: esoterically it's not in order to anaesthetise oneself but to reach a higher elevated stage, to approach the Absolute, God if you will. Then again, Jünger says, "you can only approach the Absolute, not live there". If you open the door completely you can't return. That's the human condition.

In other words: in ecstasy you don't leave reality, you go and visit it – Reality with a capital R. But did Jünger himself actually reach this clear-minded stage with the help of drugs? No, he didn't; he never saw God or the Absolute when inebriated but he kept trying and that was a noble cause in itself, since he in later years stressed the need for esotericism per se, warning against atheism and the unreflected life.

Drugs as a means to reach the divine is a risky path, a somewhat crude and cumbersome path, as Castaneda for instance can testify. This Hispanic American starts his journey into shamanism by taking peyote, mushrooms and Jimson weed but later on he leaves the drugs behind, approaching the Absolute by dreaming and other, more subtle ways. And when asking his guru don Juan why he made him take the drugs in the first place don Juan answers: "Because you're dumb..." I won't label all drug romantics as inferior but for the true esotericist drugs are something of a bypath.

You could say: if you want mysterious, first-hand relations of drug sessions, read Castaneda's *The Teachings of Don Juan* or *Confessions of an English Opium-Eater*. Jünger talks in some length about this last-mentioned book of de Quincey's. But Jünger's own drug session never reached the outright esoteric and occult stages of these gentlemen's outings. *Annäherungen* is a fine, well-studied book on drugs and then some, like passages of memoirs of Jünger's life before and after the First World War, plus reflections on the divine and everything else. It's a good read whether you're interested in drugs or not. Clearly one of the top ten Jünger books, if I could put it that way.

16. EUMESWIL

I see that *Eumeswil* has been published in English. That was by an American label called Marsilio in 1994. That gladdens me. That makes up for other instances of neglect in translating Jünger works into English, this novel being a central piece of his œuvre along with *On the Marble Cliffs*, *Heliopolis* and the World War Two diaries. As for myself, I have a weak spot for *Eumeswil* since it was the first Jünger book that I ever laid my hands on.

ANARCH

Jünger is an anarch and the anarch is Jünger. The anarch is always right, standing as he does in a special relationship to reality and the essence of things, something of a worldly saint and seer. How then does he succeed in this? Simply by being – and being Jünger, or being Manuel Venator, the narrator of *Eumeswil*, this novel from 1977. The anarch always seems to land on his feet, like a cat or maybe like a fox, since Jünger to me had many vulpine traits to his character. And it's not just me, even Jean Coctaeu saw it, once naming him The Silver

Fox. It was something of a put down but I think the name is apt; in his old age Jünger also had silvery grey hair as a distinguishing trait. Clearly something of a Silberfuchs.

The anarch and what he stands for is a main feature of *Eumeswil*. The anarch for one is smarter than the common anarchist, the latter being bent on destroying the power and thus only strengthening it. The anarch furthermore is a counterpart to the monarch, something of an adversary but not hostile to the bone as the anarchist, no, the anarch can – as Manuel Venator – be content with serving the ruler and observe him in his daily duties, thus getting a sense of Grandeur and History. Venator also happens to be a historian, employed at the university and in that function being able to observe even more on the essential side of history, myth and culture.

Thus the narrator bowls along in his musings on history, politics and myth, effortlessly giving metaphors and images of times past and times future, and of life in the never-never-land of *Eumeswil*, partly something of an north African town, partly something European, partly something Mexican. It is, in other words, *Eumeswil*, the city being named after the Alexandrian diadoch Eumenes. As for Venator's view on history it's guided by images, symbols and scenes, by some kind of tangibility in contrast to abstractions, programs and sterile dissections. Seeking out the Eros of history he wants to feel wonder and awe, he wants to find the ideal essence of things not only in history, but also in nature and myth – in everything. And his guides in this endeavour are his own teachers, Vigo and Bruno. The former can see the recurrent dramatic forms of history, beyond the particular styles of each epoch, and the latter sees the ideal form existing in the copy and the timeless in the ephemeral. Thus both of them are some kind of idealists, advocates of the perennial Platonic philosophy, and that was by the time of the book's publishing – and still today – rather unusual if not heretical. Materialism, scepticism and irony are the ideals of the west but this book of Jünger is a welcome counterbalance to that.

LENNART SVENSSON

THE CASTLE

Eumeswil takes place in a undefined future, in a sort of post-apocalyptic world with city-states in a fragile state of peace. That's only the background since no ordinary action takes place in the novel, we just get Venator's musings on this and that. But it's a vivid account nonetheless of Venator's life as a historian and a bartender in the night-bar of Eumeswil's ruler, the Condor, a sort of South American warlord. In his castle or casbah Venator pours drinks and listens in on the Condor's talks with his military commander, his doctor and diverse invited guests.

Living in this castle is like living on a ship: the ruler commands, no women are allowed, and more than that it becomes a timeless symbol of the state: "sail on, ship of state". As the Swedish critic Göran Lundstedt has noted the ship is one of the Leitmotifs of the story, representing the temporal and the human, the other Leitmotif being the forest representing the myth, the eternal and the natural. And if the Condor is the symbol character of the ship then his doctor Attila is the symbol character of the forest. Attila had been dwelling in the southern outback after the great debacle, after the furious wars and destructions intimated here and there by Venator in his narrative, and what Attila saw in these woods we get to know at the end of the novel. And to wait for that is well worth it. The chapter on the forest is a bit unclear and vague in its meaning, however brilliantly executed. A bit of obscurity is needed when you venture out in the Myth and the Dream. Jünger in this chapter stands out as a myth maker and a fantasist – a fantasist not in the today generic sense, but in the original sense of the word.

In the climactic chapter of *Eumeswil* Jünger has boldly gone where no man has gone before. And all is topped off with Venator returning to his ordinary narrative, saying that he's going off with the Condor for a hunting expedition to these woods. If I'm allowed

159

a personal reflection, this passage carries some meaning for me as a Jünger reader. For when he died in 1998 I thought: Manuel Venator has left Eumeswil... It's hard to convey that special feeling, but my basic message is that *Eumeswil* serves to capture its reader in spite of – or maybe because of – its simple, neue Sachlichkeit type of style. *Heliopolis* (q.v. Chapter 11), his comparable 1949 novel about another future city state, was more traditional in its narrative style, more embellished and comforting but at the same time emotionally less gripping. *Eumeswil* on the other hand is a true artistic triumph, an authentic and genuine novel in spite of its slightly academic tone and utopian setting.

VIGO AND BRUNO

As I said one of Manuel Venator's teachers is Vigo, an idealist historian. Vigo has taught his pupil to see the presence of the eternally beautiful, to see the magic quality even in everyday objects. Without sentimentality and romantic overtones the world-view of Vigo is conveyed to us, a form of a latter-day esotericism to use as an instrument in the study of art and history.

Vigo is said to be a man of the woods: the Eumeswil wood, discussed above, is Vigo's mythical biotope, a symbol of the organic and living in nature and culture. Then we have Bruno, Venator's other noteworthy teacher, also a man tending to the abstract side of things, being guided by ideas. Bruno however is said to be a man of the catacombs, technical grottoes situated beneath the city, mysterious "Mauretanian" archives and storerooms with computers that know all, the Mauretanian in this case being a specific Jünger label on things titanic and life-threatening but at the same time learned and systematic.

So there we have another dimension to this novel. To a reader steeped in materialism and nihilism Vigo and Bruno tend to merge; concepts like spiritual, gods, idealism, essence and ideal forms are related now here now there, tending to be aspects of one and the same system, of the esoteric and hermetic, the arcane and the occult. It comes as a consolation that even the narrator, Jünger/Venator, sees it thus sometimes. Not even he can tell Vigo and Bruno apart all the time.

HERE AND NOW

A central idea of *Eumeswil* is that no transcendence is needed, everything exists here and now – a sort of immanent transcendence like the one Julius Evola taught, the Italian however dealing with it in more abstract terms since he was a Buddhist, affected by the force-field of the nihilistic idea of an-âtman. Jünger for his part makes it all tangible for the everyday person. Everything is revealed, trust your senses as Goethe said. That's Venator's basic message.

A bit hard to translate is the relevant Eumeswil sentence, in German: "Das Urbild is Bild und Spiegelbild" – in English, "the idea is both the original image and the mirror image". However that's the axiom summing it all up. The Platonic idea, das Urbild, the guiding archetype is mirrored in its copy, its earthly image. This earthly image however is no mere shadow since it has the Platonic idea immanent. The idea is both transcendent and immanent, existing both in its temporal copy and in the timeless ether beyond the Beyond.

The fantastic lives here and now, the idea lives in the temporal copies, in the everyday objects in our kitchen sink world. Aristotle called this "universalia in re" - the universal concepts exist in the objects. It's only in our own private, temporal view they tend to exist "afterwards" (post rem), having looked at the objects and found out

their ideal ground. (Universalia ante rem, for its part, was the third element of this Aristotelian axiom, signifying the eternal existence of the universal in God's thought.)

Everything corresponds, as Swedenborg said. Everything has its ideal counterpart, the material coil only being there for the ideas to have something to present themselves in. This could explain how sometimes in the world we are overcome by a timeless sense of wonder and beauty: it's the eternal idea revealing itself, be it in a sunrise, a nocturnal landscape with a lake before a mountain or whatever.

They say about Hollywood: "Beneath all that glitter of Tinsel-town there's real glitter." There is something magical about the town after all, in spite of what all the cynics say. Hollywood has an existence that – to borrow Goethe's concept – is "tangible-intangible" (sinnlich übersinnlich), at the same time real and surreal. We thus have a kind of double aspect theory for the transcendent. And the concept of "the idea mirrored in a temporal image", of "das Urbild is Bild und Spiegelbild", is that kind of double aspect theory.

BRUNO: THE EIDOS

A synonym for "Platonic idea" is eidos, the Greek word in question. And Venator thanks his teacher Bruno for having brought eidos back to the outer appearance, letting the wonderful exist here and now and not in some remote world of ideas. This is what Aristotle and eventually Plotinos gave us: a better view than the strictly Platonic one, the one with the metaphor of the cave reducing the visions of our daily life into being mere shadows.

Plato said that we live like cave-dwellers staring into a wall, with a fire behind us projecting shapes onto that wall. Thus the extreme idealism of Plato. But life isn't shadowy, not so extremely shadowy

as Plato intimated. We still can experience beauty in this world: universalia in re, remember. Jünger's exemplifying all this in *Eumeswil* is highly valuable for a student having been misled that idealism is about dreaming about eidos in a remote ideal world, the common view of idealism given to us in our textbooks. On the contrary true idealism is about living and loving here and now, not like a hedonistic moron but as a conscious aesthete knowing the fundamentals of existence.

THE ANIMAL AS A SYMBOL

Jünger applies this here-and-now-approach in several ways in *Eumeswil*. Manuel Venator for example tells us about his fascination for animals: living differently than we do and having no freedom, at the same time they have no angst, being instead guided by their instinct and ultimately by God, the animals in a sense standing closer to God than we do. Therefore the image of an animal face is enriching, saying us more on the animal way of life that the study of development patterns of the species and musings over ideas such as "the struggle for existence".

Jünger-Venator says this and more, like: animals may be uprooted and exterminated but nevertheless they will live on in images and symbols, in heraldry and star constellations – as eternal ideas. The lion in the Swedish coat of arms, the bear in Berlin's and the bull in Uruguay's: voilà living examples of archetypes, symbols that never die.

Then Venator has this to say about the charms of bird watching:

The eye resting on the richness of the palette, having its fill, however not in some expectation but in "the here and now". No progress: universalia in re.

163

This Aristotelian idea can't be exemplified any more pregnantly.

The most mysterious this concept of Urbilder becomes in a discussion about waking the dead, like a certain shell Venator holds in his hand, the stoned remains of a trilobite, with Venator wondering whether he by projecting the Urbild can reanimate the stone, once again giving life to the sea it once swam in. It would be a kind of resurrection like when an old text is read anew. "The rock lies awaiting the touch of Mose's staff", Venator sums it up, utilizing a striking image to convey his "imaginist" look on life.

A UTOPIAN CITY STATE

Like Heliopolis, Eumeswil is a utopian city state. In the former novel the place and setting was conveyed by poetic prose and a rhetoric stance, in this latter work we have a more low-key style. Eumeswil as such may be a celluloid plaything in the hands of its neighbours, an outlived wreck of a city with lethargic intellectuals, but in all the Eumeswillains can't complain: they have food on the table, there's races and entertainment, and there's beautiful surroundings like the river Sus with its marshes rich in bird-life. As for races, Jünger can give the vision a timeless quality when referring to "quarrels among the race drivers", making you both think of 6th century Constantinople with its blue and green race teams and of present times with its horse and formula 1 races. The Eumewsil setting allows for "multi-temporal" associations like these.

Eumeswil is a city state, Venator himself comparing it to Florence and to ancient precursors like Athens and Corinth. These Greek states were once ruled by tyrants, governors ousting the old-style monarchies and paving the way for democracy. And this gives Venator the chance of juxtaposing the archaic times to the modern, with examples from both antiquity and our times. As for antiquity

he has a trump card in the Anatolian city state once ruled by the Alexandrine diadoch Eumenes, something of an ideal ruler in this context, the city of Eumeswil deriving its name from him. The suffix is a French –ville, "city", with German pronouncing and spelling, like in the Swiss Amriswil.

In *Eumeswil* everything flows together in timeless harmony à la Eliot: "History is a series of timeless moments." A fine example of the style in question is this one, with Venator speaking about his historical kaleidoscope, his panopticon of historical images and reels called the Luminary. For example to get an image of the renaissance history of Perugia he evokes in the Luminary...

(...) the Perugian chronicle of Matazzo, the history of a city among cities in a land among lands; in between I tune in pictures of Etruscan gates, of the Pisano chancel, of the Baglioni family, Pietro Perugino, the twelve year Raphael. Even this selection leads out into the limitless – and that goes for every source, for every point of tradition that I touch upon. I hear it creaking, then a light; it's the historical build-up in its continuous, undivided power. Friends and enemies, perpetrators and victims have contributed with their best to it.

Eumeswil may be a bit hard to get into, with the Jünger style at first glance seeming a bit devoid of charm and readability. There's a certain lack of feeling here, every emotion being held in firm control. But there's emotion under the surface, and this novel even comes through as a pious document at times. Like when Venator says that "the glass of water you give to a thirsting is greater than the ocean", and when he – without sentimentality – suffers with the victims of history, and when he reaches out a hand for nameless generations. They are all brought forth in the Luminary and all have their say:

We partook of their hopes, the ever elusive hope being inherited from generation to generation. Sitting in our midst it was often impossible to tell friend from foe; we could speak as they did through their actions. We became their counsels for the defence. And each one of them was right. We gave each other our hands; they were empty. But in them there was something we gave over: the fullness of the world.

17. MINOR WORKS

Jünger wrote many books, numbering about 55 during his lifetime. You just haven't got time to read them all. But I've read most of them and here are my notes on the minor works I find interesting.

BLÄTTER UND STEINE (LEAVES AND STONES), 1934

This collection of essays contained many texts, among them the controversial *Über den Schmerz* (*On Pain*, recently translated by Telos Press and published as a paperback). Among other things Jünger here seems to say that the ability to endure pain is a sign of nobility. On the other hand, trying to lessen the human suffering would be nothing but a liberal prejudice. Now that could be taken as a mean philosophy. Of course we have to alleviate pain among our fellow citizens. But it's not all we can do. In some way or another the individual has to get to grips with the problem of pain. Like enduring it, somehow or other.

Like the stoics of antiquity. Escaping pain at any price makes us into comfort seeking slackers.

Blätter und Steine also contained "Lob der Vokale" ("In Praise of Vowels"). From a German standpoint Jünger meditated over the essence of the vowels, coming to diverse conclusions. Is this ingenious or nonsensical? See for yourselves:

> The A means the high and wide, the O the high and deep, the E the empty and elevated, the I life and decay, the U procreation and death. In the A we invoke power, in the O the light, in the E the spirit, in the I the flesh and in the U the motherly earth. Through these five sounds, in their purity and blendings, mixtures and percolations, the accompanying sounds bring forth the diversity of matter. With a few keys the world's fullness is unfolding, as far as language can present it to the ear!

THE PEACE (DER FRIEDE)

The German original to *The Peace* surfaced in 1943, the English translation in 1948. This might be a sympathetic piece of work, divulging ideas like preventing technology to spread at the expense of happiness, love and health, and the idea that men and gods have to be above Titans. This is a fruitful perspective, compared to the pre-war Jünger who sometimes had a predilection for the Titanic and the sterile.

The atmosphere of *The Peace* is magnanimous and Christian. Or at least Jünger wants to have some deeper foundation for his ethics, something more than just the philanthropy and altruism of the common intellectual. But even then I'd say that something's lacking here. I don't know what. It just isn't enough to read the Bible from start to finish, like Jünger did during the war (he even did it twice).

It takes more than speaking of churches and piety as the cure for the ills of the time. Jünger is on firmer ground when he speaks esoterically in more general terms, like the need for fighting nihilism within ourselves (Greek eso - means "within"), "in the heart of each one of us".

God and Christ aren't mentioned in *The Peace*. But as intimated there are Christian traits to this text, like the idea that theology once again has to be a central discipline, the idea of the value of piety and the request to return to the bosom of the church. It's well-meant but sounds a bit empty. It's easier to follow when Jünger talks about our common guilt for the war and the need for healing powers. The Christian slant of this book made people think that Jünger had converted, or that he was a born again Christian.

If he was or wasn't a formal Christian isn't important for the overall impression of Jünger's writing and creed these days, the time immediately after the war. What's important is that he had learned his lesson, becoming less Titanic, less of a fire-eater. Like Henry Kuttner said of Robert Heinlein in about the same time, in 1955 as it was: "He has accepted membership in the human race".

Christian or not Christian the post war Jünger is fully anchored in Goethe's dictum "Im Innern ist's getan" ("everything is made/decided/conceived in man's inner sense, in his soul"). That was good enough. An esoteric creed, in line with western thinkers since Plato. But to sum up *The Peace* you could say: if you aren't fully Christian in your beliefs, then don't preach Christianity.

Go within: that Jünger says in *The Peace*. Like: we have to make peace within ourselves, stand firm in our inner minds before we can have world peace. The nihilism of the times has to be fought within our souls. That's a creed that enlivens all of Jünger's post war books. And with time he toned down the Christian traits. Of course he converted in the 1990s, in secret. More on this in Chapter 23. That was a thing for itself. But he was sometimes sceptic about old school Christianity being the cure. Like in his war diary in 1942:

It's a mistake to expect that religion and religiosity will restore the order [after the ravages of nihilism]. [September 29th, 1942]

This could be seen as: conventional religiosity can't be the way for all. What the world need is a deeper sense of spirituality, an esoteric awakening where a new mindfulness and old school religions can cooperate.

RIVAROL, 1956

Antoine Comte de Rivarol lived 1753-1801. In actuality he wasn't a count (Fr. comte), having made that up himself. He was a Frenchman with Italian roots, becoming a writer in the style of "les moralistes", observing the world through epigrams and essays. Jünger often quotes this conservative enemy of the revolution, having in this book translated some of his aphorisms in German.

A fine Rivarol proverb is this one:

Generally speaking, there is more wit than talent in the world. Society swarms with witty people who lack talent.

AN DER ZEITMAUER
(BY THE TIME WALL), 1959

The creed of *An der Zeitmauer* can be seen as: back to nature. This is something of a green philosophy, however not in any way a political philosophy. In Europe we have these green parties like Die Grünen in Germany and the Green Party in England, propagating environmental issues. However, often being dyed-in-the-wool materialists, these

agents aren't exactly in for the esotericism of Jünger. And Jünger knew that, as intimated by Schwilk in his pictorial biography.

Furthermore *An der Zeitmauer* wanted a religion based on myth, not mysticism. Sounds striking but what does it mean? A religion without union with the divine (which is the school book definition of "mysticism")? Maybe Jünger isn't much of a classic esoteric, living in hope and faith and constant meditation. He's more of an aesthetic mystic, needing the presence of the divine and the mysterious in everyday life, in flowers and leaves and in the face of an animal. That's a bit like how Manuel Venator of *Eumeswil* lives. He wants immanence, not transcendence (but in this case you could remember a certain Julius Evola talking about "immanent transcendence"). More on *Eumeswil* in Chapter 16.

Except for myth the religion of *An der Zeitmauer* was to be based on nature. And irrespective of the materialism of the green movement Jünger saw this as the beginning of something new: the interest for environmental issues, for preservation and protection of woods and plants and animals, being a reflection of the Aquarian Age we're entering. Jünger himself mentioned this star sign, being generally rather interested in astrology. Changes will come, we're living in exciting times, and if we only stop seeing things one-dimensionally as world history and more fundamentally as planetary history, then we're on to something Jünger says in *An der Zeitmauer*. This is no mere play on words. Planetary history to me is an archetypal, symbolic concept leading us away from linear history, social factors and nihilism and off into elemental realms, putting us into contact with the earth, the sea, the air and the fire. With a truly elemental perspective like that we move away from being obsessed by technology and material development, instead reaching out into spiritual and mythical modes of thinking that holds a future for us all.

So then, away from nihilism and the blind faith in formal science and on to realms of myth, holistic and life-affirming attitudes. That's

the creed of *An der Zeitmauer* like many of Jünger's post 1945 books like *Eumeswil* and the late diary. So if you don't like either novels or diaries then this is the book for you.

ANTAIOS (MAGAZINE), 1959-71

The magazine *Antaios* was issued by the German publishing house Ernst Klett Verlag. The editors-in-chief were Ernst Jünger and Mircea Eliade. The paper wrote about mythology, religion and cultural history. A guiding idea was: myths go beyond history and ratio, occupying a timeless region where legends, heroes and gods rule (Neaman).

Antaios had the motto, "magazine for a free world". In Jünger's foreword to the first issue it was stated that "a free world is equal to a spiritual world". Personally I'd say that this is quite true; it can make you think of *Chândogya Upanisad* 7.23, where in a free translation it is stated: "Only in the infinite there is freedom. Try and get to know this infinity."

Jünger also said this in his foreword: "The freedom grows along with the spiritual outlook, with the gaining of firm, higher levels." And there you find outlook and overview and thereby security: "Freedom doesn't follow security, it goes ahead of it as a spiritual power."

In his *Antaios* editorial Jünger envisioned a new world of cosmic consciousness, of "growth in power and space". These cosmic elements would be balanced by a son of the Earth; from the holy depths he would constitute a counter-balance to these more ethereal forces. This earthly force was none other than Antaios himself, the giant son of Gaia who was powerful as long as he had contact with the earth but week and feeble when Hercules lifted him in the air. Jünger liked the metaphor and used Antaios as his totem and archetype from then on, substituting in this respect the figure of "the Worker". As

intimated Jünger in the early 30's more or less lived by the ethos of *der Arbeiter*, the Titanic Worker who mobilized men and machines for a Faustian, heroic endeavour. In the light of World War II's destruction and nihilism Jünger re-defined his ethos and turned to more earthly powers – to figures like Antaios as part of a new, more spiritual, life-affirming creed.

SGRAFFITI (GRAFFITI), 1960

This is a collection of shorter prose, like *The Adventurous Heart*. Among other things Jünger here talks about not having a point of view, instead having an area of view (Ger. Standfläche versus Standpunkt). This is a fine creed for a holistic mind. In the same book he answers why he doesn't show the youth the way, pointing out the marching direction. On this he says that rather than being a roadmap he's a terrain map, again a holistic solution beyond simple programs and pointers.

BESUCH AUF GODENHOLM (VISIT TO GODENHOLM), 1962

A mind like Jünger's needs images: pictures, symbols and drawings, vivid and tangible. Conversely he dozes off when confronted with abstractions like constitutions, ideologies and administrative charts. For instance, contemporary historiography often seems to focus on this, on formula, neglecting gripping images, scenes and characters.

This Jünger said in the novel *Eumeswil*, surfacing in 1977. And in the same vein the guru Schwarzenberg speaks in *Besuch auf Godenholm* from the early 60's, noting the lack of pictures in the contemporary culture, the lack of colour and form and pizazz. However there is a

remedy for all this if we move away from concepts and get back to the unspeakable, to the essence of creation. We have to move away from exaggerated reason and indifferent analysis since these only increase the insecurity, leading to technocracy and sterility. Pictures on the other hand give security.

Besuch auf Godenholm is abounding in pictures, eventually experienced by the main characters. Having met this guru on the island they had expected a clear-cut lesson, but instead they are being led into a visionary voyage where they see flowers, seas and castles, a scene from an ancient death-cult and further on into the unconscious. As a literary text this is a bit trying and vague, however, artistically it's also the case that the true, lasting works has to offer some resistance. How easy it would be for Schwarzenberg/Jünger to simply line out his wisdom in a dialogue; instead the images get to speak for themselves, the images being the main crux of it all. It's a kind of hieroglyphic writing, an example of Jünger advocating the more lasting quality of picture writing compared to abstract writing, of pictography compared to phonography.

Children read illustrated books, enchanted by the images. Concept art aside, it's pictures and forms you want as an art lover. This also brings Goethe into mind, advocating Gegenständliches denken – to think in objects, tangible things, not in abstract terms. And to get back to Jünger many of his works have the image in focus. As Gisbert Kranz once noted the mere titles reveal this: *The Worker, Heliopolis, On the Marble Cliffs, Storm of Steel, The Adventurous Heart, The Glass Bees*. It's images for the mind, in German Bildhaftigkeit, iconographic power.

As a zoology student Jünger was alienated by the abstractions, by numbers and facts. He wanted images, forms and shapes, something tangible to be inspired by. And as a Bible reader among other things he was searching for images and symbolic attitudes. Irrespective of the Bible this is an original way of reading: not being out there searching for ideas and thoughts, no, it's the forms speaking to your

subconscious you're after. In the broad sense of the word this is a Jungian way of reading. More on Jung in Chapter 20.

TYPUS, NAME, GESTALT (TYPE, NAME, GESTALT), 1963

In *Besuch auf Godenholm* Jünger was propagating concreteness and tangibility; here, in *Typus, Name, Gestalt*, it was more abstract since this was a formal treaty of sorts, however still dealing with the symbolic representation of things. It's a summing up of Jünger's idealistic philosophy focusing on the eidos (Ger. Urbild; idea) and how it presents itself in the world: on the one hand the pattern, the model, the ideal, on the other hand the copy, the common representation, the everyday object. As a side note this academic study is linguistically rather easy to read, using short sentences as Jünger always do. German syntax favours long periods but of this we see nothing in the Jünger prose. He's not indulging in it as is otherwise often the case for German writers.

SUBTILE JAGDEN (SUBTLE HUNTS), 1967

This is the story of Jünger's two favourite hobbies, plants and insects. The subject is how to collect them and everything else, giving us in this respect memories, travel anecdotes and practical tips.

As for entomology, Jünger has told us about it several times, like in the war diary. Asking himself why having this hobby he says that he needed more signs than offered by the alphabet:

I need a writing like the Egyptian or the Chinese with its one hundred thousand ideograms. I therefore adopted this writing,

allowing me to indulge in beehives of age-old learning (...) With it you're coming the things closer than with words. [Bourges, June 25th, 1940]

The way Jünger speculates over the forms and shapes of insects can remind you of Walter Benjamin, meditating over the meaning of stamps on envelopes (in *Einbahnstrasse*, 1928; see also chapter 20). It's a sort of micrology, a charming and sometimes evocative kind of pedantry. Entomology to Jünger was a hobby, something private. Jünger once admitted that. But at the same time he had to add: it's not altogether a hobby...! It's a way of life, as when it serves you as a support for the memory when traveling:

The entomological notes may be incomprehensible to the outsider but they serve to remember me of climatic details and above all emotions. The world is enlarged through a new dimension, partly as fitting engrams in review, partly as surprises. [Agadir, March 29th, 1974]

Watching birds, insects and nature thus becomes a puzzle throughout life over several continents,

(...) aided by an associative or combination of hunger. The spirit always want to be occupied; if there's nothing else to do you count the passing cars (which Jünger admits to doing sometimes, giving you a clue to the man...).

Like Linnaeus Jünger was holistically minded, seeing nature's diversity as part of a subtle Plan. Neither Linnaeus nor Jünger tended to talk about their scientific ventures as divinely led, but in the writings on nature of both of them, I'd say that the divine presence is immanently there.

LENNART SVENSSON

A DANGEROUS ENCOUNTER
(EINE GEFÄHRLICHE BEGEGNUNG), 1983,
ENGLISH TRANSLATION 1993

Paris, late 19th century. A certain inspector Dobrowsky is solving the murder of an actress. Jünger for his part began this novel in 1949 and then put it aside. As for the murder mystery it's solved in due time, on the way letting Jünger speak about topics such as the perfect crime, Paris, and Germans versus Frenchmen.

Jünger knew his milieu, Paris. He visited it for the first time in the 30's, served there in 1941-44 and returning several times in post war years. It was a home from home. He liked to stroll in the avenues and along the boulevards. In *Eumeswil* he quotes these congenial lines, without mentioning its author, on drifting alone in the Paris night:

> Tout, jusqu'au souvenir,
> tout s'envole, tout s'enfuit,
> et on est seul avec Paris, l'onde et la nuit.
> (Prose translation: "Everything, even the memory, / everything flies away and flees / and you're alone with Paris, the shadows and the night.")

ZWEI MAL HALLEY
(TWO TIMES HALLEY), 1986

In 1986 Jünger went to Kuala Lumpur, Malaysia, to get the best view of Halley's comet. As mentioned in the biographical essay (Chapter 1) he had seen it before, in 1910, as a fifteen year old before the First World War. In his 1986 book he tells about all this and his Asian journey with the hope of again seeing his old friend in the skies.

177

He does get to see it. And at the same time he gets the news of the Chernobyl accident, the nuclear disaster in Ukraine. It's a kind of Titanic disaster, spelling yet another end of technological optimism. At the same time we have spiritual reserves in our inner minds. Jünger at least have them and he knows how to convey them to his readers. His book ends on an optimistic note, with the harmony expressed by the satellite Halley as symbol. Nature has order and beauty and there's a great consolation in this.

18. ART

J ünger had a keen eye for the visual arts. When in Paris during the war he for instance met Picasso and Braque. And in his diaries he often mentions great works of art and pictures of this and that type. He knew the meaning of symbolism, a central concept for art through the ages.

SYMBOLISM

Any painting is symbolic in one way or another. Even a realistic picture has a symbolical value. A pair of shoes painted by van Gogh can point beyond itself, representing the seven mile boots, the winged shoes of Hermes or whatever, parallel to showing a common pair of shoes the artist got sight of and made into a picture. What it all means depends on what inner visions the spectator has. As I've already said: I'm Innern ist's getan.

How can you even look at art without becoming speculative, without linking it to the invisible, to the higher worlds of which our world is but a mirror? As such a mirror the German painter Caspar David Friedrich (1774-1840) saw it: the divine is mirrored in nature,

the material world being nothing but a reflection of a higher world. What we see are mere symbols of something even more real. And by looking inwards, by beholding the eternal ideas, you could create fantastic art. Simply painting what you see in front of you wasn't Friedrich's modus operandi. Friedrich painted inner scenes, inner landscapes, objects yet strangely real: monk by the sea, wanderer over the ocean of fog, two men watching the moon...

Here you can also mention Giorgio de Chirico (1888-1978). He painted inner landscapes, inspired by Mediterranean streets and plazas. He saw their metaphysical qualities, luring the secret out of porticoes, street corners and galleries in a veritable peintura metafisica.

You could say: the symbolist eye-balling Absolute Reality gains contact with the Idea; then, as an artist, he is occupied with embodying this Idea in the form of a feeling. The eternal form, das Urbild, is understood in concrete terms, expressed so that the common man can understand it – as an artistic object. This object however isn't just a simple thing but a sign for the idea that the artist has seen with his mind's eye. Thus we get an eidetic visual art, a discipline nurtured by the Platonic Ideas (Greek eidos).

This may serve as an introduction to Ernst Jünger's notes on art. He was firmly into visual arts as symbolism, as depictions of a higher reality. In *Typus, Name, Gestalt* he for instance said: "The works of art remain wonderful traces along the way to the absolute, which we can't reach. They are symbols, preliminary stages to the eternal triumph."

Art allows for transcendence, this trait existing in all art worth its name. This Jünger said in an interview with Fabrizia Lanza when visiting the Venice Biennal, copied verbatim in the late diary [Wilflingen, June 1993]. In the interview he also mentioned the magical nature of surrealism. Magical was a word he often used, like calling Picasso and Kubin magicians, as noted by Gisbert Kranz. And in *Annäherungen* Jünger says this on magical art in general:

LENNART SVENSSON

I here make the reservation that a work of art always hides a rest, unreachable by any method. Except for its aesthetic quality a great work of art has another one – a magical. Formerly this was very strong, even dominant, however declining in the same way as art began to apply rules and laws.

THE ARTIST AS A MAGICIAN

The true artist is a magician, a man in trance seeing a higher reality. Picasso himself intimated this. When visited by Jünger in his Paris studio, on June 22nd, 1942, the painter said:

My pictures would have the same effect if I, after completing them, wrapped them up and sealed them for no one to see. We're dealing with manifestations of an immediate nature.

This makes you think of the Indian sage Vivekânanda saying: "Words have a subordinate function while thoughts travel far." Thus, he went on, an enlightened recluse living in a cave can affect the world even though he sees and talks to no one. This is idealism in its purest sense.

Art creates "a spiritual native place", a geistiger Heimat, Jünger said in his first *Antaios* editorial. Furthermore art gives us a sense of direction, Jünger said in his foreword to *Strahlungen*. Strangely enough, art is depending on the world being incomplete: art makes a profile, a selection of the reality we see. For:

Art has to wither away where everything becomes meaningful. [Kirchhorst, May 23rd, 1943]

In the same way, Jünger adds, there would be no gardening if there weren't any weeds.

181

Many artists are mentioned in Jünger's œuvre. One painter who fascinated him was for instance Memling, a Dutch 15th century master. This Jünger said about his *March of the Thousand Virgins*, the picture giving you "a hint of the elevated brilliance man can reach" [Paris, November 25th, 1941]. And in contrast to the 19th century writer Huysmans who indulged in strange colours Memling had "clean jewellery colours, the clear spectrum of the rainbow". [Kirchhorst, March 18th, 1945]

Memling could stand as a symbol of all the old masters that Jünger mentions in his diaries. Moving on to modern times we find this interesting passage on Courbet, the 19th realist or was it naturalist...? Courbet himself (as we gather from the late diary on July 7th, 1987) stated that having transcended all genres he painted reality, period. But I guess all artists say that (except maybe for post modern ones, satisfied with making pictures of pictures).

To strive for Reality, True Being: Cézanne for example had the ambition to create an absolute picture. Did he succeed? All artists of note seem to reach for the eternal archetype, towards something everlasting beyond the multitude of the everyday world. Maybe Malevich got as far as you could go with "White Rectangle on a Black Ground", this attempt to catch the elusive fourth dimension.

PICASSO

As intimated Jünger visited Picasso once, on June 22nd, 1942. I'm actually no fan of Picasso and neither was Jünger it would seem, however this artist had charisma and pathos and this translates rather well into the Jünger report. Even the studio itself has an unmistakeable atmosphere:

> Except for small living quarters and some storage rooms there were two halls, the one downstairs used for sculpting and the

one upstairs used for painting. The floors were laid with bricks in honeycomb patterns, and the yellowish walls were supported by dark spars of oakwood. The ceilings too had black beams of oak. The rooms seemed well suited for work, as fecund as old attics where time is standing still.

Then we get to see pictures. Among other objects Jünger is shown "... a beach scene that by closer inspection seemed to blossom even stronger in red and yellow tones". Then Picasso also had his grotesque side, alien to Jünger the aesthete, but he makes an effort in decoding even this:

> Other pictures, like some asymmetrical heads, to me seemed rather monstrous. Then again, seeing such a master being occupied with such objects for decades, you have to acknowledge their objective value, even if you can't understand them. Basically it's about things that no one has seen yet, experiment of an alchemical nature.

Picasso himself has a magical aura. Any artist must have something of this, and here's Jünger's first impression of the man:

> I rung the bell. A tiny man in a simple working coat opened, Picasso himself. I had fleetingly met him once before, and again I had the feeling of standing in front of a magician – an impression enhanced by a conical green cap.

In this chapter I've been talking about esoterica in art, some metaphysical peculiarities that seemed to interest Jünger. As a conclusion I will give you a quote from *Heliopolis* highlighting this, a kind of synthesis over all the mystery a work of art can radiate, everything that is special for a masterful object d'art – and then some. It's about the invisible, unmeasurable effects of a picture. In the chapter "The Symposium" the painter Halder has this to say:

According to him [Halder] a master work is the most valuable possession of a household. In the event of a fire this and only this has to be saved, like the lares of old and the old family portraits. For who, in reality, knew the effect of pictures in working spaces, in the dining room, in the room of a pregnant mother. In them lay the secret of the right measure, bringing forth fecundity and abundance. Then there were pictures whose might was incommensurable to private ownership and whose place was in castles, directed at the welfare of the people. Yet others were meaningful only in churches and how disheartening it was when you found such items in the museums. Still, how grand it is when pictures become holy, with miraculous power exuding from them.

19. HISTORIA IN NUCE

istoria in nuce: history in a nutshell. The protagonist in *Eumeswil*, Manuel Venator, is a professor of history and one of his many projects is called "Historia in Nuce". There he collects fragments, quotes and anecdotes that in themselves seem to sum up history, as in a symbol or an archetype. And this could highlight how Jünger tended to see history: not as "great narratives" or sterile monographs but as enigmatic and unfathomable events. They were not wholly incomprehensible, they simply were more than transparent proofs that could be amalgamated into meta narratives – like the way the venerable Oswald Spengler made everything through the ages, any fact he found, part of his grand theory of the growing, blossoming and decay of civilizations.

Jünger, like Walter Benjamin in *Die Passagenarbeit*, would have nothing of that. Jünger never wrote a comprehensive treatise on history, and how could he. His view on history instead has this trait of "meaningful fragments", of "the street insurrection of the anecdote" (Benjamin). Jünger's attitude to history was non-programmatic.

To this we had the presence of Jünger himself where history was made. The following examples are all from the Second World War, serving as a mirror for all ages.

JÜNGER HIMSELF AS A NEXUS FOR HISTORICAL EVENTS

In his diaries Jünger becomes a sort of prism for history. He's just a man but what he sees and does sometimes rises to the rank of historical significance.

There's a lot to quote here. So where to begin...? Well, for instance we have the entry for May 9th, 1945, when Jünger in Kirchhorst has a young woman from Berlin visiting. Having fled from the east she has something to tell. Jünger:

> [H]er heartsick mother escaped the horrors of the Russian entry by taking poison. It seems as if the aristocracy of all the East Prussian, Schlesian and Pomeranian burgs have done the same. Through the windows the refugees saw whole companies of dead bodies sitting around made tables. They invoked antiquity; now they've gotten their answer.

By "invoking antiquity", what does Jünger mean? Maybe he's hinting at the architecture of Albert Speer, the Nazi classicism of die Reichskanslie, the planned Grosse Halle with its 20 meter high columns of red granite, the facade of the antiquity yearning Nazi regime being imperious and grand while at the same time the torture chambers and camps were ruled by nihilism and brutality. I can't really figure out what Jünger means, the line being a bit obscure, but it has some power. The style carries it through.

Another reference to antiquity is made in the Kirchhorst entry for September 16th, 1944, mentioning Seneca. It's an unsought passage of

186

the historia in nuce type, I'd say ["lemurs" are Jünger's code name for Nazis]:

> Having been transferred to the reserve I now await the last stages of the drama. It's still dangerous, the lemurs having begun with a great deal of executions aiming for the situation after their death. This kind of prophylactic revenge has, among others, had former Communist leader Thälmann and the Social Democrat Breitscheid as its victims. Had they been smarter you could, with Seneca, say to them: "No matter how many you kill your successors won't be among them."

HISTORICAL PRESENCE

Jünger is there, a discreet part of the historical action. He's present when history is written. And he knows it, without being overly self-conscious about it. Like when he's in southern Russia in January 1943, noting how the units are preparing a hasty retreat ("soldiers smoking geese in the gardens, on the tables whole mountains of pork piling up", Vorosjilovsk, January 8th, 1943). At the same time as an army was caught in Stalingrad another one had to retreat from Caucasus, a near run thing it was, and this is how Jünger gets his glimpse of it:

> Lunch with the army group commander, Generaloberst von Kleist, who when I entered was leaning over his map with a concerned face. How fascinating to come in from the hubbub of the square right into the centre of action. The perspective of the commander is extremely simplified and at the same time demoniacally elevated. Loosing sight of the separate destinies they are still spiritually present, forming an atmosphere that are overly depressing.

This is unsought, without self-consciousness on the author's part. But the following quote has something of Jünger the poser:

> At twelve o'clock today I relieved the main guard at the Hotel Continental with my company. Before that mustering on the Avenue de Wagram, letting the company do the manoeuvres we had been practicing for a month, followed by defilation in front of the tomb of The Unknown Soldier. We even passed by the statue of Clemenceau who could foresee all this. I nodded at him, as one oracle to another. [Paris, May 20th/21th, 1941]

Rather boastful this one, but elegantly executed: the Unknown Soldier, Clemenceau and Jünger, all in one picture.

THE INVISIBLE SIDE OF HISTORY

Jünger easily merges the past with the present. Like in this entry from June 6th, 1944, mentioning medieval crusaders on the eve of Eisenhower's crusade in Europe. Other than that the passage touches on the invisible side of history, stressing the need for a sixth sense when doing historical research. On this historical day, Jünger says, he's been reading...

> (...) *L'Histoire de Saint Louis* by Joinville. In many episodes, for example at the landing of the crusaders at Damiette, we see the sprit of man in its highest possible glory. Materialistic historiography only catches the visible side of things, not knowing the diversity giving the fabric colour and pattern. So this is our mission: to rediscover the multiformity of impulses. And for this a greater objectivity than the positivism is needed.

This is true even today. Marxist scholarship and the materialistic attitude to history may have seen its best days, however I can't detect the urge among today's historians to discover the invisible traits of history, of finding the discreet ruling powers of history beyond economy and the struggle for existence. Today's readable historians are like glorified journalists, writing readable books but devoid of any deeper meaning.

The popular historians of today sometimes succeed in painting broad pictures, like Anthony Beevor depicting the eastern front (for example in "Stalingrad", 1998). The ideal has come to be the long book, the best-seller thick as a brick. But true history writing should be more of drawing than painting. Thus Jünger has it:

> The historian must know the recurring patterns; only thus history can be seen as a science. The anatomy then will fit, the proportions becoming meaningful. However the historian is more of a draughtsman than a painter; he is captured by the categories that the plan is partitioned in, the great lines.

20. GERMAN GURUS

E rnst Jünger was a German. And he was influenced by some other great Germans, like Goethe and Nietzsche. Moreover he had traits in common with contemporary Germans, like Walter Benjamin and C. G. Jung.

GOETHE

As I said in Chapter 17 Jünger liked the Swedish botanist Linnaeus. And Linnaeus for his part was more than a systematizer and a pedant. He had a keen eye for the wholeness of nature, how flora and fauna, minerals and men affect each other mutually, playing together in a concert of interdependence. Nature is an organic system, not a machine. Linnaeus was into this kind of holistic and so was Johann Wolfgang von Goethe (1749-1832), another of Jünger's household gods.

I admit to never having read the words "Goethe", "the Weimar Apollo" or the like in any of Jünger's books. But for instance the last words in Jünger's *Jahre der Okkupation*, "Im Innern ist's getan", are a Goethe quote, the phrase originally occurring in Goethe's

Wilhelm Tischbeins Idyllen. Moreover the attitude of Manuel Venator in Jünger's novel *Eumeswil* is genuinely Goethean when dealing with das Urbild and die Urpflanze, the original forms of plants and animals, the essence of everything alive. Seeing the world around you as animate, seeing the mystery of an animal's face, of a flower cup – I call that Goethean and we find elaborations on all this in *Eumeswil*.

A good overview of Goethe's animate science ("Metamorphose des Pflanzen", the colour theory etc..) is written by Paul-Henri Bideau: "Goethe (Que sais-je)". Goethe's approach to science can be summed up as: "My observation is a thinking and my thinking is an observation." He made his lines of thought concrete, anchoring ideas and concepts in the shape of flowers, minerals, clouds and colours. However, he didn't like maths or theories. And the same traits we find in Jünger. According to Gisbert Kranz he wanted to see symbols and totalities rather than discursively dissecting the problems.

HUGO FISCHER

Hugo Fischer (1897-1975) is a central name when looking at Jünger's German masters and inspirations, Fischer being steeped in the same idealistic holistic as sketched above. With Plotinos and Goethe Fischer for instance could see a flower as "a spontaneous and massive confluence of life", "a totality of shape and colour, growth and origin" in sync with both itself and its surroundings. In the same vein a cathedral was to be likened to a fugue accompanying itself, a structure with inner rhythm where the part is mirrored in the whole and vice versa. This is what Fischer said in *"Die Aktualität Plotins – Über die Konvergenz von Wissenschaft und Metaphysik"* (1956).

Jünger and Fischer were both children of the same perennial philosophy. They also met in real life, for instance studying in Leipzig in the same class (see chapter 1). In *The Adventurous Heart*,

the short story "Die Vexierbilder", the character of Nigromontanus is said to have traits of Fischer. That's also said of the Schwarzenberg character in the novel *Besuch aud Godenholm* (more on that story in Chapter 17). And in *Myrdun* Fischer starrs as Der Doktor, Fischer accompanying Jünger on that Norwegian trip.

Fischer was a life-affirming esoteric, a teacher with a keen eye for the invisible in nature. His world view is summed up in the above mentioned "Die Aktualität Plotins". Criticizing reductionism and the mechanical world-view Fischer paints a holistic, systemic picture that we today also see among science writers like Paul Davies and David Bohm and before them among scientists like Haldane, Eddington, James Jeans and Alfred North Whitehead. Moving away from materialism and nihilism science has begun to see nature as a flow with implicit order (Bohm). Nothing is isolated, everything affects everything else.

SPENGLER

Jünger had a metaphysical world view but he never systematized it. Oswald Spengler (1880-1936) on the other hand made his Anschauung into a system. It's not as fruitful as the Jünger approach, Spengler's work being something of a grand palace that not quite holds together: interesting to experience but here and there you can see the cracks. Jünger's work for his part is less systematic and more eclectic, having no easily surveyable master plan, however, thus having more inherent strength, more organic vitality.

Jünger once sent Spengler a copy of *Der Arbeiter*. Spengler didn't like it, saying that Jünger had neglected the role of the farmer in it. Without comment I think this anecdote says something of the difference between the two, on many levels. Moreover you could say that the late Spengler was a nihilist pessimist, envisioning a world

ruled by war, technology and colonisation, a world caught in a struggle against nature that man had to lose. Jünger in his comparable works (e.g. *Der Arbeiter*) wasn't exactly an optimist but he seemed to have made room for human endeavour and willpower. As you see Spengler and Jünger had differences but in my book they will always be of the same ilk. They both made me see history as animated, as a living organism. History isn't a preconceived march towards The Liberal Enlightenment, it's an ongoing struggle and a drama.

These days I personally get more out of reading a random Jünger book than looking into Spengler's tomes, but Spengler nevertheless holds a certain place in my heart as a history philosopher. In addition you could say that both Spengler and Jünger affected the culture of the Weimar Republic, mostly for the better.

WALTER BENJAMIN

"I have nothing to say. Only to show." This Walter Benjamin (1892-1940) said in his *Passagenarbeit*, a study of 19th century Paris. This reminds me of Jünger's modus operandi, more so than the Spenglerian attitude does. Jünger and Benjamin had one tendency in common: the ability to connect distant, unrelated phenomena with each other, the art of making a surprising synthesis. And the ability to delve into abstruse disciplines and yet find them revealing: beetles, stamps. Benjamin's *Einbahnstrasse* and Jünger's *The Adventurous Heart*, in certain moments, to me seems two of a kind.

NIETZSCHE

Jünger mentions Friedrich Nietzsche (1844-1900) now and then: by name in his late diary, by the codename Pulverkopf ("Gunpowder Head") in *Heliopolis*. On the surface these two Germans were rather dissimilar, at least judging from their writings. Nietzsche for one could be boastful and funny, overusing the word "I" (as noted by Rüdiger Safranski). Jünger on the other hand is the born gentleman, more discreet and almost never funny (on Jünger and humour, otherwise see Chapter 29).

Jünger's reflections seem to stand the test of time a bit better than Nietzsche's. At least personally I can endure the Jünger style better than Nietzsche's style. Jünger has openings towards the esoteric and the invisible. Nietzsche has this tendency too, but at the same time he goes on with his fabled "philosophical hammer" judging this and that, leaving the reader exhausted and alienated.

Nietzsche "danced on the edge of volcanoes" and Jünger seemed to do the same in *Der Arbeiter* and *Storm of Steel*. But Jünger is saved by a sense of measure, even in the most incandescent, nihilist surroundings. *Der Arbeiter* is no mere cult of industrialization and modernization, it's a reflective essay. And even in the combat zone Jünger could read old masters and meditate over life. Nietzsche on the other hand often lacks these cultural moorings, his spirit soaring away into a space devoid of gods. He's the god, having dethroned the original one.

In *Thus Spoke Zarathustra* Nietzsche speaks about the passing by: "where you no longer can love – just walk on by" (to be found in Part Three of the book). Instead of complaining at the ills of civilization you should leave the city and seek out the green islands of the sea. And didn't in fact Jünger, instead of Nietzsche, really find his way there...? Be that as it may; the island plays a vital part in the Jünger myth, both in real life and fiction, with works like *Atlantische*

Fahrt, Ein Inselfrühling and *Besuch auf Godenholm* plus the distant Hesperides and the more close Vinho del Mar in *Heliopolis*, all of them islands depicted with warmth. Jünger has been called a veritable nesofile, a lover of islands.

C. G. JUNG

Last but not least in this study of German gurus and like-minded authors I feel like mentioning Carl Gustaf Jung (1875-1961). There isn't any direct connection between this Swiss psychologist and Jünger (apart from the magazine *Antaios*, see below), but they seem to share a common attitude: to be influenced mainly by old masters, old writers and old scriptures. Now of course Jünger knew modern writers like Trakl and Benn, he had his feelers out among expressionists and others, but all things considered he seems to have liked the company of dead writers the best. Again and again he mentions figures of the 18th and 19th centuries like Léon Bloy, Rivarol, Hamann and Poe, and then there's his reading of the Bible, Herakleitos, the church fathers, les moralistes and others. Jung for his part was rather familiar with writers like Goethe, Shakespeare and Nietzsche, these he could analyze and more or less understand, while – it is said – a modern spirit like James Joyce was a hard nut to crack for him. Other than this Jung of course felt at home in archaic works like the *I Ching*, the Bible and everything dealing with gnosticism, hermeticism and alchemy.

Jung and Jünger also shared an interest in dreams. Jung's autobiography for its part even in the title mentions dreams (*Memories, Dreams, Reflections*), this being a unique personal recollection sprinkled as it is with detailed dream narratives. They differ from Jünger's dreams in their analytical approach but other than that you have to notice the similarity. To dream and be able to intelligently relate what you've dreamed is a rather unusual talent.

Jünger and Jung also had this in common: an interest in myths and legends and related esoterica. This was demonstrated, above all, in Jung's contribution to Jünger's and Eliade's magazine *Antaios*. More on *Antaios* in Chapter 17.

21. THREE COMPARISONS

It's interesting to compare Jünger with other writers. Here I've gathered three diverse authors, a Japanese, an American and an Italian: Yukio Mishima, Carlos Castaneda and Julius Evola. In one or other respect they can serve to highlight certain traits of the Jünger Gestalt and the Jünger oeuvre.

MISHIMA

Was Yukio Mishima (1925-1970) the Ernst Jünger of the east...?

The similarities are there: they were both subjects of Axis countries, they saluted the Warrior and other traditional ideals and both were mentioned as Nobel prize candidates. Then we have the obvious differences: Mishima was thirty years younger than Jünger and his books had a broader appeal to the mainstream reader (see for example the female characters of *After the Banquet* and *The Marquess de Sade*). Mishima wasn't a "better" writer than Jünger but he had the ability to translate his insights into a conventionally more readable form, carrying his fiction to a wider audience. At the same time

Mishima was more nihilistic than Jünger, something that might have helped his sales at least in the short run.

A similarity: both Jünger and Mishima advocated suicide as a viable option. However Jünger in time seems to have become negative to the idea, considering it as a misleading solution. You have to live: il faut essayer de vivre as Valéry said, to me seems to sum up Jüngers attitude on all this. Mishima on the other hand seems to have lived his whole life thinking about suicide. His wife is reported to have said: don't pity his destiny, because in taking his life (as he did in November 1970) he for once did something he really wanted to do.

Mishima never served in the armed forces. But wasn't it so that he in 1967 enlisted in the Japanese Ground Self Defense Forces? However, this wasn't about active service or any kind of service, I gather. Nevertheless Mishima was an avid fan of all things military, Japanese style. He adored the lives of the samurai, the kamikaze pilots and the army soldiers of the Russo-Japanese war of 1904. The latter are given a heroic salute at the beginning of the *Sea of Fertility* series, with Mishima depicting a scene of soldiers departing for war in front of a Shinto shrine. In a post war context that's about how far a Japanese author could go in these matters – heroism, martial traditionalism – without being censored. And this Mishima trait may remind you of Jünger's ventures into warlike heroism. Now Jünger was the professional here, Mishima the amateur. But he confessed to being an amateur, liking to dress in the fancy uniform of his Shield Society. Still, he cut a dashing figure in this uniform and that image somewhat endures, as does the one of Jünger in his gray World War One uniform.

Both Jünger and Mishima dabbled in politics, Jünger in his early career, Mishima at the end of his life. The snobs here tend to forgive Jünger's radicalism as a folie de jenuesse while Mishima is condemned as a madman, his political venture seeming to cloud his oeuvre.

Mishima once wrote the play *My Friend Hitler*, about Ernst Röhm and the Night of the Long Knives, a play never played in the west as

far as I know. Jünger for his part could have written the imaginary script to *My Friend Goebbels*. Imaginary or not, in a way he did: after the war he remembered the days when he knew Goebbels, now eternalized for us in an entry of the 1945 war diary. Jünger didn't much care for this anti-Semite demagogue but at the same time he noted his rhetorical strengths, like the trope "the workers of the fist and the forehead" which was more efficient than "the workers of the hand and the head". Jünger also noted Goebbels pre-1933 salon, a fecund meeting place for people of the right, the left and the arts. Jünger aptly says: "In those days we lived in the insides of Leviathan".

CASTANEDA

In 1998 the world lost two men of distinction, two great authors and magicians.

On March 17th we were reached by the news that Ernst Jünger had died, 102 years old. Some days after I personally remember reading a fine essay in the Swedish daily Svenska Dagbladet, with Peter Luthersson looking at the *On the Marble Cliffs* from many angles, not exclusively the obvious Nazi one. Luthersson saw the timeless aspects of the novel, catching the elusive symbolic character of the work.

That was early in 1998. Then, by Midsummer, another important message reached me: Carlos Castaneda is dead. In fact he died already on April 27th (and he was born in 1925). However the Swedish media outlets were mostly silent on this, not feeling the need to post an obituary or a review of his work. But you can't have everything.

Dying in the same year, what other similarities are there between Jünger and Castaneda...? I would say; dreams, drugs and the tendency of styling yourself into a myth. In German the last propensity is called Selbststilisierung. Jünger clearly had some poser traits, like the predilection to be photographed in profile. By cutting a dashing

figure in uniform and in costume, and with all his diaries where he talks about himself doing this and that – it all becomes part of rising a monument of yourself, of painting Jünger as a mythical figure. He doesn't lie about his exploits but it becomes a process of mythification nonetheless. Now Castaneda was more secretive, eradicating on the way the traces of who he really was. However they are both writers of the existential kind, having led interesting lives, partaking in the storm of events and thus getting something to write home about.

Additionally they were esoterics with an interest in the invisible, the obscure and the occult. "Either everything is enchanted or nothing is", Jünger for his part said. And Castaneda, even though he was a more formally schooled mystic, could have agreed to that.

Both were dreamers, Jünger an unsystematic, Castaneda a systematic one, however not conveying his dreams as artistically vivid as Jünger did. But he came close now and then, giving us memorable moments from the dream world. Castaneda's *The Art of Dreaming* (1993) for its part is a fascinating account of the guru led dreaming activity of a sorcerer's apprentice, Castaneda being the apprentice and the Indian don Juan being the guru. Jünger on the other hand never had a teacher leading him through the dream world but for a student of the occult both Jünger's and Castaneda's dream passages are enlightening.

Jünger has some notes on dreaming in *Annäherungen*, his book on drugs. And drugs were another common trait between the two, Castaneda and Jünger. And both seemed to have reached the conclusion that drugs are an ineffectual means of reaching the higher spiritual stages. That said this subject is fascinating; for the bourgeois mind, satisfied with wine, tea and the likes in the way of stimulation, the drug experiments of the German and the American (Castaneda was Spanish-American) are milestones of 20th century literature. Jünger among other things had a keen eye for the Mexican lands of psychotropic drugs, the selfsame twilight zone of Castaneda's experiments in *The Teachings of Don Juan* (1968).

EVOLA

Yukio Mishima was treated at the beginning of this chapter. And if Mishima was the Jünger of the East then the Jünger of the south must have been none other than Julius Evola (1898-1974). You shouldn't take the Jünger-Evola comparison too far but the similarities are certainly there: conservatives partaking in the First World War, during the mid war years drawn to both experimental art and right wing politics, never members of the governing parties in question but honoured by them as pillars of society, and during the post-war years faced with the task of slightly redefining and reformulating their creeds.

If we start from the end Julius Evola in the 60's regrouped and admitted that his previous assertion, made in such works as *Revolt Against the Modern World* (1934) and *Men Among the Ruins* (1953), that the world could be reformed on traditionalist grounds, was a bit naive. He retained his belief in traditional values anchored in the transcendental realm but he realized that today's materialist, nihilist civilization was rotten to the core and had best run its course. But when this Iron Age was over then the discreet but undeniably existing traditionalist avant garde, the aristocrats of the soul, could re-surface and take control of this emerging new world, this emerging Sat Yûga of truth being thus helped on its way by these operators still versed in tradition and guided by the ideas of a world gone by, a world steeped in idealism and esotericism.

Evola's work delineating this development, this handbook for latter-day esoteric agents, was called *Ride the Tiger* (1961). And it's similar in attitude to the late Jünger, the Jünger criticizing the nihilist, atheist Leviathan that our current world system has become. Jünger like Evola didn't believe in partisan politics and furthermore, also here like the Italian, he envisioned the person as the saviour of culture and civilization, like in his symbol of the forest walker – der Waldgänger (see Chapter 12).

You could also say: the symbol of Evola's *Ride the Tiger* was the tiger-rider, the aristocrat of the soul meeting the attack of the nihilist modern world's tiger by jumping up on its back and riding it, letting it run itself tired. Finally, when the tiger lies down exhausted, the tiger-rider can step off and take command of the situation, implementing a world of Traditions, the ideals of which the tiger-rider has borne within him all the time. The Jünger counterpart to the tiger-rider could be said to be the anarch, another spiritually apt operator acting in the shadows in these nihilist times, however with a command of history, myth, traditions and faith that soon will surface again and affect society as a whole.

There were other similarities between Evola and Jünger. They both lauded war as a spiritually fulfilling experience, Evola for his part discussing this and other related topics in *Metaphysics of War* (2011). This is no mere militarist manifesto; instead Evola talks about the need for the soldier – any soldier, even a democratic soldier fighting tyranny – to have a creed, a personal, transcendentally anchored creed. The soldier has to stay in his heart, being able to access inner, spiritual reserves. Otherwise he will crumble, either on the battlefield itself or in his post war peaceful existence. Because having no spiritual creed he will become the victim of the gruesome memories every soldier has to deal with. And these ideas of battle as an inner experience are what Jünger was hinting at in his works too, most vividly in *Der Kampf als inneres Erlebins* (q.v. chapter 6).

As for experimental art Jünger, as I said in chapter 1, dealt with some expressionist poets after the First World War (Hannover's Klabund). And the one surviving example of Jünger's avant-garde poetry is showed in chapter 32 of this biography. Evola for his part was an abstract painter of no mean skill, echoing the works of Balla, Severini and Russolo. Before 1921 Evola also wrote Dadaist poetry and to that enjoying avant-garde poets like Rimbaud and Mallarmé. Unlike Jünger, Evola didn't destroy his experimental pieces and a retrospective exhibition of all his futurist paintings was held in Rome

in 1963. If you Google "Evola paintings" you can see these works for yourself: abstract they are, in no way traditional as was Evola's subsequent ideal in life, but nonetheless fresh and vital.

TRADITION

Jünger and Evola to me seem to show that it's still possible to stand for a reflected conservatism, a conservatism footed in truly traditional values, a creed where the past lives on within us – the past of our forebears, of our fathers and mothers way back. Jünger and Evola did that, in post war years taking into account that we live in a world officially hostile to such attitudes. But in realizing this, that the tradition is officially dead, they seem to say: "Fully dead, at last, and wondrously alive...!" As long as there are aristocrats of the soul admitting to the reality of the values of tradition – values like courage, self-restraint, piety, responsibility and self-sacrifice – then tradition will live on. It only takes "a few good men".

Neither Evola nor Jünger were academics in the ordinary sense but they wrote for the studied reader. And Evola for his part noted the ideas of Ernst Jünger, like when he has this to say about an unnamed author who is unmistakably Jünger, from a text in *Metaphysics of War* originally printed in 1950:

One of the most highly praised contemporary writers in Europe has written things about modern war which he experienced thoroughly and actively (he volunteered, was injured eighteen times, and was awarded the highest German military decoration), whose value will become more and more obvious in the times to come. He has said that modern man, by creating the world of technology and putting it to work, has signed his name to a debt which he is now required to pay. Technology, his creature, turns against him, reduces him to its own instrument and threatens

him with destruction. This fact manifests itself most clearly in modern war: total, elemental war, the merciless struggle with materiality itself. Man has no choice but to confront this force, to render himself fit to answer this challenge, to find in himself hitherto unsuspected spiritual dimensions, to awake to forms of extreme, essential, heroism, forms which, while caring nothing for his person, nevertheless actualise what the aforementioned author calls the 'absolute person' within him, thus justifying the whole experience. [Evola, 2011, p 138-139]

22. ERNST JÜNGER AND SWEDEN

I, the writer of this book, am a Swede. And now I'm going to look at Jünger from a Swedish perspective, with comparisons of the man with Swedish authors.

It's true that Jünger never visited Sweden. In the 30's he traveled in our neighbouring country Norway (q.v. "Myrdun", 1943). That's as far as he got because he never set foot in this country of mine. Then of course he met Swedes sometimes, like the expatriate Prince Lennart Bernadotte living on his castle on Mainau, the flower lake in the Bodensee. A visit to this place is noted in the late diary. Another notable Swede in the Jünger oeuvre is the Ingrid character in *Eumeswil*, described as a typical specimen of our kind: a cool blonde in cornflower blue, underlining her appearance with a hint of lavender.

LINNAEUS

In *On the Marble Cliffs* Jünger hails Carolus Linnaeus as the one bringing order to the seeming chaos of nature with the marshal's baton of thought. The Linnean classification system of plants became

a virtual home for Jünger along with the Prussian army, the court of Louis XIV and other phenomena based on order. This he stated in an interview with Kristian Petri in the Swedish daily *Expressen* in 1988 (q.v. the bibliography). Moreover Jünger all his life studied and collected plants, along with his entomological interest (q.v. the notes on "Subtile Jagden" in Chapter 17). This makes Jünger into a fine disciple of the Swedish botanist.

LARS GUSTAFSSON

Lars Gustafsson (1934-) is one of Sweden's most famous contemporary authors, having worked as a professor in Austin, Texas for several years and receiving the Goethe prize in 2009. More than ten Gustafsson works, among them novels and poem collections, have been translated into English.

I find several things in common between Gustafsson and Jünger. They both deal with high flying allusions, the reader being supposed to know what the author is talking about. Nothing is unnecessarily explained since the style, if anything, is supposed to convey the meaning. Gustafsson and Jünger don't teach the basics, and in this way both are approaching the role of the prophet and the glorified guru.

A sympathetic Gustafsson trait among others is the absence of anti-Germanic feelings. And this he has in common with Jünger. They're both inspired by the German scholarly and artistic tradition, and that's rather unusual for the other western authors I met as a reader in the 70's, 80's and on.

Gustafsson and Jünger are educated, scholarly authors lacking a certain common appeal. They're in a sense academic authors; that Jünger left the university world early on and that Gustafsson is a professor is of no significance here. What I mean is that the works

of both are filled with references to ideas and books, to philosophers and authors. A sample of the Gustafsson style in this respect is when in a poem he speaks about how certain minerals may enclose age old water, residues of an ancient ocean. A similar fascination of geology could be found in Jünger's work, like these lines in *The Adventurous Heart* (*Das Abenteuerliche Herz*, zweite Fassung, 1938):

> In the mineralogical institute of Leipzig I once saw a rock crystal, a foot long, mined from the inner of St Gotthard during the tunnel boring – a very lonely and exclusive dream of matter.

Minute observations, appalling metaphors and speculative allusions, but with an esoteric depth stopping them from becoming pedantry and micrology: that's the forte of both of them, Jünger and Gustafsson. They're a kind of authors' for authors and both, at the same time, considered controversial. Jünger was too right and Gustafsson somehow shared that role, however in a shall we say Swedish 1970's context since now he is seen as a pillar of society by all and sundry.

As for differences: as an author Gustafsson might be more easily accessible, having slightly more stylistic charm. And he's a poet of no mean skill (while Jünger's poetic harvest is interesting but minimal, see Chapter 32). And then of course there's the age difference. Furthermore this is a common mark between them: an overall lack of angst. It seems to me that in every other 20th century author there has to be fear, ressentiment and uneasiness abounding, as a main chord throughout every work. To thrive, be happy and occupy yourself in fruitful endeavours – that we seldom see in post war serious fiction.

Jünger and Gustafsson are delightfully free of this syndrome, without at the same time becoming awkwardly cheerful and trivial. I mean, consider a Gustafsson title like *Stories of Happy People* (1981): these unsought short stories seem like a revelation of another world, the visions of an alien mind compared to what other modern writers usually give us. And consider the first line of the novel *The Tennis*

Player (1977): "Yes. I remember it as a happy time." Looking back at his days as a visiting professor in Austin Gustafsson without lying can speak about happiness. Jünger isn't so outspoken but the level of energy, the general tenor of his books remind me of Gustafsson: an atmosphere devoid of angst.

BERTIL MALMBERG

Bertil Malmberg (1889-1958) was a Swedish poet very much influenced by the German Kaiserreich and German romantic poets, like Stefan George (1868-1933) and German art and philosophy in general. Malmberg lived in Berlin for a while before the Great War and in München during the 20's. The similarities between the Swede and Jünger are all there: born about the same time, aesthetes, conservatives and wary of the Nazi challenge, nevertheless allured by it at the same time. At least they couldn't ignore it, having to relate to it somehow.

Malmberg visited Germany some time after 1945, watching the ruins of Munich and reflecting on the war and all, concluding his essay: "And over endless fields of ruins a Wagner theme flew" [from *Ett författarliv (An Author's Life)*, 1952]. That's a stylish, and true, way of looking at it, vaguely reminiscent of Jünger's sketchy review of the Third Reich in *Jahre der Okkupation*. Both Jünger and Malmberg were a sort of aloof dandies glancing down into the abyss, resorting to spirituality and introspection when the abyss got too dark. And that's how it should be since introspection holds a key to Reality. Moreover, dandyism proper can be a preamble to nihilism as Jünger once said.

Both Jünger and Malmberg grew up in a culture dominated by the German Kaiserreich, a world without radio and cars (almost), without jazz and frenzy. When growing old Jünger said that he and his wife Liselotte spiritually remained in this pre-war era. Malmberg for his

part often returned to his childhood in poems, memoir essays and a novel about a kid, all in but name equal to Malmberg's childhood existence in a northern Swedish coastal town, the Little Puddleton of Härnösand (Åke och hans värld/Åke and His World, 1924).

By the way Malmberg translated *On the Marble Cliffs* into Swedish in 1950, being perfectly familiar with the poetic prose and the archaic style. He also occupied Chair No. 18 of the Swedish Academy 1953-1958.

HEIDENSTAM

"Any polemic proclamation we withhold we can consider a gain, the more so the more substance it has." [The war diary, June 10th, 1940] This uttering of Jünger's remind me of Verner von Heidenstam, a member of the Swedish Academy and poet who died in 1940. Heidenstam for instance had every chance in the world to fight it off verbally with his arch-enemy August Strindberg but Heidenstam declined, considering himself to be above petty feuds. He knew he was right; what need to argue then...? This of course incensed Strindberg even more.

In Paetel's biography there's another Jünger proverb that I find very Heidenstamish in this respect: "Few are worthy of being opposed" (wenige sind wert, dass man ihnen widerspricht).

Heidenstam was a genuine nationalist author like Jünger, and moreover they both had something of the poser in them. The common trait of having their portrait taken in profile is my indication of that. In addition they both had their unsought ease, their désinvolture (Jünger) or the nobleman's inborn manners (Heidenstam), but this can be a bit posing too. They knew how to stylise themselves, like in their novels: Jünger in *Eumeswil* and *Heliopolis* (and somehow also in his diaries) and Heidenstam in his novel *Hans Alienus* (1892),

about a pilgrim journeying from Rome to a mythical East, on to Hell and then back home to his northern native land. Of course you have to dramatize your persona when you are a novelist, however, Heidenstam took it a bit too far when he had his picture painted, expressly posing as *Hans Alienus* in white shroud and staff. And in profile of course.

Both Heidenstam and Jünger liked to travel in the Middle East, Heidenstam widely in the 1870's and Jünger to Agadir in Morocco in 1969, 1974 and 1975. It was the charm of the archaic world with carpet sellers and little carpentry, tinker and pottery shops, of the markets with all their smells and impressions, mirrored in Heidenstams poetry collection *Vallfart och vandringsår* (*Pilgrimage and Journeyman Years*, 1888) and for Jünger in *Eumeswil*. This is a viable orientalism, the respective authors appreciating the Orient as a timelessly heartwarming symbol of Terre des Hommes – the world of men, with both Jünger and Heidenstam having the ability to see the uniqueness of the environment and use it as a trigger to dream yourself away.

23. JÜNGER THE PIOUS

Throughout his life Jünger was inspired by religion. He was a pious esotericist in his own right, a stout free-thinker and at the same time drawn to the power of organized religion. Maybe the motto extra ecclesiam nulla salus – "without the church no salvation" – affected him. However, with or without organized religion Jünger above all raised a finger of warning against atheism, and in this he was rather unique as a 20th century author.

THE IMPRESSION OF BRAZILIAN MONKS

In the 30's Jünger went to Brazil. He wrote about it all and eventually, after the war, published it as *Atlantische Fahrt*. A central episode in the book is a visit to German monks in a Benedictine abbey, the brethren impressing the visitor with their joy in spite of having relinquished life and all its pleasures. Strange indeed – isn't the cloister life supposed to be about hardships and suffering...?

Jünger is amazed. At the same time he can relate to it like in the subservience, with monks obeying the monastic rules like a soldier obeying his orders, the monk life becoming a sort of spiritual body-building and the abbey a training camp for the inner mind. There's order and joy here, what more to ask for...?

At this stage in life Jünger himself had moved away from titanism and militarism, areas where order was ever present but joy in a lesser degree, so this rendezvous with religion was rather significant. His conversion would take another 60 years. But that event in itself isn't so important in my book. What's more important is the Jünger preoccupation with spiritual attitudes that sometimes touch upon those of conventional religion: he was a free-thinker and an esotericist, playing the role of prophet and catalyst, along with and sometimes in opposition to organized religion.

The chief contribution by Jünger in the discussion at hand is this: his warning against atheism. In *Eumeswil* and the late diary he is crystal clear on this issue. Atheism is a vice, a mental sickness. One may object and say that faith in God and/or gods isn't everything in the esoteric realm, with for instance taoism and Buddhism being somewhat atheistic in nature. The answer to that is: no they aren't, they don't deny the existence of gods. Buddhism, in putting the emphasis on the personal spiritual development, doesn't state that gods for that matter are totally non-existent. Gods exist on a higher level than we, however still subjected to the laws of karma. That's the Buddhist theology in nuce.

Of course everything isn't solved by automatically starting to worship gods. That's not what Jünger means. But he means that the central ontological foundation of Christianity, Hinduism, Judaism, Islam and shamanism is true. The existence of God is an ontological reality, there are gods out and about, the divine presence in reality is real. The atheist on the other hand is like a ship without anchor, the mind of him (and the current culture as a whole) being the victim of a kind of cross-section paralysis, a total lethargy of the intellect leading out into a sterile desert.

That's Jüngers basic message as I see it. Then it's not so important if he himself was or wasn't the epitome of piousness, faith and charity. He understood like no one else the ills of our culture. And by not being steeped in the common parochial and sanctified language his message came across more pregnantly.

START THE DAY BY PRAYING

The hero of *Eumeswil*, Manuel Venator, warns against atheism. And he himself, without being a Bible beater or a church goer, lives his life with some pious foundations. Like when he talks about his starting the day by praying, remarking that it's a central human incentive, even stronger than the sex drive. Both have to be cultivated and released, not suppressed, because if suppressed horrifying things will ensue. – Jünger here comes forth as a strong advocate for the pious life, stronger than any latter-day church person I've met.

Jünger-Venator is an anarch (see chapter 16). And there is something religious about this, something esoteric, something meditative and in a state of trance, something like saying I AM like the Christ of S:t John's Gospel (I am the true vine, I am the door, I am the light of the world etc). Alright, the "I am" dictum isn't mentioned in the novel. But Uwe Wolf (in Figal and Schwilks *Magie der Heiterkeit: Ernst Jünger zum Hundertsten*, Wolf's chapter being called "Dichten, danken, beten") calls the condition of this anarch Gottesunmittelbar, i.e., "in direct connection with God". And that's a central Christian idea, advocated by St. Paul and Martin Luther as well as Christ himself, the idea of man not needing a priest as mediator between himself and God, not any more than reason or other systematic means are needed. They can't do the trick here. You meet God by wanting to do so, by realizing your freedom (and limitations) as a man and by letting your intuition guide you. That's being Gottesunmittelbar and

the Jünger speaking as Manuel Venator to me seems to embody that life form.

Wolf moreover has a keen eye for Jünger's role as a spiritual author. Wolf states that churches and priests are needed as vehicles for the Word and for Tradition, for continuity and for keeping the flame burning, but additionally we need desert prophets and free spirits to come with impulses, new interpretations and reminiscences of forgotten usages. Jünger, spending most of his author life as an agent free from ties to any organisation, in Wolf's eye played this role. And I agree with that. Jünger to me represents the eminent free-thinker, a pious but independent prophet helping us to see the religious concepts in a new light.

24. JÜNGER & ESOTERICISM

Ernst Jünger was an esotericist, an author interested in the invisible patterns that govern our reality. Ontology and metaphysics were at the centre of his works. His creed was influenced by German idealism but he was no ordinary academical thinker. His terminology was rather peculiar at times. He was an author of belles lettres, not a systematic philosopher.

THE ADVENTUROUS HEART

Jünger was first and foremost an author with the aim of writing readable texts, not a scientifically occupied academic. A well sounding sentence was more important to him than a dry, unobjectionable thesis. Jünger for example didn't waste time defining words and discussing their scientific meaning, no, the stylistic value of the words was more important. You could say that he was a philosopher in the spirit of Nietzsche, not of Kant. And that's fine with me. I'm no professional philosopher. I only want a good read. And this we get from Jünger, sometimes with a philosophical slant and truly original to that.

ERNST JÜNGER – A PORTRAIT

For a look at the Jünger philosophical method you could of course go to Gisbert Kranz's *Ernst Jünger's symbolische Weltschau* (1968). This is a fine work for the systematic mind, like the career academic who wants impulses for his own dissertations on the Jünger way of thinking. As for myself I'll satisfy myself with a look at one of the outings of Jünger himself into the philosophical realm, *The Adventurous Heart* of 1938. I'll then move on to the novel *Eumeswil* and the war diary and look at their metaphysical traits.

Jünger was an idealistic thinker. Maybe his days at Leipzig university in the 20's steeped him in this thinking, maybe (and probably) he was like this even before. Anyhow, the idealistic world view says that the world at its essence is spiritual in nature. "There's more than meets the eye." Holism and a look at the big picture is the basis while reductionism and dry analysis leads you wrong. Of course you can and must analyse the world but you can't just leave it in shambles, you have to have a vision of the whole, of a harmoniously cooperating cosmos.

This is more or less the idealistic creed. And we see some of it mirrored in *The Adventurous Heart* – not systematically, but in glimpses. There are specifically three texts in this book that deal with metaphysics in the Jünger way and they are "Die Überzeugung", "Der Hauptschlüssel" and "Das kombinatorische Schluss" ("The Conviction", "The Master Key" and "Combinatory Conclusion"). They follow suit, all dealing with the invisible side of things and forming a sort of philosophical sub-theme as they stand.

"Die Überzeugung" for its part makes a distinction between merely knowing and being convinced of something. The former is a transparent lesson learned, the latter the wisdom you gain, "a spiritual act completed in the darkness – a secret influence and an inner concordance" (Jünger), free of the mere urge to learn something. You get wise by contemplating what you've gathered, sleeping on it, waking up a wiser man after this nocturnal lesson. Thus we get access to "the secret doctrine hidden in every noteworthy language".

216

What this secret doctrine is Jünger doesn't elaborate on. But of course he means something like idealism, esotericism and perennial philosophy like Plotinos, the *Vedas*, the *Upanishads*, gnosticism, the great Tao, Goethe, Meister Eckart and the like.

The same goes for the essay "Der Haputschlüssel", its coda being that a genius seems to have a master key providing him "access all areas", while ordinary spirits only have keys to separate chambers. The latter stand beside looking in envy at this playing Orpheus, this dancing Dionysus being endowed with the ability to make a combination of conclusions, not to confuse with common, mechanistic conclusions that even animals can make. For instance a dog sniffing a trail and coming to a road fork where he doesn't find anything on the one trail automatically comes to the conclusion that the prey is on the other trail, taking that one instead.

The dog can make Aristotelean conclusions. But the deeper form of conclusion discussed in the third essay is about what Jünger has already touched upon, namely wisdom instead of mere knowledge. It's the idea that you have to reach beyond the things themselves to arrive at the essence, that the world is more than meets the eye. You need intuition. And, as a writer, style. Nietzsche knew that and Plato too.

Combinatorics (Jünger says) sees hidden connections, going beyond the superficial similarities of pedantry. Combinatorics sees both the part and the whole while the logician only sees the separate parts. Then combinatorics is hailed by Jünger in different ways, like being able to multiply and potentate while ordinary minds only can add; combinatorics is like a field marshal outflanking his enemy who only can advance in lines. Any great professional, any master of his trade, any genius must have this combinatory trait.

EUMESWIL

I've already looked at the metaphysics of *Eumeswil* (see Chapter 16). Here's a repetition.

No transcendence is needed, everything is revealed here and now. Trust your senses. Goethe said that and Jünger reminds us of it.

Idealism for its part is about recognising the idea. And the ideal form is copy and original at the same time: "das Urbild is Bild und Spiegelbild" as the German original of *Eumeswil* has it. The transcendental image or idea is copied in the everyday object, living on in the copy as well as being transcendent. It's immanent and transcendent at the same time. This we have from Plotinos, elaborating and refining the Platonian philosophy of mere transcendence. And in *Eumeswil* Jünger has the character Bruno teaching us this.

Everything is guided by its innermost essence, by its idea, the things existing for the ideas to have something to show themselves in. The idea is what makes the objects, the flowers, animals, everything, live, visible in any garden, forest or whatever. Jünger dedicates some pages in this novel to bring this argument home.

THE WAR DIARY

The Jünger war diary is replete with Jüngerian idealism, differing in style if not content from Cambridge Platonism and German Idealism. As I've already said: Jünger brings us the metaphysics of everyday, making the abstractions of idealism tangible for the common man.

Like for instance: what's in the chessboard king? In this, Jünger says, the magic of the archaic kingdom is preserved, the chess piece in question being a discreet symbol of a lost world. The same goes with hunting trophies: they are no simple wall decorations, they are carriers of magic power, talismans there to accumulate happiness and

life force, mana, for the hunter. Even artists may need talismans like these, like the painter Braque whom Jünger met in Paris on October 4th, 1943, his studio being graced with certain objects d'art that weren't motifs to be painted but rather magical objects assembling artistic mana.

Jünger looks at everyday objects decoding their meaning. For instance oil in a barrel is dark but a spilled out drop is a psychedelic palette, this being due to its thinness [Kirchhorst, November 5th, 1945]. The thinner the more etheric. It's like Goethe said tangible-intangible (Ger. "sinnlich-übersinnlich"), living on the edge between the material and the immaterial.

The war diary also says that the way to the Southern Paradise can be found by maps, but a better way is to let oneself be guided by images of opulence and riches, of grapes ripening in the sun and the like [Kirchhorst, September 16th, 1945]. This to me is a simple and striking example of Jünger's symbolic world view.

25. ARCANE OUTINGS

You find many esoteric passages in the works of Jünger, many arcane and occult references. And these are often hard to systematize. So I hereby give you this collection of shorter and longer fragments in the region of arcane outings and probings into the occult, Jünger style.

I THINK

"I'm not thinking differently than you. I think."

Jünger is quoting this in the late diary [February 28th, 1985]. A quote by whom? It doesn't say. Or is it his own aphorism? It could have been. Anyhow, in the same region we have his notion in *Eumeswil* about how grateful we are to the teacher who has learned us how to think. As for myself I'm thankful for Jünger having learned me to see things differently, how to see the effects of the invisible in everyday life and the workings of discreet forces beyond space and time. An ability to see the wholeness of life, to see a world in a grain of sand. Jünger may not be the only teacher I've had in this respect but he sure is one of the most rhetorically memorable.

LENNART SVENSSON

CREATING OUR WORLD OURSELVES

We're creating our world ourselves, creating the situations we meet, maybe even the people and things we see; everything is realized (made real) by us in a somewhat solopsistic vein. We create our world in order to learn, in order to become freer and better men. Jünger adheres to this philosophy, for example in his notes for June 23rd, 1940 when learning that he has received the Iron Cross for a certain rescue mission. He finds it petty next to his World War One assaults rendering him the Blue Max, the highest order of the Kaiserreich. But it is what it is and as Herakleitos said you can't go down twice in the same river. In Greek that'll be "potamoisi tois autoisi embainomen, esmen te kai ouch esmen". And Jünger:

> Herakleitos is right: no one goes down in the same river twice. The mysterious in such a transformation is that it corresponds to changes within ourselves – we are the creators of our world and what we experience doesn't come randomly. The objects are selected and affected by our state of mind: the world is such as we are. Each one of us then is capable of changing the world – that's the enormous significance given to each one of us. Therefore it's so important that we work on ourselves. [German: es is wichtig das wir an uns arbeiten].

See also the entry for August 5th, 1945: "We don't randomly see the images we see, they are structured according to our frame of mind."

INVISIBLE PRESENCE

This is from the essay *Am Kieselstrand* (1951), elaborating on the presence of the invisible, a central feature of Jünger's metaphysics:

The world may seem incomplete, often cruel and almost always unfair. Then again, can't we liken our ideals, our judgements and corrections to the games the cat is playing? We don't know the other side, yet inferences of its unfathomable riches seem to invade our world like shadows. Time has something meaningless, something prearranged over it; there should be an additive loosening it from this curse. The time is the scene but in the wings we change ourselves in ourselves.

WHOLENESS

Holistic: to see the big picture is the crux, this giving you security and perspective, in life as well as in science. Thus you don't get caught up by irregularities and coincidences, these becoming redundant:

> What matters is the ambiance, electrifying all the way into the capillaries. Dreyfus, the diamond necklace caper and the shot in Sarajevo should be seen in their contexts, not in their details. [Agadir, June 7th, 1975]

Wholeness is the norm. Conversely this constant "what if" is fruitless ("what if Princip had missed" etc.), things you tend to think about before falling asleep as Jünger says in his war diary. It's like the eternal nagging and fussing in a 24 hour bar.

Coincidences don't exist; instead our lives are governed by totalities. We're not ruled by particularities, like missing the bus and thereby happen to meet completely other people than those you otherwise would have met. Rather we're ruled by:

> (...) the results making up the sum of life, the destiny that is in store for us and which, seen chronologically, seem to be assembled

by innumerable chance points. Metaphysically however no such points exist on our course of life, as little as in the course of an arrow. [Paris, March 7th, 1944]

Some sense of security is needed in your life, whether through prayer or meditation or whatever. Anything but this constant worrying about the life changing implications of having tea or coffee in the morning. This belief in chance, Jünger says, is related to bacillophobia, the witch scare of our time. The remedy of all this, I'd say, is some spiritual common sense.

BENEFICENCE

"The glass of water you give to the thirsting is bigger than the ocean." Thus a Russian monk quoted by Jünger in *Eumeswil*. More of the same from the war diary:

> Two Russians chopping wood for us, in the kitchen told Perpetua that this was the first time during three years of captivity they had been offered food in a house they were working for. This is even more disconcerting than the cruelty. This time, so well versed in the energy processes, has nonetheless forgotten the enormous powers disguised in a piece of bread you share with others. [Kirchhorst, February 26th, 1945]

In the same vein is Jünger's mentioning of a pilot, having saved himself by parachute, who was at the risk of being killed by a Dutch refugee. He was saved by Jünger's neighbour Rehbock who saved the airman "thereby risking his own life" [Kirchhorst, November 27th, 1944]. At the same time two other airmen, dead, had landed by parachute. They were buried at the cemetery. [November 28th, 1944]

What we see here is the power to forgive, inherent among the common people. The airmen were there to bomb them back to the stone age, but people forgave them this when they were at their mercy. In defense of the airmen it could be said that they probably hadn't started their lives with the intent of going off to bomb Germany. In, say, 1935, did future airman NN dream of pouring out phosphorus over Germany...? I doubt it. He was drawn into the war. The responsibility is on those who have started the war, not the soldier in the ranks.

A GLIMPSE INTO THE INTERIOR OF MEN

Journey through the burned out cities of Western Germany, lined up like on a dark chain, and again this thought: This is how it looks in people's brains. This impression was enhanced when listening to my fellow passengers; the sight of this ruin world in them only awoke the desire to enlarge it, hoping to see London in the same state, whispering about the enormous batteries now installed on the Channel coast in order to fire at this city. [June 17th, 1943]

A Christian thought: free yourself of feelings of revenge. And then the esoteric quality: everything is decided in man's interior.

ON THE OTHER SIDE OF THE TIME WALL

In the late diary of November 5th, 1991, we read:

To be or not to be? Rather both. Our phantom world is seen on the back of a mirror. This mirror is the Time Wall. [continued on November 20th] (...) The Time Wall as a mirror in the sense of

Corinthians becomes transparent and also permeable. Is irony still possible here? Maybe conversely. This you often find in words on the death bed, but before the break: "the most holy in the storm" on which Hölderlin was hoping. And with him Novalis:

I feel the invigorating
flow of death,
waiting in the storm
for the full confidence of life.

The mirror refers to St. Paul in the *New Testament* Letter to the Corinthians, the words about on the one hand seeing things as "through a glass darkly" and, on the other, about seeing clearly. Other than that I have no clear-cut interpretation to give you, leaving this Jünger quote standing as an example of the obscurantism he has been accused of.

DREAMS

One day during the phoney war Jünger dreams about a marvellous shop, one where they,

(...) sold such treasures as turtle shells, corals and mother of pearl. I had entered the palaeontological department where they had display cabinets with exquisite fossils, these natural works of art being chiselled by the aeons. I saw fascinating things: on blue samite trilobites of pure gold next to fishes of green and violet metal, and mussels with deeply furrowed shells resplendent in all the colours of the rainbow. Next to me count Pignatelli was standing selecting red marble plates for his city hall. [The Reed Hut, February 14th, 1940]

225

There's an undeniable clarity to Jünger's paleontology dreams, this he admits himself referring to this one:

> This night dreams of trilobites that I bought at the Leipzig institute of Rinnes the mineralogist, ordering them after a catalogue and offering the missing examples in casts exquisitely well made, some in pure gold, some in red sealing-wax. [Paris, May 8th, 1944]

This brings to mind what Armance, the millionaire wife Florence Gould, says to Jünger after a trip to the Mediterranean sea: "When looking at mussels, octopuses and jelly-fish I've often thought about you." [Paris, August 4th, 1943] As an author to be associated with certain symbols, that's what I call immortality – like J. G Ballard and swimming pools, Ray Bradbury and "old man sitting on a front porch" and Philip K. Dick and talking machines.

Dreams. There are many of them in Jünger's diaries. Picking one at random, a mysterious and enchanting one, I give you this:

> I conversed on the style of Cassidorius with a hunting knight from early medieval times, a fine connoisseur of the classics. During the conversation I had no problems with at first being contemporary with the author, then with the knight and finally with the 20th century. I was looking as if through a glass in which three colours merge. [Bescheid, May 21st, 1940]

Jünger now and then dreams about his parents, be they dead or alive. About the father he for example dreams one year before he dies [January 10th, 1942], and about the mother he has a dream "(...) making me extremely lucky and warming me long afterwards when standing on the cold loading dock supervising the unloading"; this was when serving as occupation troops in France [February 18th, 1941]. Here we again see the for others unusual, but for Jünger common habit of speaking about happiness (more on this in Chapter 30).

In Paris, February 23rd, 1942 he has a dream that he can steer, a known phenomenon among some dreamers, leading him into reflections on the art of dreaming: "The world is a dream and we must dream more intensely when needed." This is echoed in *Eumeswil*, thirty five years later: "We're not defeated because of our dreams but because we haven't dreamed intensely enough."

DANTE

"Dantean atmosphere: horrifying without fear." This Jünger says in the entry for Wilflingen, June 2nd, 1986. And I would say that precisely this, the absence of fear, of the feeling of danger and drama, is what makes me a bit indifferent to Divina Commedia. Even when climbing over the Devil in the interior of the Earth it's like a picnic.

THE MUSIC

During the visit to the eastern front Jünger spends the new year in an army HQ. The festive spirits are absent, both here and there this time. "Festive joy isn't possible these days" he says. [Kutais, December 31st, 1942]

So what then is a feast, what is joy? True joy has got to have music; the Muses, goddesses for arts like dance, music and epic poetry, is the etymological root to "music". In German they have the word "musisch" along with "musikalisch", the latter having to do with music specifically and the former – musisch – with the joy of art in life in general, a glorified, creative sense of mirth. English doesn't have this distinction, only having the word "musical". Jünger often talks about die musische, of the need for musische joy, musische living. From his brother Fritz (in *Griechische Götter*, 1943) he had learned of the

Olympian gods having parties which the titans didn't, the latter only having work and toil: all work and no play made the titans dull. In short: the titans had no music, they weren't musisch but the Olympian gods were.

This becomes something of a sub-theme in Jünger's later works: the difference between gods and titans, and especially how our technological times often seem titanic in nature. And the symbol for the anti-titanic, olympian lifestyle is music, the talent for being musisch. We have the word in Swedish too – musisk – and it says a lot more than simply "cultural", and especially "working with culture" as the jargon goes – for against this Jünger would say that it's a contradiction to "work with culture". The musical soul of art has got nothing to do with work and toil, it's about divine inspiration and Apollonian ease. Apollo for example is said to build a city with the tones of his harp.

This world needs to understand the musical attitude. And Jünger has the clues to it, q.v. *An der Zeitmauer, Eumeswil, The Glass Bees, Heliopolis, Strahlungen* and the late diary.

SHIMMERING SURFACES

In the late diary of June 12th, 1992, Jünger is sitting in the garden blowing soap bubbles, seeing how they fly off, intermingle, reflect the light and disappear. The surface of the soap bubble indeed has a fascinating lustre and these shimmering surfaces was a standing feature of the Jünger oeuvre. He never tired of delving into their magic.

For this subject you could start with the war diary entry for February 16th, 1944. Having mentioned an hourglass he has received, the object being from the 15th or 16th century, Jünger depicts how

"age has made the glass opalizing so that the reddish dust trickles down behind a veil weaved by time". Jünger has a soft spot for things transforming and refining with age, like well worn books and old wooden tools. A prime example of the shimmer of worn and weathered objects we find in relation to the figure of Vigo in *Eumeswil*, a wise historian:

> During his lectures Vigo usually shows trinkets, holding them forth or just holding them – not as evidence but as bearers of the substance in question, often nothing more than a shard or a piece of a brick. This morning he brought a plate of faïence with an arabesque motive of flowers and writing. He indicated the colours: a pattern of faded saffron, rose and violet, and above it a shimmer neither made by the glazing or the brush but by time itself. Such is the existence of glass, dreaming away after being buried in a Roman trash pile or, on desolate backyards, brick roofs whose colour have faded through a thousand summers.

Returning to the war diary we have a certain passage on how the shimmer of a spilled out drop of oil surpasses that of oil in a barrel:

> Oil in a barrel is matt, opaque and lacking lustre. But when a drop of it falls on the road it spreads out on the humidity as a wondrous palette. All we know as colour is rough and material. It's the play on the finest of membranes, close to Nothingness, the matter indicating that it's approaching the secret state and is on the verge of transition. [Kirchhorst, November 5th, 1945]

As I've already intimated it's the thinness that does it, matter being on the borderline to the immaterial, "tangible-intangible" as Goethe said.

Finally we have "Die Vexierbilder" (Puzzling Pictures) of *The Adventurous Heart*, with the fascination of Nigromontanus before this divine lustre of things:

229

He loved changing materials, iridizing glass and fluids, whose colours shimmer or change with the light, his favourite stone being the opal and the polished tourmaline.

PROVERBS

In volume IV of the late diary you find three good, esoteric proverbs scattered throughout the text, starting in Wilflingen, October 25th, 1986: "The Talmud says: When the tenements reach higher than the temples the end of the world is near." This in regard to skyscrapers.

Then we have Eurydike, five years old, baptized in champagne with Jünger attending on the Rue de Seine. She sends him the proverb: "Only God knows if he exists or not." [Wilflingen, January 27th, 1987]

Later on in the book Jünger gives us his own proverb: "The twin duties of art are identical: to approach the godhead and chase away the anxiety of death." [Wilflingen, October 27th, 1987]

NIETZSCHE'S IMPROBABILITY

Nietzsche was inconsistent. You can't have it both ways, both saying "God is dead" and advocate the idea of the eternal recurrence. Jünger intimates this in the late diary [January 30th, 1945] and rightfully so: if something eternally recurs, if something eternal exists, then there should also exist eternal beings, embodiments of eternal principles – like gods. To connect "God" with "dead" is absurd. A god is an immortal being; even if he dies (Bacchus, Balder, Mithra) he has a tendency to return.

When speaking about the divine you have to accept certain presuppositions. You can't violate the inner logic.

STYLE

In the entry for January 1st, 1992 we read: there's a fashion trend in feelings, however, the spirit externalizes. This could mean: so long as your work is based on ideas, concepts and visions then they will last, while the purely sentimental won't last. How to achieve good style, then, is about having something to say. That's how Matthew Arnold, a 19th century scholar and poet put it. You don't have to experimentally come up with some unique literary attitude, no, just write down what you have on your mind in the most efficient way.

Goethe said something similar in *Dichtung und Wahrheit* (*Writing and Reality*, 1833): the quintessential content of a text is what makes it come alive, not the outer shape or style.

DÉSINVOLTURE

According to Heimo Schwilk a defining feature of Jünger's attitude was distance: as a person Jünger could be distant, taking the role of the observer. And this attitude could be said to have carried Jünger through the storms of the 20th century.

The Anarch, a theme in Jünger's novel *Eumeswil*, is a sort of embodiment of this distance (more on this on Chapter 16). We also see it in the concept of désinvolture which Jünger wrote about in *The Adventurous Heart*. It's a concept with roots in court circles in medieval southern France, according to Jonasson to be defined as "unconcerned attitude" and "elevated tranquility" in a worldly context, that is, taking part in society you still have a private space within that doesn't partake. It's like Jackie Kennedy who said: "I am here and yet I am not here." As a socialite this role of hers seems to rhyme with the désinvolture of Jünger.

231

Désinvolture is like the stoic concept of apateia (tranquility), equanimity. Désinvolture could be seen as an attitude for dandies of today, however without the nihilism that alwas seem to accompany the dandy. Désinvolture is coolness with an ethical sounding board.

Of course you shouldn't be a robot. You have to live, to feel and all that. But you always have to have some distance. You can't be too engaged. Becoming too engaged could be dangerous. A line from the German TV-series "Heimat III" springs to mind here: "He who marries die Zeitgeist soon becomes a widower."

THE BEST OF WORLDS

When Leinbniz said that "this world is the best of worlds" he didn't mean planet Earth but the whole universe. Therefore the question of life on other planets is misleading, according to Jünger in his late diary [Agadir, October 18th, 1959]. In the same spirit he says in *Grenzgänge*, an essay collection from 1966: the question of life in the universe is wrongly posed, because anyone gazing up into the night sky can se that the universe is alive. This kind of intuitive holistic is what the world needs today, Jünger being a sort of master of the obvious in this sense.

ETHICS AS AESTHETICS

Jünger:

> The good stylist. He was about to write: "I acted right", however, he wrote "wrongly" because it sounded better. [Paris, April 3rd, 1943]

Voilà - an ethic grounded in aesthetic values.

26. JÜNGER AS A FANTASIST

Jünger isn't ordinarily considered as an author of science fiction or fantasy. Authors of his calibre don't need a specific genre as a creative or commercial support. That said it wouldn't be totally irrelevant to apply a genre specific view of his novels taking place in future settings. Does Jünger have a talent for the craft of science fiction? That's the subject of this chapter, looking at Jünger's inventiveness as a gadget maker. Then I look at other Jünger works and their meditations over technology and machines. Lastly I make some general comparisons between him and other authors of fantastic fiction, namely Heinlein, Tolkien and Ballard.

JÜNGER AS AN INVENTOR

Ernst Jünger was a remarkable man. He had a brain of his own. He was a genius of sorts, a man with the ability to amaze his audience. And that quirk is definitely there in his science fiction novels.

It's like this: science fiction taking place in the future needs speculative settings, it needs inventions and technical gadgets of the one or the other kind. Of course it's about more than that, you have

to have characters enacting a viable plot, but as for technology it has to be explicitly present throughout. You just can't throw in a simple "three glass window" and leave it with that. You have to invent things and sprinkle them over the pages, creating a futuristic atmosphere. And Jünger knew this art, employing it in *Heliopolis, Gläserne Bienen* and *Eumeswil*. His inventing activity in these novels is so prolific that I have to make a survey.

Starting with *Heliopolis* you find things like:

- The permanent film, both a kind of TV showing moving pictures and a sort of computer showing "rolling text and numbers". This last feature home computers were unable to do even in 1980, so this strikes me as kind of prophetic for a novel from 1949.
- The Phonophor, a hand-held computer functioning as a telephone, passport, ID, ticket and insignia of rank. Additionally it can download music and text from "the Central Archives", that is, a kind if internet – not bad a vision being conceived by a layman in 1949. The phonophor was worn in the breast pocket partly visible and the different colours of its shell indicated the wearer's rank.
- Thermic metal, a mysterious element heating things with its internal heat. It's an invention of the magical kind, a thing you would like to have without being able to explain it. That's how many SF authors work, throwing in things like soaring cars and space travel faster than light: without being explained in detail they still seem probable and give the tale a futuristic feeling.

Additional technical gadgetry of *Heliopolis* are beam weapons, a metal melting device (thermic concave mirror), soaring vessels and then some. Even if the machines in question aren't central to the plot they embellish it, giving it atmosphere and futuristic ambiance.

Moving on to *Gläserne Bienen* we at first find these glass bees as a symbol of technological marvels. They are an early example of micro– if not nano technology. Miniature insects in this future setting are occupied with cleaning ducts, counting money, handle radioactive material etc, even sucking nectar out of flowers. The latter however was a sign of their limitations since the flowers died after the act.

As intimated Jünger early on was into the achievements of information technology: the principle of internet, to have access to all the collected cultural treasures of mankind in your pocket, is fully realized in the world of *Heliopolis*. In *Eumeswil* he developed the concept even further; there, in the Luminary (das Luminarium), you could punch in a time and a place on the keyboard and then have it played before you. It was like an advanced, graphic google search; for instance, punching in "Normandy, dawn, June 6th 1944" you would see the allied invasion fleet approaching the sandy beaches in a virtual reality fashion.

Jünger used this library of historical scenes to elaborate on historical presence and the role of the historian, making the novel – *Eumeswil* – a rich storehouse of historical images and historiographical attitudes (more on this in Chapter 16). As for conjuring scenes out of history today's computer technology is able to do that, portraying scenes of historical figures with real-life actors and having the face computer animated. Then, in the ensuing production, you could for example see Rommel as real as IRL walk over a desert battlefield.

MACHINE DREAMS

The symbol of today's information technology (computers, internet), someone has suggested, is the net, maybe seen as a spider's web with concentric circles connected by spokes, thus having everything in contact with everything else. This kind of summarizes our age, this is how we live: there's no single centre, any point in the net having the potential to be the centre.

ERNST JÜNGER – A PORTRAIT

This is our age. But the previous age, what symbol summing it up was there? I'd say the machine was the archetype of the bygone era. The past 100-200 years had the machine as its leading hieroglyph. And as for science fiction, the subject of this chapter, the SF I grew up with had a wealth of machines: space ships, soaring cars and robots, even whole cityscapes of mighty machines. Everything you did could be done better by machines, that was the gist.

This epoch is now ending. Now we live in subtler times, venturing out in conceptual landscapes instead of tangible ones, moving towards brain building instead of bodybuilding. In urban circles the computer is now a bigger status symbol than the car. However dwelling for a moment in the land of machines we soon encounter Jünger himself there. He always had a keen eye for machines, like these lines in *Feuer und Blut* (*Fire and Blood*) from 1925:

> The machine is beautiful. And it has to be beautiful for the lover of life in all its fullness and violence. (...) Haven't we noticed it when seeing a bullet train flashing through the landscape, race drivers heading for the straight after the banked curve; when metal birds have circled over our cities and when in large glass-covered halls we've been standing between crank shafts and shining flywheels, with the mercury pillars of the manometers rising and falling and the red pointers of the instruments on the wall trembling – haven't we noticed that in all these actions there must be an abundance of life, of luxury, of a will of totally transforming life into power.

This machine poetry is reminiscent of Thea von Harbou in her novel *Metropolis*, which surfaced at the same time. However she was more of a sceptic, seeming to have an aversion against the world of machines while Jünger, here at least, embraced it. The master of this romantic view of machines to me is Eugen Zamjatin whom I look at in the next chapter.

LENNART SVENSSON

TECHNICAL ENCOUNTERS

As we recently saw the Jünger of the 20's was romancing the shapes and forms of the machine world. But he soon changed his attitude, becoming more of a sceptic. Like when in France 1940 seeing some tank wrecks he clearly is a stranger: "I crept inside them and as always I have to admit that I don't feel at ease inside these creations smelling of oil, petrol and rubber." [May 29th, 1940]

So then, the author of *Der Arbeiter*, envisioning a totally industrialized world, doesn't like machines...? Maybe his techno-romance, as long it lasted, was more of the theoretical kind. He wasn't a hands-on practical man. In the First World War he preferred bayonet and sabre, only grudgingly accepting the more technical weapons of hand-grenades and machine guns. Mines for its part he avoided. And as for cars he never learned to drive, as far as I'm informed.

You could say: the young Jünger loved machines and what they represented but then the love abated. Nevertheless he still could write technologically credible science fiction, well into the post war years. *Eumeswil* for instance appeared in 1977 when he was over 80.

And speaking of his personal distaste for machines and his love of "natural" technology there was one old artifact he came to adore: the hour glass, dedicating a whole book to them (*Das Sanduhrbuch*, 1954). In his war diary we find these lines on the subject:

This object [the hour glass] suits me well when the presence of mechanical things becomes unbearable, especially during conversations, reading sessions, meditations and studies, whose length you don't want to measure to the minute – instead letting the sand in a little glass pour out. The hourglass time is another one, connected to life: no peals are heard here, no hand is moving. It's time that flows, passes, runs off – untightened, unrhythmisized time. [Paris, February 16th, 1944]

237

Jünger was a complex man. You could find a lot of complaining in his late diary of how modern technology has destroyed the earth. At the same time he liked watching TV, he liked to travel by jet to distant countries and he acknowledged the complexity and heroism of the Apollo project, putting a man on the moon. So I leave the question of where he stood on the question of modern technology versus olden lifestyles and move on to some comparisons with other fantasists. I begin with the American Robert Heinlein.

HEINLEIN

> A human being should be able to change a diaper, plan an invasion, butcher a hog, conn a ship, design a building, write a sonnet, balance accounts, build a wall, set a bone, comfort the dying, take orders, give orders, cooperate, act alone, solve equations, analyze a new problem, pitch manure, program a computer, cook a tasty meal, fight efficiently, die gallantly. Specialization is for insects.

This is a quote from the novel *Time Enough For Love* by Robert Heinlein (1907-1988). All things considered it describes Heinlein himself rather well. He (and Jünger) was this kind of man, versatile and educated and with the military background as a defining experience. Heinlein for one had been a lieutenant in the US Navy. Both also had their early radical periods, Jünger as a nationalist, Heinlein as a man of the left. Heinlein in this respect is said to have supported Upton Sinclair's socialist Californian reform movement in the beginning of the 30's.

Both Jünger and Heinlein came to be known as men of the right. From my SF reading days in the 80's I learned that Heinlein was something worse than Hitler. Such was the sentiment of the left in those days. It doesn't matter much now, I just came to remember it.

More interesting to note is how these men of diverse talents, Jünger and Heinlein, found writing to be the ultimate field of activity. Can't do anything properly, being a jack of all trades, master of none...? Well then, try writing books.

Both Jünger and Heinlein were living condensations of knowledge, being able to state their opinion on everything. An author should be able to do that. Now any journalist or politician can do the same, however an author hopefully does it in a stylistically memorable way. Finally I would like to say that Jünger and Heinlein both exhibited a humane character; I avoid the word "humanistic" since it's kind of platitudinous in these matters. Without being great portrayer's of men you still meet human beings in their works. "He has accepted membership in the human race" Henry Kuttner once said of Heinlein and a comparable Jünger quote could be: "I enjoy taking part in the life of men." [Paris, May 10th, 1943]

TOLKIEN

Jünger had his enmities towards modern technology and J. R. R. Tolkien (1892-1973) even more so. When paying his back tax once in the early 70's he added the note: "Not one penny to the Concord project", the supersonic endeavour at the time being the symbol of expensive Big Science.

You could compare Tolkien's *Lord of the Rings* to Jünger's *On the Marble Cliffs*. Both writers served in the First World War, both became or were conservatives, and both wrote fantasy stories of idyllic lands being threatened by evil forces. Both books have the same atmosphere: the main characters feel the approaching darkness, in time getting the resolve to stand up against evil and fight it in open combat. After the fight there's a slight sense of resignation but the final chords speak of confidence in things eternal, mirrored in everyday life.

239

Like Jünger Tolkien was a World War One veteran. Tolkien actually was an officer too, participating in the battle of Somme (like Jünger, see chapter 1). Tolkien soon caught a fever and was sent home and while recuperating he started to sketch his fantasy masterpiece. You can see traces of Tolkien's military experience in the work; both "Bilbo" and the trilogy has a fair share of fighting and pitched battles in them.

BALLARD

A certain James Graham Ballard (1930-2009) had been a technical journalist before becoming fiction writer. He had also been a pilot. So he knew his way around things technical. As for the similarities with Jünger he had the ability to write a tight and condensed prose. Jünger's style can be elaborated at times but mostly it's a wonder of concentration, even more so than Ballard's.

In addition to this they both had a penchant for symbolism, jungles and enchanted nature. As if that wasn't enough they both had a keen eye for the titanic culture, secretly enjoying desolate techno landscapes. They were both witnesses to how a seemingly safe and secure world is literally bombed to pieces, Jünger in his war diary and Ballard in his semi-documentary novel *Empire of the Sun* (1984). As a prisoner of the Japanese the boy Ballard sees American B-29 bombers level Shanghai just as in war-torn Germany Jünger sees the B-17's and B-24's head off to demolish Hannover and Hamburg.

Last but not least both Jünger and Ballard did experiments with LSD in the 60's. Jünger relates this in *Annäherungen – über Drogen und Rausch* (see Chapter 15). Ballard tells his LSD story in *The Kindness of Women* (1991), taking the drug in a similarly controlled fashion. An example of Ballard's drug influenced prose can be seen in the short story "Memories of the Space Age".

As for Ballard's and Jünger's science fiction it shares the common trait of taking place on earth. "Earth is the only alien planet" Ballard once said and Jünger could have said the same. Except for the moon crater scene referred to at the beginning of *Heliopolis* (see Chapter 11 for details) all of Jünger's fantastic stories are firmly set on earth.

27. THE RADIO VALKYRIE

In one respect there's a remarkable shift from dream to reality in Jünger's war diary, beginning in *Gärter und Strassen* and being accomplished in *Strahlungen*. I mean: first Jünger gives us visions of a future war, of dreamt bombers flying over a burning world; Jünger had these dreams both before and during the war. Then he sees the same bomb machines in the real world, flying over his German house. To give some extra perspective to this fascinating phenomenon I'll start this chapter by looking at Evgenij Zamjatin, a Russian fantasist.

ZAMJATIN

Once upon a time I encountered something called science fiction. And it was in the shape of American SF, an American variety of this fantastic story. The yanks wrote efficiently, exuding ideas and opinions in the process, but the stylistic side of it often got neglected. Then it was interesting to meet older, European SF like Wells and Harbou and last but not least Evgenij Zamjatin. His 1921 novel *We* had a stylistic level out of this world with daring metaphors and a romantic feel to

it, at the same time dealing with an unromantic utopia reminiscent of the Bolshevik one just emerging. It's great to delve into Zamjatin's technotopia with its artefacts like the Ackumulator Tower, the Music Factory and the Rocket Integral, the latter about to integrate the infinite equation of the universe.

On the spaceship Integral there's a certain women signaler, the Radio Valkyrie. This is how she is described during a test run of the rocket, the narrator looking for her:

> Where is she? (...) She? Over there? In the radio compartment. – I went to the place in question. Having arrived I saw three people in there all wearing earphone helmets, looking as if they had wings on their heads. She seemed taller than usual, winged and shiny, soaring like an ancient valkyrie, seemingly filling the room with a light, fresh scent of ozone.

The Zamjatin world was a world rich in forms and shapes, images and pictures, as compared to the relative sterility of the environments of SF writers like Asimov or Heinlein, these writers tending to give you nothing but talking heads in nondescript rooms. Luckily the abundance of forms and shapes is there in the Jünger prose, in his depictions of dreams of the technological kind. Not only did he write science fiction (*Heliopolis*, *The Glass Bees*), he dreamt it. Machines and planes of an unseen kind soar through his dreams, like in the war diary of November 9th, 1942:

> This morning dreams of a future air raid. A machine construction, as big as the Eiffel tower, flew over a community in heavy gunfire. To the side of it flew a contraption looking like a radio mast and equipped with a platform. A man stood on the platform, now and then making some notes which he threw down in smoke cartridges.

Equal to Zamjatin or not, I would call these Jünger passages European SF with a surrealist tinge. And more of the same is given on July 3rd, 1939:

> In the dream I saw a division of fighter aircraft above a dead landscape. By the third salvo from an AA battery one of the planes fell burning to the ground. The drama took place in a totally mechanized world and I watched it with sardonic pleasure. The impression was deeper and more thorough than during the world war [the First World War, this being written in July 1939] since the procedure had become more rational. Nothing was episodic, the airplanes moving like electrically charged objects over a world which also was highly charged. It was the direct hit that brought about the lethal contact.

A truly prophetic dream this one since war would break out two months later.

CHOICE OF CAREER

These dreams of planes come to Jünger more or less involuntarily. It's a god-given metaphor. But he uses SF metaphors deliberately too, like when on 28th May, 1944, Jünger talks about flying in his spaceship when venturing into the virtual worlds of myth and religion, war and dreams. As for techno symbols we also have this one: "Choice of career: I'd like to be a star pilot." This is an efficient line in its context, coming as it does in April 1943 when no end of the war is in sight, no light at the end of the tunnel, however this selfsame metaphor becomes a light in the dark. Thus the power of the metaphor.

Now on with some more SF dreams, leading us eventually to a coda. Another SF style dream is this one of March 14th, 1944:

During the night dreams of worlds having made additional progress in the current direction: standing by the table in a giant airplane I was watching the pilot, starting the machine by another table. He was absent minded, sometimes risking to touch the mountain crests over which we flew. Only my complete equanimity, while speaking to him and watching him, avoided the catastrophe.

Now things start to get weird. The dreams come alive. From 1942 on the allies launch massive air raids against Germany. In his pre war dreams Jünger saw a burning world and now it's here in the airspace above his house. The wolf's at the door. The fantastic flight dreams slides over into reality. The same day as he noted the "Eiffel tower craft" dream, in November 1942, we get this directly after:

Tonight visit by the neighbours, however just as the conversation was starting the sirens went off in Hannover. Gathering in the basement room, with outdoor clothes and bags as in the cabin of a ship in distress. (...) Through the window I saw the red and colourful projectiles fired off towards the cloud-cover, also the flaming lustre of the downings and the glowing ruddiness from the fires in the city. At some instances the whole house was shaking in its foundations, despite the bombs falling far off from here. The presence of the children gives it all a closer, more distressing feeling.

The SF visionary had dreamt so intensively that the dreams had become real.

BOMBERS IN THE SKY

I just quoted a passage from a 1942 air raid. Horrible as they were these raids were a bit modest, the allies still only having bombers with two motors like Hampden and Wellington. By 1943 however the four engine bombers became operative (Lancaster, Halifax, Boeing B-17) and the war went into a new phase. It was total devastation from the air, whole air battles being fought in the skies. It was SF in real life in an unpleasant way. In Kirchhorst, April 7th 1944, Jünger and his son Alexander see a B-17 or a B-24 (the models aren't named but its by daytime and the Americans flew by day) being downed by AA:

> The machine lost height and made a turn over us while three parachutes were released from it. Now, being pilotless, describing a grand spiral it rapidly grew bigger. We thought the machine was going to crash in the vicinity of our house when it slid away towards the Lohne forest where, immediately after its disappearance, a dark, coppery sea of fire cascaded up, soon to transform into a smokescreen. Who ever in this quiet village could have imagined such a drama? After the famous emptiness on the battlefield we are now entering a war theatre with actions visible far and wide, the air battles being observed by hundreds of thousands, maybe millions.

November 26th of the same year Jünger sees new bomb raids, new armadas in the sky, new downings, the air being full of fragment and shrapnel. Reflecting over the nature of the vision he notes how it "upsets the reason". It's like a dream – like dreams he has already had, although he himself doesn't make that conjecture, not explicitly.

Depictions of the horrors of war become the most effective when made from aside, indirectly so to speak. I for one find this one rather unsettling, giving you hints, giving you trivial details adding up to a vision of a dark time in the history of mankind. It's about Jünger

listening to the radio during an air raid, a night raid with his family placed in the shelter while as for himself...

(...) I now and then go inside to see if everything is in order. How curious to see how the demonic forces slowly eat away the genius of the house, undermining its stability. I feel like making my way through the cabins of a ship, above all when I happen to see the shining scale of the radio which except from the glowing lustre of the stoves is the only light visible in the rigorously darkened rooms. The sexless voice of a female announcer informs about the movement of the squadrons until the moment when they "fly in over the city and bombing is immediately at hand". [Kirchhorst, November 4th, 1944]

And there – I figure – we have her, the complete Radio Valkyrie whom Zamjatin saw in a vision: cool and correct, divulging cainitic information to the listeners, exuding "a light, fresh scent of ozone..."

28. DER ARBEITER – SF NOVEL IN DISGUISE

Jünger's essay *Der Arbeiter* lives in a grey area between being a social science treatise, a warning, a prophecy – and a novel. Now, it isn't in any way a story or a narrative, but it's open for speculation how the text would have fared had it been conceived as fiction instead of, as now, a dissertation. What form of text is the most efficient when dealing with matters like these, controversial things like industrialisation and technological mobilization? I'd say that Jünger, when choosing his seemingly objective stance as essay writer, at the same time seems to place himself at the wheel of the modernist steamroller he's writing about. Had he written a novel he would have been freer.

CHARACTERIZATION

The Jünger essay *Der Arbeiter* – why didn't he make a novel of it?

Given the theme he should have taken greater liberties, inventing a plot and characters and having them act out The Worker Drama on a grand scale. How about an SF story with the Modern Titan,

the worker, homo faber, as the main protagonist, with lots of milieu, mimesis and characterization of the men and machines, the lands and environments where it all takes place. A symbolic vision living its own life, thus being more beyond criticism than a formal treatise tends to be. As it is we are given a lot of visions and symbols but not enough. The chosen form – the essay – offers the possibility of lecturing, of putting things to order, of commanding this complex subject, making it seem plausible and feasible from some angles and from some other angles not. I here think about the ideas of a ruling elite, of armies of workers and work as war, these controversial ideas having been better suited for a novel where the writer could have exposed them and shown them for what they were instead of making it all seem practical and an optimal way of ordering society as it is.

In this matter I agree with Thomas Nevin. In *Ernst Jünger And Germany – Into The Abyss* (1997) he notes that Jüngers *Heliopolis* and *The Glass Bees* being novels have become timeless, independent of the historical contexts that engendered them. But *Der Arbeiter*, being an essay with factual, IRL leanings, has been stuck in the "controversial" file. That's the crux.

But someone might say that Jünger in those days didn't write novels. He wrote real life monographs on war and exotic travels, and essays on diverse subjects. Then I say, true, but he did write the short novel *Sturm* in 1923. And in *The Adventurous Heart* (first version, 1928) he had some short stories. So he could write fiction. And – as intimated – if writing *Der Arbeiter* as a novel it would have reached another level of artistry, maybe having it become another *Brave New World*, *We* or *Kallocain*.

MAGIC ZERO POINT

Now of course there's a time for everything. There's a time for writing essays, and there's a time for writing novels. I don't blame Jünger for having made *Der Arbeiter* into what it is. I'm just speculating on the nature of texts, on the nature of textual forms.

So then, Jünger had a feeling for images, for symbols and visions. You find them in all his works and you find them in *Der Arbeiter*. So what do we find in this respect in the essay at hand, what are the novelist elements of it?

To begin with we have the plot of a development going towards a magic zero point, a defining moment, a crisis spelling the end of the archaic era: away with castles and churches, away with wells in the squares and the pétit bourgeois lifestyle, all giving place to a heroic style overwhelming in its proportions. Skyscrapers is one way, the vertical way to build; another is the horisontally outstretched way, the tendency to cover whole landscapes with industries, store houses, shopping malls and offices. Everything thus becomes, as Jünger says, a landscape of factories, a Werkstattlandschaft. And for sure we can see them realized today in and around every major city, and in giant scale in mega cities like Tokyo-Nagasaki, Ruhr-Benelux-Northern France and the New York-Washington area, to mention but a few of these urban creations stretching for miles and miles with almost no greenery in between.

In the Jüngerian Worker's world you work, not as a slave but as a duty fulfilled, dedicated and heroically as during a pitched battle. In the obedience there's a freedom. Leaders of it all is a cadre of rock-hard individuals, commanders of the working armies. No single dictator exists but truly this order of warrior-engineers, cold men who know how to steer and govern vessels, factories and armadas of machines.

Its about dedication and duty, working and conquering, but there's no room for joy. No, here "even the coitus has been reduced to a

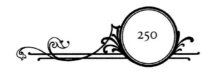

working process..." The sexes themselves are transformed into "the third sex".

How fascinating this would be in a SF context. A cosy nightmare like Zamjatin's *We* or Huxley's *Brave New World*. Zamjatin showed the way with his Chief Engineer, the hero of his novel, the true Worker come real on the pages of a novel.

Zamjatin did it, reaching deathlessness by envisioning a grand if chilling future. Jünger then, the Jünger who never wrote this Worker novel – he fared as good since he had more strings to his bow, moving away from the cainitic landscapes of the Worker and eventually settling on The Mountain of Flowers and Fruits, like some latter day Wu Ch'eng-en. That is to say, he left the stale, sterile Worker's world and went up *On the Marble Cliffs*. More on that in Chapter 10.

That said there still is a time for everything. There's a time for studying flowers and there's a time for organizing industrial armies. At least artistically the authoritarian, steely visions of Boye, von Harbou, Zamjatin and Huxley will never die and they had a brother in spirit in Jünger.

29. FUN

The words "fun" and "Ernst Jünger" doesn't easily come together. He wasn't a clown, you seldom laugh when you read his books, but he can give you smiles. He had a sense of humour – a dry, stiff upper lip kind of humour. It's all there, mostly in the diaries.

THE MARK OF EXCELLENCE OF AN AUTHOR

Kann Ernst Jünger auch mal lustig sein? Nein, Jünger ist immer Ernst.

This untranslatable line is given by Rossnagel in his compendium. But of course Jünger could be funny. His œuvre has some humorous passages, if you just give yourself time in finding them. Generally I'd say that without being ha ha-funny all the time, having humour is the mark of excellence of an author. Simply writing decent and profound

things tends to get a little tedious. In every deck of cards there's got to be a Joker, and in every great authorship there should be something to smile at. And we find this in Jünger's works.

For example, this episode in the late diary is rather heartwartming and fun. Jünger, once on his way to visit Mitterand in France, noticed that he had forgotten his passport. Luckily in his pocket he had an envelope with a stamp depicting Jünger himself, Jünger intending to show this to the President as a novelty. So Jünger showed the envelope at the customs, the officers seeing the stamp and acknowledging that he was indeed the famous author. No passport needed. [Wilflingen, April 5th, 1993]

Another elegantly funny episode in the late diary [Düsseldorf, December 9th, 1981] is this anecdote. When France had fallen Hitler once visited Paris incognito, an early morning this June, 1940. This is a historical fact, Hitler among others being accompanied by Arno Breker who was the one who told it to Jünger. Hitler for example wants to see the Paris Opera and on the way they meet a paper salesman approaching the car. But he runs away scared when he recognizes Hitler. Later on they pass by Les Halles where a market-woman recognizes Hitler. Unlike the paper salesman she keeps her calm, simply exclaiming: Voilà le bel Adolphe!

This could be seen as an example of "the voice of the people".

SELF IRONY

With the years Jünger developed a mild sense of self irony. When hearing that an American collector wanted to buy his Second World War uniform he asked himself why, does the buyer want to start a horror cabinet...? [late diary]

Another one in the same vein. From the war when the allies were bombing Germany, we have this dialogue on the home front:

A talk by the fence: – Me: "It's lively in the air today." The neighbour: – "Yes, they say that Osnabrück and Chemnitz have been ruined." But I only meant the mosquitoes swarming for the first time this year. [Kirchhorst, February 16th, 1945]

The following is not a self irony but ironical nonetheless. When the Americans invaded Germany this was, among other things, noted:

A worker passing by had his cycle stolen from him by some stray Poles, this having become the norm. An American patrol interceded and gave him back his property. The man said thank you, saying farewell with a "Heil Hitler" as he had been taught. Then he got beaten up and they once again took his bike from him. [Kirchhorst, April 15th, 1945]

GOEBBELS ANECDOTE

I find these lines starring Joseph Goebbels rather funny.

In May 1945, Jünger sits at home summing up the Nazi epoch in his diary. He remembers it all, among other things how the Nazis came to power. Jünger did meet the Berlin Gauleiter Dr. Goebbels now and then before 1933, visiting his home at parties and the like. They used to debate politics, dissenting on this and that. Then:

I met the Doctor once more, by this time he was a minister. It was at the premier of Johst's play "Schlageter" who served as the debut of the new regime in high society. "Now what do you say?" were his last words to me, a question – would I be able to answer it today? You always tend to answer too early.

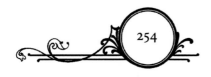

254

I find this comment hilarious, very subtle and elegant. Jünger knows that he has triumphed over the Nazi's but he sort of gives it the benefit of his doubt.

JOKES ON JÜNGER

I started this chapter with an untranslatable Jünger joke out of Rossnagel's anthology. As a conclusion I give you three additional ones:

Letztes Jahr sagte Heinz Rühmann zu Ernst Jünger: "Ich bin Rühmann, ich bin 93." Dann antwortete der Schriftsteller: "Ich bin Jünger, ich bin älter."

Was ist der Unterschied zwischen Jesus und Wilflingen? Jesus hatte zwölf Jünger, Wilflingen nur einen.

Welche Frage hat Helmuth Kohl dem französischen Staatspräsident Francois Mitterand in Wilflingen gestellt? Ist das dein Ernst? Oder ist das meiner?

The author of these jokes is one Olivier Schmitt.

30. OPTIMISM

There is a discrete sense of optimism throughout Jünger's Second World War diary. There's darkness and despair, true, but through it all there's a guiding light of what the Germans call Zuversicht. The word is hard to translate, conveying a feeling in the area between enthusiasm, optimism, expectation and positivism. "Zu" means "to" and "ver" is like "vor" that is, "for". And "Sicht" means "what you see", the word Zuversicht thus bordering on the English concept "to foresee" and then on to what you forefeel, presciently know and have a hunch about. The following is what I've found in the Jünger diary that present the reader with a dubious, uncertain and yet hopeful feeling: a light in the dark so to speak.

1939

The first part of Jünger WWII diary is *Gärter und Strassen*, beginning in the spring of 1939. The atmosphere is if not hopeful and cheery then at least not far from it. It's almost blasphemous to read a 1939 narrative so biased. But the under-text, with the reader knowing

that Jünger is who he is – among other things, not a Nazi – carries it through into "living literature" and not simply "a relict of the Third Reich".

There's a common, pétite bourgeois enjoyment of everyday life with a Jünger reading, writing and poking about in his garden:

> In the afternoon been doing the garden, sowing radishes and sweet cicely. Been reading Thornton Wilder's *The Bridge of San Luis Rey*. [Kirchhorst, April 4th, 1939]

Some months later he is visited by a reader, an unnamed corporal serving in Braunschweig, this man however seeming to suffer quietly. And this is a symptom of the anguished world situation.

But Jünger seems debonair. He gives the impression of well-being and ease, here and in the late diary as well as in *Storm of Steel*. In the latter he says somewhere: I knew that it would all work out for the better. That's divine grace if you're asking me.

He may of course have days of unease. But the main chord is an atmosphere free from angst, from the constantly grinding fear which Kierkegaard spoke about and which Heidegger construed into a whole ontological category. To me that category could be described as darkness: the presence of the dark, real or imagined, makes you constantly scared.

But in Jünger's world there's an unmistakable light, shining from within his being. Again: "I'm Innern ist's getan" ("it's decided within"), as the final words of the WWII diary says "Jahre der Okkupation" (see Chapter 14).

Another example of the quiet joy of Jünger's existence is this, about a visit to the neighbouring town of Burgdorf:

> This afternoon in Burgdorf which I always like to visit. The town is characterized by an indestructible dryness whose substance seems to withstand all the illusions of history. And for that matter there's

no sign of higher culture. When seeing the old houses I'm filled with the hope that mankind won't be obliterated just like that. However late I've clearly come to realize what persistence in life means." [May 26th, 1939]

The sight of an ordinary town making your heart warm: that's optimism.

Moving on to 1941 this is of course a hectic time, the battles having ground to a halt before Moscow and Jünger thinking about Poe's *The Maelstrom*. Even so there's a greater sense of hope with him:

Still how odd that I'm enlivened by optimism in the core of my being. Through the waves and clouds the guiding star shines. I don't mean that just for my own sake but generally. During these weeks we have passed the zero point. [Paris, November 18th, 1941]

The Paris of 1943 is a place of light and shade, this we learn from Jünger's diary. A ray of light shines on him May 7th, saying that he likes to take the Métro in the direction of Place d'Italie...

(...) since the trip often goes above ground. The house fronts, seemingly dead and fading in the sun, always make me glad; seeing them an old saurian bent is awakened within me. Behind the stillness of the sunlit walls I see people relaxing in their apartments, dreaming away or making love. You're riding along a gallery with secret still lives: tables on which stand misty glasses and cut up melons, a woman in a red gown opening a novel, a nude bearded man sitting comfortably in a recliner dreaming about sublime things, a couple sharing an orange after the amorous interlude.

Enjoying the moment, experiencing happiness here and now: that's grace. Like in Paris, June 11th, 1944, just after the Normandy invasion who brings uncertainty to Jünger's current existence:

Yet again been walking from Saint-Cloud by Route de l'Imperatrice to Versailles, even this time sunbathing in the small meadow between the chestnuts. During these walks I always think: It could be the last time.

That's how you always should think: this could be the last time...! Kon-fu-tse for one said: "A man should live so that he any moment is prepared to die." That's how you learn to appreciate life.

1944

The summer of 1944: the ground burning beneath the feet, the 20th July plot has come and gone and everything floats. But still we have the Jüngerian quiet sense of joy in his doings:

> The last luncheon with La Doctoresse. Home by Rue de Varenne where I as always was gladdened by the high gates typical of the old palaces of Faubourg Saint-Germain. They were built that way so that highly loaded hay carriages could enter the stables. A burst of rain made me visit the Musée Rodin, a place which normally doesn't attract me. [Paris, July 30th, 1944]

Of course Jünger has mentioned boredom, unease and exhaustion during his Paris war years, but the moments of well-being gives the whole narrative a peculiar "light and shade" character.

Even during the retreat from France there are moments of quiet:

> The Americans entering Paris. This afternoon again at Meurthe. The rounded hilltops and dark rocks of the Vosges have a calming effect, making you aware of the earthly stability. [Saint-Dié, August 23rd, 1944]

Jünger eventually comes home to Kirchhorst, living the civilian life in the uncertain post-1945 times. The war is lost and occupying troops and liberated prisoners of war are out and about, but on the whole life goes on. There's no panic attacks or desperation in Jünger's world. There are reports of violence and outrages, however, Jünger keeps his internal calm because this is the only way of creating order around you, as Pound said. The entry for May 12th, 1945: "The golden rain is blossoming, a fountain of earthly abundance." This is the picture worth a thousand words.

You might protest and say that any writer living in his own country house is happy. But that's not the case. There's a spontaneous sense of happiness in Jünger's existence. Spontaneous means "happening without external cause, self-generated". That's why it's so fascinating to follow this trait in his diaries. – The next alluring passage is from the winter of 1945, with troubles of heating the houses. But Jünger has his ways around that:

> Due to the cold you can hardly hold a book so during evenings I construct a sort of tent with two covers, leading an electric lamp into it. During such circumstances I once again with the greatest pleasure read *A Thousand and One Nights* in the Insel edition. What luck having saved this treasure of my library. These are exactly the times to enjoy that which Stendhal has said about it, repeated by Hugo von Hofmannsthal in his preface: "A book making a prison into the most lovely place to stay." [Kirchhorst, December 13th, 1945).

This is what I call talent for living.
Earlier this fateful 1945 Jünger by the way visited Burgdorf again, the nondescript burg that gave him such a warm feeling before the war. This, in my view, is an informal epilogue to the Second World War of Jünger, a simple picture rich in meaning, with all the pain and joy implicit:

This afternoon I was in Burgdorf to buy seeds. The roads are uncertain. I also visited the graveyard by the workhouse where roses and irises shone quietly on the graves. [Kirchhorst, May 26th, 1945]

We have seen how Jünger can feel a sense of grace, joy and optimism even in the presence of danger. I now feel like giving you a quote on this without comment, from the advance in 1940 when Jünger takes some time in between events to catch insects:

The paradoxical in such doings in the middle of catastrophes haven't escaped me, nevertheless I found it reassuring – here we have rich funds of stability. In addition I've learned since 1914 to work in the presence of danger. In our time you must have a salamandrian calm in order to reach your goal, this especially being the case during successive reading during good as well as bad times. If you daily lay down some bricks, after sixty or eighty years you can live in a castle. [Bourges, June 25th, 1940]

1945

Recently I've mentioned an event from the spring of 1945. And now let's look at April 14th, 1945, when the Americans have come and gone and peace is imminent. To be sure Jünger isn't overall elated by the prospects, bearing in mind that peace for him as a soldier means defeat, this one his second. No soldier wants to be defeated. However, at the same time he can appreciate the anarchic situation, making the pressure of civilization go away and seeing how...

(...) life becomes more opulent; supplies, even foodstuffs, arrive. Thus I was sitting in my room between all the carpets and books

like in a desert tent, being absorbed in my Brazilian notes. Beside me was a bottle of bourgogne that Löhning has deposited here. It would be a crime to let such a wine fall into the hands of the guys from Kentucky; my good friend will agree with me. In order not to get tired Perpetua or Louise now and then brought me extra strong coffee, the parting gift of the Americans.

This has essentially nothing to do with either editing a travel diary, having coffee brought or anything else; that would be a trivial, materialistic point of view. Of course it doesn't hurt to have the essentials and then some, but that's not the main issue here – for what it's all about is the ability of through it all feeling quiet, the ability to enjoy the moment as such. And for this a kind of willpower is needed: the will to peace. Wille zur Macht over the moment: thus you get the "impression of being on a constant vacation" that Jünger mentions in *Eumeswil*.

Before I move on into post war years I give you this timeless quote from Paris, comments unnecessary:

This afternoon street studies behind the Panthéon, on the Rue Mouffetard and adjoining back streets where something of the life in the overcrowded, pre revolutionary 18th century still lives on. There was even mint on sale, making me remember a wondrous night in the Arab quarters of Casablanca. Market places are always rich in revelations, like the land of childhood and dreams. Again I experienced a strong sense of joy and thankfulness that this city of cities has escaped unscathed from the catastrophe. How many wondrous things are we not to keep if it like an ark, loaded to the rail with old and precious cargo, reaches the harbour of peace after this deluge and is kept for centuries ahead. [Paris, August 7th, 1943]

LENNART SVENSSON

1994

After the war Jünger stopped keeping a diary. But in the 60's, with Klett Verlag having just published his collected works, he started anew, the new journal being called *Siebzig verweht* (*Beyond Seventy*). He had just turned 70. And by the reading of this late diary you're again struck by the existential joy gleaming forth here and there. It's an unmistakeable sub-theme of it all.

Now of course the old Jünger was something of a pessimist too, the late diary having its share of railings against the modern world and its faults. Nevertheless there are more positive tendencies too, Jünger in his individual life on the whole being rather contented. He travels the world, he reads interesting books, he even enjoys the odd documentary on that strange new medium, television.

So then, some pearls from this treasury in the vein of optimism and Zuversicht. For instance we have this dream of December 12th, 1994:

> This night on a hill planted with vine; the bushes replete with green grapes – and in between trees of medium height like date palms, the branches bowing down under the load of raspberries with a sign saying: "Picking allowed."

And Wilflingen, August 30th, 1970:

> In the garden where it had rained during the night, fog hanging in the bushes. Alone with the leaves, the flowers, the fruits...

Then we have the subtly joyous passage from Agadir, on his birthday on March 29th, 1974, while doing research for *Eumeswil*, a kind of summing up of his situation:

263

I'm 79 now, moreover full of ideas, even disturbing ones, generally in every moment my head is like an associating mill, finally optimist. Like the sculptor Marks, still older, said of himself: Kaum zu glauben, / Trägt noch Trauben. ["Would you believe it, still carrying grapes"]

Jünger himself admits that this Agadir visit was slightly euphoric (on board, April 8th, 1974): "Brisk walks in the morian landscape between the sea and the mountains with its plants and animals, by inner calm." And then he went home to write *Eumeswil*; a novel as fresh and vital as *On the Marble Cliffs* if not more so. He blossomed in old age like the painter Rubens.

31. ON WRITING

I n his diaries Jünger now and then mentions the craft of writing, what it's like to be an author and such. These passages are never self-conscious and esoteric, having instead an interest for a wider audience. Therefore this chapter.

IN BURGDORF

A good quote to start with could be this one. It's about how an author has certain difficulties in explaining his craft, what exactly he does during his workdays:

> This morning in Burgdorf, at the doctor. I get slightly embarrassed when questioned about my books. I guess it depends on that the nature of what I do is hard to convey in speech. Actually there's no point in me being an author – I could do the same but differently, for example by meditating. Books are the residual matter, the rest product of life. More than that there's a secret quality to it, akin to the erotic sphere: You love to show your kids but you don't want to

talk about details during the conception. [Kirchhorst, December 14th, 1944]

This was fairly modest: his books are merely rest products...! But that's how an author often sees his books since he seldom or never rereads them. Then, as for the problem of talking about your life as an author, you could say that an author when asked about his craft could "make up something" because that's what novelists do, don't they...? People don't want to hear that you half the time surf on the net or do the other thing. So make something up: I get my ideas from a brownie in the woods, he comes everyday at ten o'clock and leaves his notes in my drawer. Or whatever. To create is to play, that's not so hard to say. "Artistry is systematically regained childishness" as Baudelaire said. This the writer could say to enquiring people.

A fine quote on style is the following, from a conversation with a Frenchman:

> Léautaud hates images, comparisons, rewordings. An author should express what me means with the utmost precision and economy. He mustn't waste time perfecting rhythm and polishing. "J'aime plutôt une répétition qu'une préciosité." [untranslated in the original, the French meaning "I prefer a repetition before an artificiality".] If you want to say that it rains, then write: "It rains." When Paulhan objected that this could be submitted to an office clerk to perform, he answered: "Alors, vivent les employés." ["Long live the crew."]

This is a good lesson in efficient prose, contrary to the elaborated style that Jünger himself sometimes had a predilection for, indulging in images, metaphors and spending time "perfecting rhythm and polishing". Now Jünger could write efficiently too, abstaining from elaborate passages (as in most of his war diaries). However, he did use to revise his published works several times, like *Storm of Steel* and *The*

Adventurous Heart, and his diaries went through a thorough editing process before being printed. And just because Jünger's stylistic ideal was somewhat different from the overt simplicity of Paul Léautaud it's generous of him to recapitulate the Frenchman's thoughts.

At the same time you can find other Jünger lines lauding simplicity. In the late diary of November 8th, 1982, he says that pedantry should be avoided, "fresh out of the pan is best". So then, no embellishing, no reworking...? But great artists have the right to contradict themselves: "I contradict myself? Well then, I contradict myself" as Walt Whitman said.

EXPENSIVE BOOK

When your books have been published they start to live a life of their own, like certain editions becoming rare and expensive. In January 1992 Jünger for example heard about a book of his having become overpriced, a certain edition of the travel book *San Pietro* being sold for a "fantasy price", Jünger commenting: "Even though I only played the role of Midas here it gladdens me."

An aspect of being a writer is the reception and the possible admiration of your work and your person. Jünger, saying that he doesn't want to be admired, prefers moderate, critical appreciation [Paris, July 18th, 1943]. To meet nothing but praise bores even the best of authors. And if everyone agrees with you, then you might start to doubt yourself (as Oscar Wilde said).

Now some words on inspiration, of people who have been inspired by Jünger's work. A certain artist once wrote Jünger saying that she hadn't read any of his works but she was still inspired by it. That's what comes form making yourself into a symbol, an archetype if you will, as Jünger has. A somewhat risqué method, even if it inspires people. Then we have a pupil in a more poetic vein, writing and saying: "I've

never seen your garden but I've felt the fragrance of it." [October 24th, 1982] Jünger's mentioning of his garden in his diary had thus borne virtual fruit. A fine picture of what it's like to be an author: to envision scenes and vistas and have the reader smell the scents of it.

LÉON BLOY

In the entry for Paris, May 4th, 1943 Jünger says this on the French writer Léon Bloy (1846-1917):

> Bloy is no classic but he will be. It takes a while for the works having the temporal disappear from them. They too have their purgatory. Then they grow above and beyond criticism.

This could be applied to Jünger himself. He has been criticized and lambasted, has been called controversial and dangerous, even today, at least in my home country Sweden. But the acclaim and recognition has always been there and this eventually seems to carry the day. The works of Jünger tend to discard their temporal qualities and become immortal, growing into classics. There's nothing stopping this, no matter how many brilliant intellectuals try to make him into the eternal bad guy (more on Jünger's role as an outsider in chapter 4).

The works of Jünger live and change character as time goes by. The people of the inter war years read *Storm of Steel* and *Der Arbeiter* differently than we do. And his less distinct, less clear-cut books like *The Adventurous Heart* and *Eumeswil* tend to get clearer over the passage of time. Jünger knew intuitively what he was after in those books and now the reading public seems to catch up. Jünger had an inkling of this phenomenon when he wrote that in his works "(...) there are passages that still aren't true, but a secret existence builds them up to reality." [Paris, April 11th, 1943]

THE READER

Above and beyond wanting to be famous and become a household name, writing is about communication. You write for yourself, for God – and for the reader, the one reader. "One reader counts for a thousand" Jünger says somewhere. This is truly wise. No need counting copies, never mind the prizes and ovations; having at least heard from one reader that this and that book really nailed it, really meant something – those moments in a writer's life are precious.

32. JÜNGER AS A POET

It isn't widely known that Jünger wrote poems. But he did. There are some surviving examples of his lyrical activity.

OUR LIFE

Jünger might have been the greatest German author since Goethe, but unlike the Weimar Apollo writing lyrics didn't come easy to him. Jünger's poems are few and far between. However, they exist. And his first ever published text is a fine example of verse.

In Schwilk's 1988 pictorial biography there's a facsimile of a poem Jünger wrote as a German Scout, a Vandervögel. Published in 1911 it's a vivid, enlivening survey of life as a wandering, camping and singing boy in this particular framework, die Vandervögel movement. I personally know my limitations so I won't even try to translate its rhymes and meter, hoping that a prose version is enough. First I give you the German original, *Unser Leben* (*Our Life*):

Noch eh' der erste Hahnenschrei verklungen,
erhebt der Vandervogel sich vom Stroh,
in seinen klaren Augen blitzt es froh,
denn heute wird gewandert und gesungen.

Wie flieht die Zeit beim Wandern und beim Schauen!
Am Bache wird ein warmes Mahl bereitet,
des Feuers Knistern mit Gesang begleitet.
Und weiter geht's durch Fluren und durch Auen.

Wenn dann die Sonne hinterm Berg verschwunden,
wenn dann die Müdigkeit ihn übermannt,
sein fröhlich Herz ist jedem ja bekannt,
ein schützend Obdach hat er bald gefunden.

So spart er für des Alltags Treiben
ein Füllhorn goldner Lieder auf,
die stets ihm in Erinnerung bleiben,
und schmücken seinen Lebenslauf.

What, then, do we actually read here? In English prose the first verse goes something like this: "Even before the first rooster call the scout arises from his night quarters, a fire lit in his eyes since now it's time for wandering and singing."

Verse two: "Time flies when you walk about, seeing the sights! By the brook a meal is cooked, by the fire we sing. And then ever onward through flowery lands."

Verse three: "In the setting sun, weary by the walk, the scout is glad to find shelter."

Verse four: "In his everyday life the Scout can gladden himself

271

with golden memories of hiking songs, melodies forever staying with him."

This poem of Jünger's was a fine examination work in the literary realm, a promise of things to come. Even if he did become a prose writer, not a lyrical poet.

ON KUBIN'S PICTURE MAN

Jünger was a friend of the painter Alfred Kubin (1877-1959), once visiting this Austrian in his medieval estate Zwickledt. That was in 1937. Kubin for his part drew the picture on the cover of *Myrdun* (1943), this image of a Nordic skogstroll, a forest dwelling ogre. Other than that Kubin was a modern artist with visions of decay and misery, of tormented people in the confusion of existence. This might not exactly seem to be in Jünger's taste, but it's true that he had an eye for modern art as well as for traditional art.

In Schwilk we find the only extant poem of the earlier times of Jünger's professional career. Jünger somewhere in his late diary said that he wrote a lot of expressionist poetry, eventually destroying all he could lay hands on. The surviving piece was quoted in a letter to Kubin in 1921. As for the style it's a bit pedantic, there's some lack of rhythm, but it's an honest piece. These are Jünger's impression of Kubin's picture "Der Mensch" ("Man"):

Zu Kubins Bild: Der Mensch

Traum, hindurchglüht, wird Vision, Krystall,
Urfrage Sein zu Wahnsinn, Katarakt:
aufrechter Mensch, geschleudert in das All,
Orkan im Haar, bleich, einsam, nackt.

Ausschnitt endloser Kurve dämmert Welt,
Absturz in Dunkel, transzendenter Schwung,
Aufschrei das Leben, jäh aus Nichts geschnellt,
ein Rampenlicht zu irrem Zirkussprung.

And how to translate this? I suggest this:

Translucent dream becoming vision, crystal,
the burning question of reality turning into a mad cataract;
man upright, thrown into the Cosmos,
hurricane hair, pale and desolate, naked.

Segment of an endless curve hiding the world,
going down into transcendent nothingness,
screaming for life, then projected out of the void,
limelight for a stupendous circus act.

SINAI

After this venture Jünger seems to have totally given up on his poetry, only writing prose for the rest of his career. But the trait lay dormant for in his late diary [Wilflingen, August 1st, 1991] we again find some traces of the lyrical poet and this with the untranslatable *Sinai*. I was on the brink of saying "unreadable" too but I won't. It's an experiment, trying to get the poetical value out of the words themselves, without metaphors and embellishments, almost like Pound and the imaginists but unlike them a bit lacking in rhythm and melody. Jünger said that it should be read out loud, declared like a mantra, not read quietly like ordinary poems.

And here it is. I won't translate it, only saying that "ich klopfe an" means "I'm knocking (on the door)", "Zwerge" means "dwarfs" and "Waage" "waves":

273

Sinai

Ich klopfe an.
Ich klopfe an.
Ich klopfe an.
Im Namen des Vaters,
des Sohnes,
des Heiligen Geistes
und der Erde.
Amen, Dank.

Zwerge, Zwerge, Zwerge.
Waage, Waage, Waage.
Sterne, Sterne, Sterne.
Waage, Waage, Waage.
Sinai.
Sonne, Sonne, Sonne.
Dank.

PROSE POETRY

As for Jünger and poetry there's more to be said. I mean, the man sometimes went to great lengths to "weave a necklace for Cleopatra" in his depictions of nature, insects, flowers and cityscapes, interiors and all. His novels and diaries are full of them. So I think I'll pick three examples. And to be honest they aren't all embellished and ornamented. Some are but not all. I begin with this exemplary piece from the outbreak of the Second World War: no rhetoric, no goody-good moralisms here, only the weight of the words depicting the mobilization town where the author happens to be at the time:

At ten I went to an appointment at the Schlossbrücke. The old moor town was in darkness and the people were moving about like wraiths in a minimum of light. The castle, steeped in a matt, blue light, rose like a palace in a fairy city. Like weightless dancers people drifted by on their bicycles in the dark. And now and then a carp splashed in the moat surrounding the castle park.[Celle, September 1st, 1939]

Talk about efficient prose. There's nothing to add about this style, it is simply right as someone said about the Icelandic sagas.

The following is also from the war, from the phoney war of the autumn 1939. The Germans are deployed facing the French but nothing happens. It's a grey area of peace and war, succinctly illustrated like this:

The French show themselves without being shot at by us, and vice versa. Between the concrete bunkers and the trenches the farmers are ploughing and gathering in turnips. On the way to Rastatt, just passing by my bunker, cars are racing by – maybe with businessmen or loving couples. This existence of zones now touching, now intermingling with each other remind you of images in a dream and is typical for our world, whose dangerous tendencies are rather amplified by this. The scenes and their atmospheres blend with each other as in a movie. [Greffern, November 15th, 1939]

In short: these are discreet examples of good prose: simple but not facile. You don't have to "weave a necklace for Cleopatra". However, Jünger is doing that also sometimes. We'll make do with one last example, still from his diaries. (If I sought out the novels for juicy quotes I'd never be finished. Then again, I have quoted from the novels elsewhere in this study, like when I treated *Heliopolis* in Chapter 11.) This view from the World War Two diary is almost surreal, like a drug dream:

The half moon was surrounded by a pale gloden aura, this in its turn lined by a circle in the colour of the milk opal. And in between, like a second skin, a picrinous brown circle. The village and the field were also steeped in the colours of the moon palette. To realize what here slumbers in its opulence you have to have the eyes of an oleander sphinx-moth. The faint vibrations in these creatures suggest a world of exquisite pleasures, with colours, smells and sounds our senses can't reach. Inachis ios and catocalas swarm over the violet beds which they moisten with nectar; the dream rules the world. [Kirchhorst, June 18th, 1945].

CODA

As a serious writer you always hear: don't use Wikipedia...! Wikipedia is unreliable...! And I more or less agree with that. I don't use this online encyclopaedia as a main source in my writings, only having it for checking dates and such. The sources of this biography have been other biographical books and studies and then of course Jünger's own works.

That said, in uncontroversial subjects Wikipedia is fairly reliable. And when reading the English Wikipedia entry "Ernst Jünger" I was reminded of this and that, of info on him and his life that I can corroborate from other sources. And no, I won't mention those corroborative sources. I just know that these facts happen to be true. And I got them from Wikipedia. So this is a kind of anecdotal survey of certain things worth mentioning (if you want to check the facts I direct you to the entry which overall is correctly annotated). Among other things the entry says that Jünger's second son Alexander committed suicide in 1993. I noted the same thing in chapter 1 and now I have it confirmed; however, this death is still somewhat shrouded in mystery.

In the Ernst Jünger Wikipedia entry it then says that "[i]n Germany, an important entomological prize is named after him: the

Ernst-Jünger-Preis für Entomologie". That would be something to strive for, wouldn't it? If you were an entomologist, that is. In the late diary Jünger reprinted the speech he held for each recipient of the prize. Wikipedia:

> In 1985, to mark Jünger's 90th birthday, the German state of Baden-Württemberg established Ernst Jünger Prize in Entomology. It is given every three years for outstanding work in the field of entomology.

In 1965 Jünger had his collected works published, as I said in chapter 1, and Wikipedia tells us that only three other German authors have enjoyed such an event in their lifetimes: Goethe, Klopstock and Wieland. The dictionary goes on to say:

> He [Jünger] remained highly controversial, though, in the eyes of the German Marxist Left, both for his past, and his ongoing role as conservative philosopher and icon. When German Communists threatened his safety in 1945, Bertold Brecht instructed them to "Leave Jünger alone."

This Brecht dictum is interesting, somewhat echoing Hitler who back in the day reigned in Goebbels when the minister of culture wanted to prosecute Jünger for atavistic tendencies.

Wikipedia then names Jünger as a forerunner of magical realism. I usually don't deliberate on genre labels and what they intrinsically mean, but "magical realism" actually rings true to me in describing the Jünger literary attitude: the dreams, the futuristic novels, the metaphysical trait. Jünger along with Borges and maybe such names as Phil Dick and Jim Ballard (authors sometimes mentioned as magical realists) indeed have a certain real-unreal atmosphere in their works. They are not merely depicting everyday reality like Heinlein, le Guin and other notable SF authors tend to do, even when writing

about other worlds. So if you really need to put a label on Jünger's work then "magical realism" says a lot. However, putting labels on great authors is mostly a useless and fruitless activity. Jünger was a genre of his own.

Wikipedia finally gives this criticism, for what it's worth, being a verdict without annotation but still a valid observation: "there is an excess of emotional control and precision in his writing". True that: Jünger executes control in every moment, making his writing a bit lacking in resilience. The Jünger style is something of its own, "a hard, lucid prose" as Chatwin said, a prose that it takes a while to get used to.

On the Wikipedia site about Ernst Jünger it says: "Ernst Jünger appears as a character in the 1974 French film "Black Thursday"". That's interesting and maybe worth checking up. Other than that I guess it would be hard for an actor to interpret a character like Jünger on the silver screen. A correct, stiff upper lipped officer with a predilection for beetles and esotericism, how on earth do you make that seem real...? So attempts to characterize Jünger on the screen should best be left alone. Then again, if you'd like to have your private Jünger film festival I'd suggest these films, which don't feature Jünger but their style and content are vaguely Jüngerian:

- "The Blue Max" (John Guillermin 1966), about a German fighter pilot in World War One and his heroic career. Jünger for his part never flew but as I said in chapter 1 he attended a course in flying in the 30s. And as a soldier he had an impulsive, cavalier trait that should have translated well into the role of a fighter pilot. And of course he was also initiated into the order which is the title of the film, "Blue Max", i.e. Pour le Mérite.
- "Rome, Open City" (Roberto Rosselini 1945), a drama about the Nazi occupation of Rome, echoing that of contemporary Paris where Jünger was part of the Wehrmacht occupation army. This is a realistic piece about hostages, patrols and searches, about civilians being caught in the power struggle

between Germans and the resistance, not an uplifting film in itself but well played and directed and catching the mood of the times.

- "Valkyrie" (Bryan Singer, 2008), about the 20th July plot that Jünger didn't participate in but in which he was, as I said in chapter 1, the spiritual center, at least of the Paris leg of the conspiracy. The Paris part of the plot isn't depicted here, the film instead focusing on the Kreisauer and Marburg circles (and on the events in the Führer HQ and Berlin on July 20th), but the film is well crafted and like the two above mentioned pictures catching the mood of the era, without taking resort to cliches. The hero of "Valkyrie", Stauffenberg, was a complex man and overall – if Hans Bernd Gisevius is to be believed – a stern military man bent on continuing the war against Russia at all costs. So Stauffenberg was no saint, in contrast to what the post war interpretation of him tends to be. However, the film in question is rather hands-on and doesn't make him into more than he was. Tom Cruise's interpretation of Stauffenberg is as good as you can demand and it could give Jünger fans a hint of German army life in those days, and of the lives of German conservatives caught up in the struggle between loyalty to Germany and opposition to the nihilism of the Nazi regime.

When it comes to actual Jünger movies I now recall that there is one good example, a Swedish documentary. It's called "102 Years in the Heart of Europe – A portrait of Ernst Jünger" (1998). It's a hands-on factual film with an interview with Jünger, stills etc., in all a fine effort doing him justice.

The battle rages on, pro or contra Jünger. But again I quote Wilde: "Diversity of opinion about a work of art shows that the work is new, complex, and vital." So Jünger's work will live on. I gather that the interest in him is steadily growing, in Germany and Sweden as well as in the English speaking world.

Oscar Wilde: as I said in chapter 1 Jünger read this Irishman during the First World War along with Laurence Sterne's *Tristram Shandy*. And focusing on English and American writers dear to Jünger, what else is there? At least I can mention one American, Edgar Allan Poe, being mentioned by Jünger now and then in both the war diary and the late diary. For example the short story "The Maelstrom" Jünger held as a masterpiece, this narrative of a natural phenomenon on the Norwegian coast where water is sucked into a seeming abyss. Poe dramatized the occurrence well, Jünger seeing it as a symbol of approaching dangerous times and living through them. One of Poe's protagonists actually makes it through while his friend is lost in the vortex. In Chapter 30 I mentioned that Jünger came to think about "The Maelstrom" in late 1941, the defeat before the gates of Moscow coming to him like a similar "nexus of the crisis". When it's over the pressure eases, so to speak, like in the conclusion of Poe's story.

Jünger somewhere in the late diary mentions a chance passage from another Poe story, "Thou Art the Man". The story has a somewhat intricate plot about a man falsely accused of murder. Jünger cites the end of the story as exemplary, of how it's possible to go on with your life after having been in dire straits. Poe:

> Mr. Pennifeather was released upon the spot, inherited the fortune of his uncle, profited by the lessons of experience, turned over a new leaf, and led happily ever afterward a new life.

I personally used to see this as merely a way of putting a happy end to it, of patching up a complex story, but maybe there's more to it, maybe this Poe passage is profound – a symbol of the light and shade we experience in our lives. Jünger in quoting lines like this helps us see things differently.

This chapter is labeled "coda". Coda means "ending part of a piece of music or a work of literature", "something that ends and completes something", "something that serves to round out, conclude, or

summarize". I first thought of this chapter as one where I could say whatever I wanted that didn't fit in with the other chapters, like the dissertations on the Anglo-American angle and films above. Well, now I've done that. And so, more in line with the essence of a coda – if I should sum up Jünger in a few words, deliver a conclusion of his oeuvre or repeat the most important lesson he has given me, what would that be?

Maybe this: "Everything is decided within".

In this book I've often returned to this line, occurring in itself in the last paragraph of *Jahre der Okkupation*. In German this sentence runs: Im Innern ist's getan. As I've already said it's from Goethe and originally to be found in *Wilhelm Tischbeins Idyllen*.

So then: you're governed by your inner mind. What does this mean? Among other things it means that your personality has to evolve internally, in your inner mind, your soul or spirit or whatever you choose to call it, and in time this lessons can be practiced and "realized" (made real) in the outer world. This is elaborated by Jünger now and then, for example when he in Bourges, June 23rd, 1940 notes that in the First World War he got the Blue Max for having been in the combat zone for four years, now he gets the venerable Iron Cross for a dangerous but brief encounter:

> Herakleitos is right: no one goes down in the same river twice. The mysterious in such a transformation is that it corresponds to changes within ourselves – we are the creators of our world and what we experience doesn't come randomly. The objects are selected and affected by our state of mind: the world is such as we are. Each one of us then is capable of changing the world – that's the enormous significance given to each one of us. Therefore it's so important that we work on ourselves.

This is a rather unique wisdom, coming as it does from a writer of the 20th century, otherwise an era steeped in nihilism and materialism.

As for summarizing Jünger's creed I also have this. When reading Rudolf Steiner's *Atlantis and Lemuria* (1904) online the other day I stumbled upon an enlightening passage. It's about the mythical island of Atlantis and how Steiner envisioned life in that realm. The Atlanteans thought in images and symbols, not in ideas:

> The man of the present day has the advantage over the Atlantean of possessing a logical understanding and an aptitude for combination; but on the other hand his memory power has waned. We now think in ideas, the Atlantean thought in pictures; and when a picture rose in his mind he remembered many other similar pictures which he had formerly seen, and then formed his judgment accordingly. Consequently all education then was quite different from that of later times. It was not intended to provide the child with rules or to sharpen his wits. Rather was life presented to him in comprehensive pictures, so that subsequently he could call to remembrance as much as possible, when dealing with this or that circumstance.

And this reminds me of Jünger, a man who thought in symbols, not in abstract ideas. On a deeper level, beyond the structure of ordinary language, his books are written in hieroglyphics. For example, as Gisbert Kranz has noted, the titles of Jünger's books are symbolic, suggesting tangible images (*Heliopolis, Storm of Steel, The Worker, The Forest Passage, The Glass Bees*). They are not abstractions or vague concepts. Moreover, in his diary Jünger was often contented with having the image speak for itself, not feeling the need to explain his thoughts. Like in this picture of a German town when World War Two is about to break out (Germany had attacked Poland this day and Britain and France declared war two days later):

> At ten I went to an appointment at the Schlossbrücke. The old moor town was in darkness and the people were moving about

like wraiths in a minimum of light. The castle, steeped in a matt, blue light, rose like a palace in a fairy city. Like weightless dancers people drifted by on their bicycles in the dark. And now and then a carp splashed in the moat surrounding the castle park. [Celle, September 1st, 1939]

No reflections, no thoughts, no complaints, even though he must have had some at the time. He had feelings, that I surmise...! But he embodies them all in a concrete picture. This is what makes the Jünger style so resilient and durable. It's like the ideal of American poet William Carlos Williams: "Say it! No ideas but in things." This is modern hieroglyphics in nuce.

BIBLIOGRAPHY

JÜNGER IN ENGLISH
(Selected bibliography, with the site "Ernst Jünger in Cyberspace" as the main source.)

Storm of Steel (*In Stahlgewittern,* Chatto & Windus, London, 1929)
Copse 125 (*Das Wäldchen 125,* Chatto & Windus, London, 1930)
On the Marble Cliffs (*Auf den Marmorklippen,* John Leman, London, 1947)
The Peace (*Der Friede,* Henry Regnery Company, Hinsdale, IL, 1948)
African Diversions (*Afrikanische Spiele,* John Lehmann, London, 1954)
The Glass Bees (*Gläserne Bienen,* Noonday Press, New York, 1960)
A Dangerous Encounter (*Eine gefährliche Begegnung,* Marsilio Publishers, 1993)
Total Mobilization (*Die Totale Mobilmachung,* 1993)
Eumeswil (*Eumeswil,* Marsilio Publishers, 1994)
The Adventurous Heart (*Das Abenteuerliche Herz,* Telos Press, New York, 2012)
The Forest Passage (*Der Waldgang,* Telos Press, New York, 2013)

DIVERSE STUDIES

Bideau, Paul-Henri, *Goethe* (Que sais-je), P.U.F., 1984
Evola, Julius, *Metaphysics of War,* Arktos, London, 2011
Evola, Julius, *Ride the Tiger,* Inner Traditions, Rochester, 2003 (originally 1961)
Fischer, Hugo, *Die Aktualität Plotins – Über die Konvergenz von Wissenschaft und Metaphysik,* C. H. Beck, München, 1956
Kiesel, Helmuth, *Ernst Jünger: Die Biographie,* Siedler Verlag, München, 2007

ERNST JÜNGER – A PORTRAIT

Kranz, Gisbert, *Ernst Jüngers symbolische Weltschau*, Pädagogische Verlag Schwann, Hamburg, 1968
Lundstedt, Göran, *Makten och minne*t, Symposion, Stehag, 1990
Nevin, Thomas, *Ernst Jünger And Germany – Into The Abyss, 1914-1945,* Constable & Co, London, 1997
Neaman, Elliot Y., *A Dubious Past – Ernst Jünger And The Politics of Literature After Nazism*, University of California Press, Los Angeles, 1999
Paetel, Karl O., *Ernst Jünger in Selbstzeugnissen und Bilddokumenten*, Rowohlt Verlag, Hamburg, 1962
Rossnagel, Alois and Lupard, Moritz (editors): *Von null auf hundert: einhundert Jahre Jünger: ein Erinnerungsbuch*, Schwäbisches Verlags-Gesellschaft, Stuttgart, 1995
Schwilk, Heimo, *Ernst Jünger – Leben und Werk in Bildern und Texten*, Klett-Cotta, Stuttgart, 1988
Schwilk, Heimo, *Ernst Jünger: Ein Jahrhundertleben*, Klett-Cotta, Stuttgart, 2007
Wolf, Uwe in Schwilk, Heimo och Figal, Günther (editors), *Magie der Heiterkeit: Ernst Jünger zum Hundertsten: "Dichten, danken, beten"*, Klett-Cotta, Stuttgart, 1995

MAGAZINE ARTICLES

Hood, Stuart, *On Meeting and Translating Ernst Jünger*, Ernst Jünger in Cyberspace/ Essays, 1945
Chatwin, Bruce, *An Aesthete of War,* New York Review of Books, 5/1981

JÜNGER IN GERMAN

Hereby a list over all the books Jünger published, based on a list given by Thomas Nevin.

In Stahlgewittern: Aus dem Tagebuch eines Stosstruppführers, Robert Meier, Leisning, 1920 [the first edition the same year was on Jünger's own imprint Gibraltar]
Der Kampf als inneres Erlebnis, Mittler, Berlin, 1922
Das Wäldchen 125: Eine Chronik aus den Grabenkämpfen, 1918. Mittler, Berlin, 1925
Feuer und Blut: Ein kleiner Ausschnitt aus einer grossen Schlacht, Stalhelm Verlag, Magdeburg, 1925
Das abenteuerliche Herz: Aufzeichnungen bei Tag und Nacht, Frundsberg, Berlin, 1929
Die totale Mobilmachung, Verlag für Zeitkritik, Berlin, 1931
Der Arbeiter: Herrschaft und Gestalt, Hanseatische Verlagsanstalt, Berlin, 1932
Blätter und Steine, Hanseatische Verlagsanstalt, Hamburg, 1934

LENNART SVENSSON

Afrikanische Spiele, Hanseatische Verlagsanstalt, Hamburg, 1936
Das abenteuerliche Herz: Figuren und Capriccios, Hanseatische Verlagsanstalt, Hamburg, 1938
Auf den Marmorklippen, Hanseatische Verlagsanstalt, Hamburg, 1938
Gärten und Strassen, Mittler, Berlin, 1942
Myrdun. Briefe aus Norwegen, Feldausgabe, Oslo, 1943
Der Friede: Ein Wort an die Jugend Europas und an die Jugend der Welt, Hanseatische Verlagsanstalt, Hamburg, 1945
Sprache und Körperbau, Verlag der Arche, Zürich, 1947
Atlantische Fahrt, Verlag der Arche, Zürich, 1947
Myrdun: Briefe aus Norwegen, Verlag der Arche, Zürich, 1948
Ein Inselfrühling, Verlag der Arche, Zürich, 1948
Heliopolis: Ruckblick auf eine Stadt, Heliopolis Verlag, Tübingen, 1949
Strahlungen, Heliopolis Verlag, Tübingen, 1949
Über die Linie, Klostermann, Frankfurt, 1950
Der Waldgang, Klostermann, Frankfurt, 1951
Der Gordische Knoten, Klostermann, Frankfurt, 1953
Das Sanduhrbuch, Klostermann, Frankfurt, 1954
Am Sarazenenturm, Klostermann, Frankfurt, 1955
Rivarol, Klostermann, Frankfurt, 1956
Gläserne Bienen, Klett, Stuttgart, 1957
Jahre der Okkupation, Klett, Stuttgart, 1958
An der Zeitmauer, Klett, Stuttgart, 1959
Der Weltstaat: Organismus und Organisation, Klett, Stuttgart, 1960
Sgraffiti, Klett, Stuttgart, 1960
Besuch auf Godenholm, Klostermann, Frankfurt, 1962
Sturm, Georg Rentsch Sons, Olten, 1963
Typus, Name, Gestalt, Klett, Stuttgart, 1963
Geheimnisse der Sprache, Klostermann, Frankfurt, 1963
Grenzgänge: Essays, Reden, Träume, Klett, Stuttgart, 1966
Subtile Jagden, Klett, Stuttgart, 1967
Ad hoc, Klett, Stuttgart, 1970
Annäherungen: Drogen und Rausch, Klett, Stuttgart, 1970
Sinn und Bedeutung: ein Figurenspiel, Klett, Stuttgart, 1971
Philemon und Baukis: Der Tod in der mytischen und in der technischen Welt, Klett, Stuttgart, 1972
Die Zwille, Klett, Stuttgart, 1973
Zahlen und Götter, Klett, Stuttgart, 1974
Eumeswil, Klett, Stuttgart, 1977

Siebzig verweht I, Klett-Cotta, Stuttgart, 1980
Siebzig verweht II, Klett-Cotta, Stuttgart, 1981
Maxima-Minima: Adnoten zum "Arbeiter", Klett-Cotta, Stuttgart, 1983
Aladins Problem, Klett-Cotta, Stuttgart, 1983
Eine gefährliche Begegnung, Klett-Cotta, Stuttgart, 1983
Autor und Autorschaft, Klett-Cotta, Stuttgart, 1984
Zwei Mal Halley, Klett-Cotta, Stuttgart,1987
Die Schere, Klett-Cotta, Stuttgart, 1990
Siebzig verweht III, Klett-Cotta, Stuttgart, 1993
Siebzig verweht IV, Klett-Cotta, Stuttgart, 1995
Siebzig verweht V, Klett-Cotta, Stuttgart, 1997

Lightning Source UK Ltd.
Milton Keynes UK
UKOW03f0803020217
293383UK00002B/437/P